D1469542

EVERYTHING

RESUME
BOOK

Great resumes for everybody
from student to executive

Steven Graber

compiled by Mark Lipsman

Adams Media Corporation
Holbrook, Massachusetts

An Everything Series Book.
The Everything Series is a trademark of Adams Media Corporation.

Published by Adams Media Corporation
260 Center Street, Holbrook, MA 02343. U.S.A.

ISBN: 1-58062-311-5

Printed in the United States of America.

J I H G F E D C B A

Library of Congress Cataloging-in-Publication Data
Graber, Steven.
The everything resume book / by Steven Graber.
p.   cm.
Includes index.
ISBN 1-58062-311-5
1. Resumes (Employment) I. Title.
HF5383 .G637   2000
650.14—dc21   99-086411

Illustrations by Barry Littmann

This book is available at quantity discounts for bulk purchases.
For information, call 1-800-872-5627.

Visit our exciting Web site at http://www.careercity.com

Contents

Chapter 10: Resume Samples for Common Jobs 143

CONTENTS

CONTENTS

Preface

Writing a resume has never been simple. And now it's more complicated than ever. Scanners, email, electronic databases. One version of your resume is no longer sufficient, now you need two. A regular one and an electronic version. Where does it all end?

And the rules for writing regular resumes are changing as well. Putting down "References available upon request" is a surefire way to let a hiring manager know you're reading from a resume book published in the eighties. Should I include my personal interests? Should I mention I never completed college? All these questions will be answered by *The Everything Resume Book*.

First of all, this book will tell you exactly what needs to be included in your resume and what should be left out. You'll learn about when to use bold, italics, and all caps and when not to. You'll read about how to write job descriptions so they seem more animated, more lively. And more importantly, you'll learn how to stand out from the crowd, how to make your resume look better than anyone else's.

Next, you'll move on to the resume makeovers. There's no better learning tool than seeing real-world examples. If you're making the same mistakes these people were, they'll stand out loud and clear, and you'll be able to make the changes before it's too late. Then go through Chapter Three, an extended checklist of items to look for before you send off hundreds of copies of your resume.

Then Chapter Four will show you how to craft a resume that can be scanned by a computer or sent by email. More and more companies are using computers to "read" their resumes and it's vital for you to know what's different about an electronic resume. If you use the wrong font or format, your resume might be read as gobbedlygook by the computer and just thrown out! *The Everything Resume Book* will help you make sure this doesn't happen.

And not only does this book cover how to write an exceptional, up-to-date resume, it also includes important information on cover letters. Even though cover letters aren't quite as important as they used to be, they're still commonplace enough that you should learn how to do them the right way.

Chapter Six is something you won't find in many other job-related books. It's all about using the Internet for your job search. It includes great Web sites for you to post your resume or just look for cool opportunities. You'll never have to leave your house to look for a job again.

And then of course comes the meat and potatoes of this book: hundreds of resume samples. Whether you're a cashier or an executive, a retiree or a parent re-entering the workforce, there's a sample for you. And even if you don't find the exact job title or situation you're looking for, take a look at some of the others. Although the jobs may be different, you just may pick up a few tips or ideas to apply to your own resume.

Remember, your resume is the first, and arguably the most important, step in the job search process, so getting off on the right foot is essential. Even though writing a resume may be intimidating, *The Everything Resume Book* will take the mystery out of the process and show you how easy it really can be. Read on, and good luck!

CHAPTER 1

Resumes

Does Your Resume Have an Accent?

Only if you want it to. All three ways are acceptable:

resume
resumé
résumé

When filling a position, an employer will often have a hundred-plus applicants but time to interview only a handful of the most promising ones. As a result, a recruiter will reject most applicants after only briefly skimming their resumes.

Unless you've phoned and talked to the employer—which you should do whenever you can—you'll be chosen or rejected entirely on the basis of your resume and cover letter. *Your cover letter must catch the employer's attention, and your resume must hold it.* (But remember—a resume is no substitute for a job-search campaign. *You* must seek a job. Your resume is only one tool, albeit a critical one.)

Both the appearance, or format, of your resume and the content are important. These are discussed in separate sections below.

Format

First impressions matter, so make sure the recruiter's first impression of your resume is a good one.

Types

The most common resume formats are the chronological resume and the functional resume. You may also see references to a "chrono-functional," or "combination," resume, but this is usually a variant on one of the other two—a chronological type with an expanded skills summary or a functional type with an expanded work-history section.

Chronological

The chronological format is the most common. Choose a chronological format if you're currently working or were working recently and if your most recent experiences relate to your desired field. Use reverse chronological order and include dates. To a recruiter, your last job and your latest schooling are the most important, so put the last first and list the rest going back in time. Remember: There is no need to capitalize "present" in "1999–present."

Functional

A functional resume focuses on skills and strengths that your most recent jobs don't necessarily reflect, while de-emphasizing job titles, employers, etc. A functional resume may be useful if you have no work experience, have been out of the work force for a long time, or are changing careers. But some recruiters may wonder if you're trying to hide something, so be ready for questions of that nature. In some cases, a skills summary section at the top of a chronological resume may be useful.

Typing

A word processing or desktop publishing program is the most common way to generate your resume. This allows you the flexibility to make changes instantly and store different drafts. These programs also offer many different fonts, each taking up different amounts of space. (It's best to stay between 10-point and 12-point type size.) Many other options are also available, like boldface or italics for emphasis and the ability to manipulate spacing. Leave the right-hand margin unjustified to keep the spacing between the letters even and easier to read.

Organization

Your name, phone number, e-mail address (if you have one), and mailing address should be at the top of the resume. Make your name stand out by using a slightly larger font size and boldface. Be sure to spell out everything—don't abbreviate "St." for "Street" or "Rd." for "Road." The word "present" (as in "1997–present") should be lowercase.

Next, list your experience, then your education. If you're a recent graduate, list your education first, unless your experience is more important than your education. (For example, if you've just graduated from a teaching school, have some business experience, and are applying for a job in business, list your business experience first.)

Typeface

Typefaces come in two general categories: *serif* and *sans serif*.

This is a serif face.
This is a sans serif face.

Serif faces are generally easier to read—the serifs and variable thicknesses of the strokes help the eye perceive the letters. They also tend to convey a more upscale image than sans serif. This doesn't mean choosing a fancy, designer typeface—something standard and conservative is best.

Paper Size

Use standard 8½- by 11-inch paper. A smaller size will appear more personal than professional and is easily lost in an employer's files; a larger size will look awkward and may be discarded for not fitting with other documents.

The important thing is to break up the text in some logical way that makes your resume visually attractive and easy to scan, so experiment to see which layout works best. However you set it up, *stay consistent*. Inconsistencies in fonts, spacing, or tenses make your resume look sloppy. Use tabs rather than the less precise space bar to keep information aligned vertically.

Abbreviations

It's advisable to spell out most abbreviations on a resume. Resumes are compressed enough as it its; frequent abbreviations and acronyms can make them nearly unintelligible.

Length

Employers dislike long resumes, so keep it to one page if possible. If you must squeeze in more information than would otherwise fit, try using a slightly smaller typeface or changing the margins. Watch also for "widows" (a word or two on a separate line at the end of a paragraph). You can often free up some space if you can edit the information enough to get rid of those single words taking up an entire line. Another tactic that works with some word processing programs is to decrease the size of your paragraph returns and change the spacing between lines.

Paper Color and Quality

Use quality paper that is standard 8½ by 11 inches and has weight and texture, in a conservative color like white or ivory. Good resume paper is easy to find at stores that sell stationery or office products and is even available at some drugstores. Use *matching* paper and envelopes for both your resume and cover letter. One hiring manager at a major magazine throws out all resumes that arrive on paper that differs in color from the envelope!

Do not buy paper with images of clouds and rainbows in the background or anything that looks like casual stationery you would send your favorite aunt. Do not spray perfume or cologne on your resume. Also, never use the stationery of your current employer.

Printing

For a resume on paper, the result will depend on the quality of the printer you use. Laser printers are best. Do not use a dot matrix printer. If you don't print out each copy individually, use a high-quality photocopier, such as in a professional copy shop.

Household typewriters and office typewriters with nylon or other cloth ribbons are *not* good enough for typing your resume. If you don't have access to a quality word processing program, hire a professional with the resources to prepare your resume for you. Keep in mind that businesses like Kinko's (open twenty-four hours) provide access to computers with quality printers.

Many companies now use scanning equipment to screen the resumes they receive, and certain paper, fonts, and other features are more compatible with this technology. Formatting a resume for scanning is discussed in Chapter 4 **[Electronic Resumes]**.

Watermark

When you print your resume (and cover letter), hold it up to a light to make sure the watermark reads correctly—that it's not upside down or backward. As trivial as this may sound, it's the accepted style in formal correspondence, and some recruiters check for it. One recruiter at a law firm in New Hampshire sheepishly admitted this is the first thing he checks: "I open each envelope and check the watermarks on the resume and cover letter. Those candidates that have it wrong go into a different pile."

Proof with Care

Mistakes on resumes are not only embarrassing, they will often remove you from consideration (particularly if something obvious, like your name, is misspelled). No matter how much you paid someone else to type, write, or typeset your resume, *you* lose if there is a mistake. So proofread it as carefully as possible. Get a friend to help you. Read your draft aloud as your friend checks the proof copy. Then have your friend read aloud while you check. Next, read it letter by letter to check spelling and punctuation.

If you're having it typed or typeset by a resume service or a printer and you don't have time to proof it, pay for it and take it home. Proof it there and bring it back later to get it corrected and printed.

If you wrote your resume with a word processing program, use the built-in spell checker to double-check for spelling errors. Keep in mind that a spell checker will not find errors like "to" for "two" or "wok" for "work." Many spell-check programs don't recognize missing or misused punctuation, nor are they set to check the spelling of capitalized words. It's important to still proofread your resume for grammatical mistakes and other problems, even after it's been spell-checked.

If you find mistakes, do not fix them with pen, pencil, or white-out! Make the changes on the computer and print out the resume again.

Content

Sell Yourself . . .

You're selling your skills and accomplishments in your resume, so it's important to take inventory and know yourself. If you've achieved something, say so. Put it in the best possible light. But avoid subjective statements, like "I am a hard worker" or "I get along well with my coworkers." Stick to the facts.

While you shouldn't hold back or be modest, don't exaggerate your achievements to the point of misrepresentation. Be honest. Many companies will immediately drop an applicant from consideration (or fire a current employee) upon discovering inaccurate or untrue information on a resume or other application material.

. . . But Be Concise

Write down the important (and pertinent) things you've done, but do it in as few words as possible. Short, concise phrases are more effective than long-winded sentences. Avoid the use of "I" when emphasizing your accomplishments. Instead, use phrases beginning with action verbs. Use present tense for your current job and past tense for previous jobs.

Also, try to hold your paragraphs to six lines or fewer. If you have more than six lines of information about one job or school, put it in two or more paragraphs. A short resume will be examined more carefully. Remember: your resume usually has between eight and forty-five seconds to catch an employer's eye, so make every second count.

Give 'Em What They Want

Employers favor certain skills. Here are the top contenders:

- *Supervising/managing skills* mean you can take responsibility for the work of others.
- *Coordinating/organizing skills* allow you to plan events or see projects to completion.
- *Negotiating skills* allow you to bring about compromise and resolve differences.
- *Customer service/public relations skills* enable you to be a spokesperson for your organization.
- *Training/instructing skills* allow you to show newcomers the ropes.
- *Interviewing skills* enable you to ask tough questions, then listen to get insight from the answers.
- *Speaking skills* involve presenting your ideas verbally in a coherent fashion.
- *Writing skills* enable you to express your ideas convincingly on paper.
- *Deadline-meeting skills* enable you to work under pressure.
- *Budgeting skills* involve the ability to save your employer money.

Avoid Catch Phrases

In the course of a job search, it's tempting to use catch phrases you've picked up from advertisements or reference materials, phrases that sound as though they *should* go in a resume or cover letter. Many people are tempted to reach for expressions like "self-starter," "excellent interpersonal skills," and "work well independently or as part of a team."

The Kitchen-Sink Sentence

Being concise doesn't mean trying to cram every facet of your job into a single sentence. Break up long, unwieldy sentences:

Example (wrong way): "Responsible for editing, writing, and production coordination of bid proposals for government, industrial, and utility engineering and construction contracts."

Example (right way): "Prepare bid proposals for government, industrial, and utility contracts, including engineering and construction. Write and edit proposals; coordinate production."

Remember that seemingly efficient strings of nouns can become hard to understand and are often better off broken up for purposes of grammar AND common sense.

The Appropriate Apostrophe

A common mistake on resumes, especially in describing your work experience, is to refer to " . . . over five years experience in. . . ."

"Years" here is a type of possessive and must have an apostrophe: ". . . over five years' experience in. . . ."

Improve on these descriptions by listing actual projects and goals. For example, rephrase "Determined achiever with proven leadership skills" as follows: "Supervised staff of fifteen and increased the number of projects completed before deadline by X percent." Once you begin working, employers will discover your personal attributes for themselves. While you're under consideration, concrete experiences are more valuable than vague phrases or obscure promises.

Job Objective

Objectives tend to sound generic, and the information they contain should be clear from your cover letter. Also, an overly specific objective may eliminate you from consideration for other positions that a recruiter feels are a better match for your qualifications.

In certain instances, an objective may be suitable—for example, if your previous work experience is unrelated to the position for which you're applying, or if you're a recent graduate with no work experience. Sometimes an objective can give a functional resume focus. One or two sentences describing the job you're seeking may clarify the capacity in which your skills can best be put to use. Be sure your objective is in line with the position for which you're applying, and don't state that you're looking for a position that will allow you to grow or to develop certain capacities. Employers are interested in what you can do for them, not what they can do for you. This is something to keep in mind throughout the job-search and interview process.

Experience

Emphasize continued experience in a particular job area or continued interest in a particular industry. De-emphasize irrelevant positions. Delete positions you held for less than four months (unless you're a recent college graduate or still in school). It's okay to include one opening line providing a general description of each company at which you've worked.

Stress your results and achievements, elaborating on how you contributed in your previous jobs. Did you increase sales, reduce costs, improve a product, implement a new program? Were you promoted? Use specific numbers (quantities, percentages, dollar amounts) whenever possible. Always avoid "etc." when presenting

Action Verbs

Action verbs make your resume more interesting to read. These are some you may want to use. (This list is not all-inclusive.)

achieved	developed	integrated	purchased
administered	devised	interpreted	reduced
advised	directed	interviewed	regulated
analyzed	discovered	invented	reorganized
arranged	distributed	launched	represented
assembled	eliminated	maintained	researched
assisted	established	managed	resolved
attained	evaluated	marketed	restored
budgeted	examined	mediated	restructured
built	executed	monitored	revised
calculated	expanded	negotiated	scheduled
collaborated	expedited	obtained	selected
collected	facilitated	operated	served
compiled	formulated	ordered	sold
completed	founded	organized	solved
computed	generated	participated	streamlined
conducted	headed	performed	studied
consolidated	identified	planned	supervised
constructed	implemented	prepared	supplied
consulted	improved	presented	supported
controlled	increased	processed	tested
coordinated	initiated	produced	trained
created	installed	proposed	updated
designed	instituted	provided	upgraded
determined	instructed	published	wrote

Conceptual Grouping

Instead of creating a long list of uncategorized bullet points, you may want to group responsibilities and accomplishments conceptually. In the following example, a resume entry is done both ways:

Director of Student Services (1993–present)
- Plan, administer, and evaluate a comprehensive freshman academic support program.
- Coordinate activities, including academic advising and placement and academic, personal, and career counseling; administer placement tests, new student orientation, parent/student workshops, cultural activities, academic tracking, and early warning system for "at risk" freshmen.
- Chair meetings of faculty/administration committee for student services. Propose new programs and changes to existing programs.
- Analyze administration data on student services to determine benefits of programs.
- Distribute evaluations to students and collate data to determine student satisfaction with programs.
- Initiated a newsletter and a recognition dinner for student achievements in academics, activities, and sports.
- Instituted cultural awareness activities, including a guest lecture series, field trips to the Boston Art Museum and the Ryder Early American Collection, and a tour to retrace the stops in Paul Revere's ride.

Grouping the bullet points conceptually makes them easier to read and understand, as do arranging the categories in logical order (planning, administration, and evaluation) and the bullets in order of importance within each category:

Director of Student Services (1993–present)
Responsibilities include planning, administering, and evaluating a comprehensive freshman academic support program.

- *Planning*
  Chair meetings of faculty/administration committee for student services. Propose new programs and changes to existing programs.

- *Administration*
  Coordinate activities, including academic advising and placement and academic, personal, and career counseling.

  Administer placement tests, new student orientation, parent/student workshops, cultural activities, academic tracking, and early warning system for "at risk" freshmen.

  Instituted cultural awareness activities, including a guest lecture series, field trips to the Boston Art Museum and the Ryder Early American Collection, and a tour to retrace the stops on Paul Revere's ride.

  Initiated a newsletter and a recognition dinner for student achievements in academics, activities, and sports.

- *Evaluation*
  Analyze administration data on student services to determine benefits of programs.

  Distribute evaluations to students and collate data to determine student satisfaction with programs.

your experiences. Don't expect a potential employer to imagine what else you mean.

Gaps in Your Employment History

You may be asked about gaps in your employment history. Although you'll need to be prepared to explain them, gaps aren't the stigma they used to be. Many people now have some kind of irregularity in their work histories—they were laid off, went back to school, took off for personal reasons, changed careers, had a baby—you name it. Because this is now so prevalent, recruiters can't very well hold it against you, as long as you have a plausible explanation and the skills for the job.

Action Verbs

In describing previous work experiences, the strongest resumes use short phrases beginning with action verbs. Remember, however, that if you upload your resume to an on-line job hunting site like CareerCity, the keywords or key nouns a computer would search for become as important as action verbs. For more on keywords in electronic resumes, see Chapter 4 **[Electronic Resumes]**.

Bullets

Bullets are useful for drawing attention to significant points, but make sure that your resume is not too bullety. A long column of bullet points in random order can lack cohesion. An alternative is to group them conceptually—in relevant categories, with a few bullets under each one—to make them easier to grasp. This may also permit you to combine several bullets into one or, conversely, to break up long paragraphs. Do remember, however, that bulleted blocks, capitals, or italics are hard to read and are best avoided. Also, periods following elements of bulleted lists are optional. The general rule is to use periods for statements that are full sentences; otherwise don't.

Avoid Excessive Jargon and Excessive Words

Some technical terms may be necessary, but try to avoid excessive "technicalese." Keep in mind that the first person to see your resume may be a human resources person, who won't necessarily know all the jargon—and can't be impressed by something he or

Volunteer Work

If you would like to include your volunteer work with your paid work experiences to give your resume a more continuous work history, make sure to title this section "Experience" rather than "Employment Background" or "Professional Experience."

The Third Degree on Your "Degree"

Cum laude, magna cum laude, and *summa cum laude* are lowercase and italic:

Bachelor of Arts in English, *summa cum laude*

"B.A. degree in . . ." is redundant. Just "B.A. in . . ." is fine. Also, don't say "Associates degree in . . ." or "Masters in. . . ." You may have an associate's degree or a master's degree (with apostrophes), but on a resume you would say "Associate in [or "of"] Arts" or "Master of Arts."

she doesn't understand. Also strive to use the fewest number necessary to convey your message. Example: "Responsible for directing" can be "Directed" (if a past experience) or "Direct" (if current).

Temporary Work

If you do your temporary work through an agency, list the company name and job description for any longer-term assignments (perhaps a month or longer) you held. For shorter assignments, use the name of the agency, but also list the names of companies where you worked.

ProTemps Employment, Houston, TX

Short-term clerk/typist assignments at the following companies:
Acme Products
Bonding Devices
Development Partners
Morrison Manufacturing
Terragard Fabrics

Skills

Most jobs now require computer knowledge. Therefore, it's usually advisable to include a section titled "Computer Skills," in which you list software programs you know. If the list is long, subdivide them by category.

Example:

Operating systems	DOS, Windows, Macintosh
Writing/publishing tools	Word, WordPerfect, QuarkXPress, PageMaker, Photoshop, Illustrator
Business [or *Financial*]	Excel, Lotus 1-2-3, Access
Languages	C++, BASIC

It isn't usually necessary to include the version number of an application. Nor do you need to be perfectly fluent with a program to list it. As long as you've used it in the past and could pick it up again with a little practice, it's legitimate to include it.

The skills section is also an ideal place to mention fluency in a foreign language. If you're listing skills other than computer

knowledge, subdivide them by category under the "Skills" heading: "Computer," "Languages," etc.

Education

Keep the education section brief if you have more than two years of career experience. Elaborate more if you have less experience. If you're a recent college graduate, you may choose to include high school activities that are *directly* relevant to your career.

Mention degrees received and any honors or special awards. Note individual courses that might be relevant to employers. (These should be at least a semester long. Shorter courses of a day or two, even a week or two, should not generally be mentioned unless they're important in your field. It's also unnecessary to list courses taken in pursuit of a degree.)

Certifications

Mention any applicable certifications or licenses you hold, such as teaching or social work.

Personal Information

Do not include your age, health, physical characteristics, marital status, race, religion, political/moral beliefs, or any other personal information. List your personal interests and hobbies only if they're directly relevant to the type of job you're seeking. If you're applying to a company that greatly values teamwork, for instance, citing that you organized a community fundraiser or played on a basketball team may be advantageous. When in doubt, however, leave it out.

Do not include your picture with your resume unless you have a specific and appropriate reason to do so—for example, if you're applying for a job as an actor or model.

Professional Affiliations

These are worth noting if you're a member of a professional organization in your industry.

It's Illegal

"Those things [marital status, church affiliations, etc.] have no place on a resume. Those are illegal questions, so why even put that information on your resume?"

—BECKY HAYES
CAREER COUNSELOR,
CAREER SERVICES,
RICE UNIVERSITY

References

"References available upon request" is unnecessary on a resume. It's understood that if you're considered for the position, you'll be asked for references and will provide them. Don't send references with your resume and cover letter unless they're specifically requested.

When to Get Help

If you write reasonably well, it's to your advantage to write your own resume. This forces you to review your experiences and figure out how to explain your accomplishments in clear, brief phrases. This will help you when you explain your work to interviewers. It's also easier to tailor your resume to each position you're applying for when you've put it together yourself.

If you have difficulty writing in resume style (which is quite unlike normal written language), if you're unsure which parts of your background to emphasize, or if you think your resume would make your case better if it didn't follow one of the standard forms outlined either here or in a book on resumes, consider having it professionally written.

The best way to choose a resume writer is by reputation: the recommendation of a friend, a personnel director, your school placement officer, or someone else knowledgeable in the field.

Important questions:
"How long have you been writing resumes?"
"If I'm not satisfied with what you write, will you go over it with me and change it?"
"Do you charge by the hour or a flat rate?"

For more information on resume services, contact the Professional Association of Resume Writers at 3637 Fourth Street, Suite 330, St. Petersburg, FL 33704, USA. Correspondence can be addressed to the attention of Mr. Frank Fox, Executive Director.

Price and Quality

There is no guaranteed relation between price and quality, except that you're unlikely to get a good writer for less than $50 for an uncomplicated resume, and you shouldn't have to pay more than $300 unless your experience is extensive or complicated. Printing charges will be extra. Assume nothing, no matter how much you pay. It's your career at stake if your resume has mistakes!

Few resume services will give you a firm price over the phone, simply because some resumes are too complicated and take too long to do for a predetermined price. Some services will quote you a price that applies to almost all of their customers. Once you decide to use a specific writer, you should insist on a firm price quote *before* engaging his or her services. Also, find out how expensive minor changes will be.

For Students and Recent Graduates

Which Type of Resume Is Right for You?

The type of resume you use depends on your job experience. If you don't have any work history, use a functional resume format, emphasizing your strong points:

Education. This should be your primary focus.
Special achievements. This could be almost anything from having an article published to graduating with honors.
Awards and competitive scholarships
Classes, internships, theses, or special projects that relate to your job objective
Computer knowledge. Are you familiar with a Mac or PC? What software programs do you know?
Language skills. Are you fluent in a foreign language? Be sure to indicate both written and verbal skills.
Volunteer work
Committees and organizations
Extracurricular activities

Show It to People

"The one piece of advice I give to everyone about their resume is: Show it to people, show it to people, show it to people. Before you ever send out a resume, show it to at least a dozen people."

—CATE TALBOT ASHTON
ASSOCIATE DIRECTOR,
CAREER SERVICES, COLBY
COLLEGE

The Punctuation Situation

Serial Comma
Standard editorial practice in a series of items is to use a comma after each item except the last item: " . . . server, lifeguard, and courier."

Colons and Subheads
It's generally unnecessary to use a colon after a subhead. The function of the subhead is to set off and describe what follows; the colon is unnecessary. Rarely are more than three levels of subheads necessary.

Recruiters like to see some kind of work history, even if it doesn't relate to your job objective, because it demonstrates that you have a good work ethic. However, it's also important to emphasize special skills or qualifications, including the above information.

Work History

When describing your work history, avoid simply listing your job duties. Focus on accomplishments and achievements, even if they're small. Consider the difference:

> *Weak:* "Lifeguard at busy public beach. Responsible for safety of bathers and cleanliness of the beach and parking areas."
>
> *Strong:* "Lifeguard at busy public beach. Rescued eight people during summer. Established recycling program for bottles and cans."

If you've held many jobs, you may choose to emphasize only two or three of the most relevant and list the rest under the heading "Other Experience" without individual job descriptions:

> *Other Experience:* Floor and stockroom clerk at university bookstore, server, lifeguard, and courier.

When Functional Is Appropriate

As indicated earlier, under some circumstances, a functional resume may be more appropriate. These may include the following:

- You haven't worked for over a year.
- You want to highlight specific skills by category that would not stand out as easily with a chronological format.
- You've held a variety of jobs.
- Your career goal has taken a dramatic turn.

In this case, a functional resume may be more suitable. It focuses not so much on what positions you've held and when but on what you've learned from your experiences that would be of use in the job.

In certain fields, it is requested that you send a Curriculum Vitae, or "CV," instead of a resume. Sometimes this is referred to as an "International Resume," since all European countries use some form of the Vitae. A CV is mainly used when applying for jobs in the education and health-care industries.

A CV differs from a resume in that it is tailored toward these industries by providing specific, more comprehensive information. It is usually longer in length, depending on the applicant's degree of experience. Typically, a CV is anywhere from two to eight pages (with those who have a master's degree or more experience at the higher end of the scale). A CV contains information such as:

- Details on educational background including degrees and certificates accrued, master's thesis and/or doctoral dissertation, honors and awards, and GPA.
- A summary of relevant work experience.
- A list of publications authored.
- A list of papers presented at conferences.
- Professional association membership(s).

The functions you served in your old jobs are the crux of this format. The actual titles and dates don't come until the very end.

GPA

Never include a grade point average (GPA) under 3.0 on your resume. If your GPA in your major is higher than your overall GPA, include it either in addition to or instead of your overall GPA.

High School Information

Including high school information is optional for college graduates, but such information should be used sparingly. If you have exceptional achievements in college and in summer or part-time jobs, omit your high school information. High school information should really only be used if the experience is directly related to the types of jobs or industry for which you are applying. If you decide to include high school achievements, describe them more briefly than your college achievements.

Keep in Touch

Put your home address and phone number at the top of the resume. Change the message on your answering machine if necessary—the Beastie Boys blaring in the background or your sorority sisters screaming may not come across well to all recruiters. If you think you may be moving within six months, include a second address and phone number of a trusted friend or relative who can reach you no matter where you are.

Remember that employers may keep your resume on file and contact you months later if a position opens that fits your qualifications. All too often, candidates are unreachable because they moved and didn't provide enough contact options on their resumes.

CHAPTER 2

Resume Makeovers

This chapter contains eight resume makeovers, to give you an idea of what goes into improving a less than outstanding resume. Each one is shown in a "Before" version, with an analysis of its shortcomings, followed by an "After" version.

Before

✖ Objective is not consistent with the rest of the resume.

✖ Job history goes back too far.

✖ Contains some irrelevant information.

CHRIS SMITH
178 Green Street
Huntington, WV 25702
(304) 555-5555

OBJECTIVE:
A position in small plant management. Willing to relocate and/or travel.

SUMMARY OF QUALIFICATIONS:
More than thirty years of experience encompassing plant management to include sales, production, plant maintenance, systems, personnel, and related functions. Hired, trained, and supervised personnel. Additional experience as Sales Counselor in the educational field. Good background in customer relations and human resources.

EXPERIENCE:
The Westview Schools, Huntington, WV
Career Counselor—1985-Present
Contact and interview teenagers, young adults, and adults with reference to pursuing courses of higher education leading towards careers in a variety of business professions (secretarial, accounting, court reporting, business management, public relations, fashions and merchandising, computer and machine operating and programming, machine accounting, etc.). Administer aptitude tests to applicants and advise prospective students as to their aptitudes and best courses to pursue. Organize welcoming ceremony and orientation meetings for new students each semester. Track completion and job-placement statistics.

Greenbriar Corporation, Huntington, WV
General Manager—1976-1985
Assumed responsibility for management of this firm which originally employed twelve. Selected, set up, equipped, and staffed new facilities; hired, trained, and supervised skilled production personnel; set up incentive plans; quality production and cost controls; systems; plant maintenance; handled payroll, billing, credit and collection, purchasing, and finance.

Rosemont Inc., Charleston, WV
Assistant Plant Manager—Laundry Company 1962-1972
Supervised all personnel in this plant which employed 250 people. Handled customer relations, complaints, quality control, and related functions.

EDUCATION:
Northeastern University, Boston, MA
BSBA degree
Industrial Relations and Accounting.

CHRIS SMITH
178 Green Street
Huntington, WV 25702
(304) 555-5555

SUMMARY OF QUALIFICATIONS
Accomplished career counselor in the educational field
Extensive experience in management, including hiring and training
Good background in customer relations and human resources

EXPERIENCE
The Westview Schools, Huntington, WV
Career Counselor   1985-present
- Contact and interview potential candidates for business courses.
- Describe school programs and provide literature.
- Administer aptitude tests; advise prospective students as to their best courses to pursue.
- Organize welcoming ceremony and orientation meetings for new students each semester.
- Track completion and job-placement statistics.

Greenbriar Corporation, Huntington, WV
General Manager   1976-85
Greenbriar Corporation is a manufacturer of stamped metal parts.
- Selected, set up, equipped, and staffed new facilities. Supervised plant maintenance.
- Hired, trained, and supervised 18 skilled production personnel, 4 executives, and 16 support staff.
- Established incentive plans and quality, production, and cost controls.
- Supervised payroll, billing, credit and collection, purchasing, and finance for this $24 million company.

EDUCATION
Northeastern University, Boston, MA
Bachelor of Science in Business Administration
Concentration: Industrial Relations and Accounting

After

✔ Bullets creates a cleaner look.

✔ Information in summary is now more consistent with last position held.

✔ Job history only has to include the last 10–15 years, so the last job listing was deleted.

Before

✖ In this case, functional resume advertises lack of experience.

CHRIS SMITH
178 Green Street
Grenvil, NE 68941
(402) 555-5555

Objective: An entry-level administrative position.

Summary of Qualifications:
ADMINISTRATION:
Accurate typing at 60 words per minute. Thoroughly experienced in all aspects of office administration, including record keeping, filing, and scheduling/planning.

ACCOUNTING:
Coordinate finances for a middle income family of five on a personal computer. Process accounts payable in a timely manner without compromising facets of the expenditure budget. Monitor checking account closely.

COMPUTERS:
Lotus 1-2-3, Microsoft Word, WordPerfect, IBM Compatible.

ORGANIZATION:
Organize a rotating carpool with five other mothers. Make several copies and distribute at least one month in advance.

Organize a monthly women's writing group. Develop writing exercises that address the hidden spiritual elements in modern women's lives. Motivate members to channel stress, uncertainty, and fear into the gift of creativity. Act as mentor and friend.

LEADERSHIP:
President of Grenvil Historical Society, an organization concerned with educating public about Grenvil town history and preserving historic landmarks. Develop calendar of events; invite guest speakers, organize fundraising events.

Coach a girls' soccer team, ages 7-11, in the Grenvil Youth Outreach Program (GYOR). Provide players with the instruction, motivation, support, and outlook that will enable them to come away from each game with satisfaction and pride.

Notable Accomplishments:
Organized fundraiser to renovate the Henry Wallace House; raised over $5,000.
Several short stories published in regional literary magazines, including *The Loft*.

Education:
Grenvil Community College, Grenvil, NE
Courses in Creative Writing, Word Processing, and Accounting.

CHRIS SMITH
178 Green Street
Grenvil, NE 68941
(402) 555-5555

OBJECTIVE
A position in administration

SUMMARY OF QUALIFICATIONS
- Thoroughly experienced in all aspects of office administration, including record keeping, filing, scheduling, and planning
- Skilled at processing accounts payable in a timely manner
- Efficient and well organized

EXPERIENCE
Freelance Writer   1992-present
Published short stories in several regional literary magazines: *Prairie Voices*, *Midwest,* and *The Loft*.

Grenvil Historical Society   Grenvil, NE
President   1994-present
Preside over meetings of this organization concerned with educating public about Grenvil town history and preserving historic landmarks. Develop calendar of events; invite guest speakers, organize fundraising events. Arrange for meeting place, materials, and refreshments. Organized fundraiser to renovate the Henry Wallace House; raised over $5,000.

Grenvil Youth Outreach Program (GYOR)   Grenvil, NE
Girls' Soccer Coach   1996-present
Coach girls ages 7-11 from September to November. Provide players with instruction, motivation, support, and outlook to enable them to come away from each game with satisfaction and pride, no matter what the score.

SKILLS
Computer: Word, Excel, Quicken
Typing: 60 wpm

EDUCATION
Grenvil Community College, Grenvil, NE
Courses in Creative Writing, Word Processing, and Accounting

After

✔ An objective is suitable, but the restrictive "entry-level" has been eliminated.

✔ Computer and typing skills are placed in a separate section.

✔ This version creates a more unified message—that this person has legitimate administrative skills.

Before

✖ Summary is too generic.

✖ Job descriptions are too sketchy.

✖ This resume does nothing to overcome the lack of direction.

Chris Smith
178 Green Street
Wise, VA 24293
(703) 555-5555

OBJECTIVE
An entry-level position in Human Resources.

SUMMARY OF QUALIFICATIONS
- Trained in basic computer skills.
- Developed interpersonal skills; excellent mediation abilities.
- Proven supervisory abilities; deal equitably with all levels.
- Function well both independently and as team member.
- Adapt easily to new concepts; adept at handling multiple responsibilities.
- Extensive experience in training.
- Charismatic, assertive personality, skilled at commanding the attention of others.

WORK HISTORY

1990–present　　　　　　　　　　ARMY NATIONAL GUARD, Richmond, VA
Assistant Section Coordinator, Sergeant/ E-5
Coordinate training of soldiers, creating schedules, overseeing adherence to rules, assisting in directing operations, and attending weekly meetings.

1997–present　　　　　　　　BENNIE WARD'S STYLE SHINDIG, Winchester, VA
- Sales Associate
- Acknowledged as one of top salespeople; consistently met/exceeded sales goals.

1994-97　　　　　　　　　　MARTELL BLUE SECURITY SERVICES, Salem, MA
Security Shift Supervisor
Handled employee ID checks; secured building; ensured other site call-ins. Worked independently on onsite assignments.

1991-94　　　　　　　　VIRGINIA SAMARITAN ASSOCIATION, Charlottesville, VA
Fundraiser
Utilized telephone techniques to raise funds for organizations.

EDUCATION
RICHMOND JUNIOR COLLEGE, Richmond VA
Associates Degree in Management Science
Major: Business Administration

Chris Smith
178 Green Street
Wise, VA 24293
(703) 555-5555

OBJECTIVE
A position in Human Resources

SUMMARY OF QUALIFICATIONS
- Developed interpersonal skills; excellent mediation abilities; supervisory experience
- Extensive experience in training; able to explain procedures and achieve significant results in a brief time

EXPERIENCE
1997–present   BENNIE WARD'S STYLE SHINDIG, Winchester, VA
Sales Associate
   Provide customer assistance and advise on selections. Develop ongoing customer relationships, enhancing future sales. Assist with promotions and special seasonal sales. Handle cash transactions. Acknowledged as one of top salespeople; consistently meet or exceed sales goals.

1990–present   ARMY NATIONAL GUARD, Richmond, VA
Assistant Section Coordinator, Sergeant/ E-5
   Coordinate training of soldiers and work assignments. Maintain personnel records. Complete performance evaluations and recommend awards. Create schedules, oversee adherence to rules, assist in directing operations.

1994-97   MARTELL BLUE SECURITY SERVICES, Salem, MA
Shift Supervisor
   Handled employee ID checks; secured building; ensured other site call-ins. Worked independently on onsite assignments.

COMPUTER SKILLS
Word, Lotus 1-2-3

EDUCATION
RICHMOND JUNIOR COLLEGE, Richmond VA
Associate in Management Science
Major: Business Administration

After

✔ Objective is appropriate because he has no prior experience in the field.

✔ Computer skills are given a separate section.

✔ Consistency of interpersonal skills and training de-emphasizes lack of direction.

Before

✖ Much too difficult to read!

✖ Lacks organization.

✖ Managers probably wouldn't even look at this one.

CHRIS SMITH
178 Green Street
Omaha, NE 68114
(402) 555-5555

SUMMARY OF QUALIFICATIONS
Successful administrative experience with major voluntary health agency ... recognized for ability to plan, organize, coordinate and direct successful fundraising programs, volunteer committees, public relations programs, educational programs ... legislative experience and knowledge ... extensive volunteer recruitment experience ... supervisory experience with both professional and non-professional staffs ... qualified to work with agencies and institutions as well as civic and industrial leaders in the best interest of the organization ... active in community affairs.

EMPLOYMENT EXPERIENCE
Nebraska Heart Society, Inc., Omaha, NE
PR Manager, 1999-present
Serve as consultant to the seven chapters in the state regarding campaign problems and activities; organize statewide and regional campaign meetings; develop fund-raising programs (bequests); conduct the 1991 and 1992 campaigns for the newly merged Central Chapter (Antelope County); 1992 Chairman for the Nebraska Independent Health Agency Committee (solicitation of State employees); 1992 Secretary for the Combined Federal Campaign (Federal employee campaign); Special Assignments: Responsible for reviewing all State legislation regarding any relationship to the Heart Society and its programs, and bringing specific bills to the attention of the proper committee or individual. Staff the Legislative Advisory Committee and follow through regarding specific bills. Act as Training Coordinator for four two-and-one-half day orientation courses held for new employees. Assist in developing the course. Speaker at several campaign conferences.

Directorial Assistant (Greater Omaha Chapter), 1997-99
Supervised all chapter campaign duties as well as assisted the Executive Director with administrative responsibilities such as personnel and budget.

EDUCATION
Dillard University, New Orleans, LA
M.S. degree, Public Relations, 1988

University of Michigan at Flint
B.A. degree, Government, 1986

PERSONAL
Willing to relocate and travel.

PUBLIC RELATIONS MANAGER

CHRIS SMITH
178 Green Street
Omaha, NE 68114
(402) 555-5555

SUMMARY OF QUALIFICATIONS
- Recognized for ability to plan and direct successful programs for fundraising, public relations, and education.
- Administrative experience with major voluntary health agency.
- Extensive volunteer recruitment experience.
- Experience representing agency interests to legislators.
- Supervisory experience with both professional and nonprofessional staffs.

EMPLOYMENT EXPERIENCE
Nebraska Heart Society, Inc., Omaha, NE
Public Relations Manager, 1999-present

Organizing
Serve as consultant to the seven state chapters regarding campaign problems and activities. Organize statewide and regional campaign meetings; speak at several campaign conferences.

Lobbying
Review state legislation regarding the Heart Society and bring specific bills to the attention of the proper committee or individual. Staff the Legislative Advisory Committee and follow through on specific bills.

Fundraising
Develop fundraising programs (bequests). Conducted the previous two annual campaigns for the newly merged Central Chapter (Antelope County). Currently serve as chairman for the Nebraska Independent Health Agency Committee and secretary for the Combined Federal Campaign.

Training
Assisted in developing four 2 1/2 day orientation courses held for new employees; acted as training coordinator.

Directorial Assistant (Greater Omaha Chapter), 1997-99
Supervised chapter campaign duties and assisted the Executive Director with administrative responsibilities, such as personnel and budget.

EDUCATION
Dillard University, New Orleans, LA   University of Michigan at Flint
M.S. in Public Relations   B.A. in Government

Before

✖ Too many bullets.

✖ Information is sketchy and repetitive.

CHRIS SMITH
178 Green Street
Burlington, VT 05401
(802) 555-5555

PROFESSIONAL EXPERIENCE

1985 to present
KATHRYN F. BELL LIBRARY   Burlington, VT
Librarian, 1993-present
- Cover the circulation desk.
- Give instructional guidance to patrons; answer reference questions.
- Shelf books, journals, and audiovisuals.
- Give instruction on use of AV equipment.
- Check new book orders to prevent duplication.
- Record incoming periodicals and microfilm and identify and strip same for security.
- Maintain Reference Search File.
- Compile statistics on door count, circulation, photocopies, and reference questions.
- Knowledgeable in library services, policies and procedures, copyright and photocopy policies and procedures, circulation, basic filing, and the NLM Classification System, ALA filing rules, mesh headings, and various indexes.

Library Assistant, 1986-1993
- Supervised the library, maintaining quiet and order.
- Supervised the evening clerk.
- Performed many general library tasks as described in current position.
- Compiled and circulated LIL (Lates in Literature) reference packet for physicians.

1980 to 1986
EAST CATHOLIC HIGH SCHOOL, Rutland, VT
Librarian/Audio Visual Coordinator
- Supervised library and aided staff.
- Responsible for all library duties.
- Ordered software, and maintained all audiovisual equipment; instructed teachers on equipment use; scheduled equipment usage.
- Supervised student assigned study periods.
- Maintained positive working relationship with teachers and students.

EDUCATION
SIMMONS COLLEGE, Boston, MA
Masters of Library Science, 1980

BURLINGTON COMMUNITY COLLEGE, Burlington, VT
Bachelor of Arts in English, 1978

LIBRARIAN

- ✔ Conceptual grouping strengthens resume.
- ✔ Redundant information is deleted.
- ✔ Focus is on most recent position.

CHRIS SMITH
178 Green Street
Burlington, VT 05401
(802) 555-5555

EXPERIENCE
KATHRYN F. BELL LIBRARY   Burlington, VT
Librarian, 1986-present
Reference
Answer reference questions and maintain a reference search file. Assist patrons in use of catalog, Internet, and AV equipment. Obtain and send books through the interlibrary loan system. Select and order new books and materials. Catalog incoming materials.

Circulation
Check out materials at the circulation desk. Shelve incoming library materials. Compile statistics on door count, photocopies, and reference questions.

Managerial
Develop and manage a $90,000 budget; hire, train, and supervise staff. Write grant proposals, resulting in $8,000 for books on health, computers, and business reference.

Community
Coordinate and publicize library reading and film series, which draw an average of 12 and 35 people, respectively, per evening. Circulation of library materials has increased 16% since these programs began. Attend meetings of the library trustees and Friends of the Library. Participate in fundraising activities. Supervise library book sale.

Assistant Librarian, 1986-93
Supervised library staff and assumed responsibilities of library director in his absence. Established Young Adult collection and upgraded home improvement and biography collections. Performed other general library tasks as described in current position.

1980-86
EAST CATHOLIC HIGH SCHOOL, Rutland, VT
Librarian/Audiovisual Coordinator
Supervised library and aided staff. Maintained audiovisual equipment; instructed teachers on equipment use; scheduled equipment use.

EDUCATION
SIMMONS COLLEGE, Boston, MA
Master of Library Science

BURLINGTON COMMUNITY COLLEGE, Burlington, VT
Bachelor of Arts in English

Before

✖ Resume lacks definition and is difficult to read at a glance.

Chris Smith
1312 Liberty Street
Lowell, MA 01854
(617) 555-5208

EDUCATION
Brown University, Providence, RI.
Bachelor of Arts degree received May 1999
Major: English Literature GPA: 3.10

Internship, Boston Literacy Program, Boston, MA.
Assisted in reading program, teaching illiterate children and adults reading skills.

EXPERIENCE
Editorial Assistant, The Bostonian Journal
June 1999-August 1999
Edited articles, features, and illustrations for monthly publication.

Editor-in-Chief, Brown U. Newspaper
September 1998-May 1999
Selected submissions, edited and wrote headlines for submissions and columns, laid out page, dealt with public, recruited columnists, trained associates.

Associate Editor, Brown U. Newspaper
January 1997-May 1998
Trained for Editor-in-Chief position; assisted in selecting submissions, edited and wrote headlines for submissions and columns, laid out page, miscellaneous other tasks.

Copy Editor, Brown U. Newspaper
January 1996-December 1996
Edited news stories, wrote headlines, assisted with layout of page, occasionally solicited advertising and helped with distribution.

COMPUTER SKILLS
Word Processing - Working knowledge of WordPerfect and Microsoft Word.
Spreadsheets - Familiar with all aspects of creating and using a spreadsheet using Lotus 1-2-3.

ACTIVITIES
Senior Class Secretary, Dean's List

After

✔ Note good use of all capitals and boldface for her name.

✔ Note use of boldface and italics used strategically throughout the resume.

✔ Reformatting helps clarify the resume—not one word has been changed!

CHRIS SMITH
1312 Liberty Street
Lowell, MA 01854
(617) 555-5208

EDUCATION
Brown University, Providence, RI.
Bachelor of Arts degree received May 1999
Major: English Literature
GPA: 3.10

Internship, Boston Literacy Program, Boston, MA.
Assisted in reading program, teaching illiterate children and adults reading skills.

EXPERIENCE
Editorial Assistant, The Bostonian Journal
June 1999-August 1999
Edited articles, features, and illustrations for monthly publication.

Editor-in-Chief, Brown U. Newspaper
September 1998-May 1999
Selected submissions, edited and wrote headlines for submissions and columns, laid out page, dealt with public, recruited columnists, trained associates.

Associate Editor, Brown U. Newspaper
January 1997-May 1998
Trained for Editor-in-Chief position; assisted in selecting submissions, edited and wrote headlines for submissions and columns, laid out pages, miscellaneous other tasks.

Copy Editor, Brown U. Newspaper
January 1996-December 1996
Edited news stories, wrote headlines, assisted with layout of page, occasionally solicited advertising and helped with distribution.

COMPUTER SKILLS
Word Processing: Working knowledge of WordPerfect and Microsoft Word.
Spreadsheets: Familiar with all aspects of creating and using a spreadsheet using Lotus 1-2-3.

ACTIVITIES
Senior Class Secretary, Dean's List.

Before

* Recruiters probably won't even read this resume.

* Too long and wordy.

* Very hard to read.

Chris Smith
1334 23rd St., #104
New York, NY 10022
212/555-5512

EDUCATION

New York University, Manhattan
Bachelor of Science degree in Management
Date of Graduation: June 1998

EXPERIENCE

John D. MacDougall, Inc., 55 East 10th St., New York NY
Executive Assistant - Assistant to the President and Senior Vice President, responsible for providing extensive and highly confidential administrative assistance and support. Due to my highly visible and important role within the organization, I ensured that top company executives were constantly kept abreast of situations, problems, etc. that arose within the company, as well as within the industry. Responsible for the complete coordination of semi-annual company meetings consisting of 250 guests; which included the site selection, attainment of desired atmosphere, planning and arranging of speakers/guests, hotel accommodations and land and air transportation, as well as ensuring the successful attainment of budgeted costs. Also coordinated company social functions including dinners, parties, and holiday celebrations; which included the initiating ideas for these functions, selection of the location of the function, coordination of all details such as reservations, transportation, etc., and also ensuring attainment of budgeted costs. Heavy involvement with the Young Executive Program; reviewed personnel reports for content, personal and professional objectives, kept records of job performance over time, and made recommendations of salary adjustments based on overall rating. Acted as the on-site computer resource with respect to the explanation and solving of all company computing problems. Working knowledge of WordPerfect and dBase programs. May 1997 to September 1997.

Tecchi Management Corporation, 833 Fifth Avenue, New York NY
Administrative Assistant/Coordinator - Assistant to the President as well as the Accounting Manager. Constantly updated my supervisor on their employees' absenteeism, tardiness, performance appraisals and disciplinary actions needed to be taken. Responsible for the orientation of new employees on all company benefits and policies; taught employees company procedures for using technical equipment such as the fax machine, typewriters, computers, copy machines, phone system, etc. Intense amount of communication with high level staff and outside agencies. Performed customer service functions, including the resolving of all consumer and agency complaints and problems. May 1996 to September 1996.

Avenue Investments, 1323 Avenue of the Americas, New York NY
Administrative Assistant - In charge of confidential communications including typing company documents, correspondence, generation of charts and data, and filing. Associate in charge of outside communications via the telephone and switchboard. Completely responsible for the travel arrangements of 10 company executives, including scheduling, coordination, and budgeting. Coordinated office supply inventory and responsible for maintaining and reordering supplies including letterhead stationery and computer disks. June 1995 to September 1995.

COLLEGE STUDENT:
MANAGEMENT MAJOR

✔ Expanded section on educational background.

✔ Easy to read—only the relevant details have been included.

✔ Reformatting creates a professional presentation.

CHRIS SMITH
1334 23rd St., #104
New York, NY 10022
212/555-5512

EDUCATION
New York University, Manhattan
Bachelor of Science degree awarded in June 1998, majoring in Management.
Courses include Physics, Biochemistry, Economics and Statistics. 3.4 grade point average in major. Honors: Dean's List.

Student member of the American Management Association. Props assistant for College Theatre. Co-captain of Intramural Volleyball Team. Actively involved in Students Against Drunk Driving.

EXPERIENCE
Executive Assistant
John D. MacDougall, Inc., 55 East 10th St., New York NY   **(Summer 1997)**
- Responsible for providing extensive and highly confidential administrative assistance and support to the President and Senior Vice President
- Heavy involvement with the Young Executive Program; reviewed personnel reports for content, personal and professional objectives, kept records of job performance over time, and made recommendations of salary adjustments based on overall rating
- Acted as the on-site computer resource with respect to the explanation and solving of all company computing problems
- Coordinated company social functions and very large semi-annual company meetings

Administrative Assistant/Coordinator
Tecchi Management Corporation, 833 Fifth Avenue, New York NY   **(Summer 1996)**
- Assistant to the President and the Accounting Manager
- Responsible for the orientation of new employees on all company benefits policies, and procedures
- Extensive communication with high level staff and outside agencies
- Performed customer service functions, including the resolving of all consumer and agency complaints and problems

Administrative Assistant
Avenue Investments, 1323 Avenue of the Americas, New York NY   **(Summer 1995)**
- Extensive typing and filing
- Generated charts and data
- Operated switchboard
- Responsible for the travel arrangements of 10 company executives, including scheduling, coordination, and budgeting

COMPUTER SKILLS
Working knowledge of WordPerfect and dBase programs

Before

✖ Objective isn't necessary.

✖ Too many bullets makes comprehension difficult.

✖ Education section shouldn't be listed first.

CHRIS SMITH
178 Green Street
Broomfield, CO 80021
(303) 555-5555

OBJECTIVE:
A challenging position in facilities engineering, project engineering, or engineering management.

EDUCATION:
University of Colorado at Boulder, Boulder, CO
B.S., Mechanical Engineering, 1992

EXPERIENCE:
Facilities Engineer
Breckenridge Company, Broomfield, CO
(1996-Present)
Supervise all phases of maintenance and engineering for this specialty steel company which employs 800, and covers a 60-acre facility.
- Direct multi-craft maintenance, utilities, engineering and construction departments.
- Supervise staff of 100 people and ten supervisors in all phases of maintenance and engineering.
- Plan and install maintenance program and directing all improvement and/or new construction projects starting from studies for justification to project start-up.
- Represented the company as general contractor on project and saved approximately $4 million of the original estimates submitted by outside contractors.
- Direct technicians and supervisor on the design, construction and maintenance of equipment and machinery.
- Established standards and policies for testing, inspection and maintenance of equipment in accordance with engineering principals and safety regulations.
- Prepared bid sheets and contracts for construction facilities and position.
- Full responsibilities for a budget of approximately $10 million annually.
- Extensive involvement in labor relations with various trades.

Project Engineer
Gibralta Corporation, Loveland, CO
(1992-1996
- Planned and implemented modernization program including the installation of bloom, billet, bar, rod and strip mills as well as the required soaking pits and reheating furnaces.
- Directed a multi-craft maintenance force of approximately 250 craftsmen and supervisors.
- Planned and installed a maintenance program which reduced equipment down-time and increased C/P/T savings, substantially.

ASSOCIATIONS:
Member of American Iron and Steel Engineers Association

FACILITIES ENGINEER

CHRIS SMITH
178 Green Street
Broomfield, CO 80021
(303) 555-5555

EXPERIENCE
Facilities Engineer, Breckenridge Company, Broomfield, CO
1996-present
- Supervise all phases of multi-craft maintenance, utilities, engineering, and construction departments for this specialty steel company, which employs 800 and covers a 60-acre facility.

Operations
- Direct staff of 100 technicians and 10 supervisors in designing, constructing, and maintaining equipment and machinery.
- Established standards and policies for testing, inspection, and maintenance of equipment in accordance with engineering principles and safety regulations.
- Manage a budget of approximately $10 million annually.
- Participate extensively in labor relations with various trades.

Planning and Construction
- Plan and install maintenance program; direct all improvement and new construction projects, from studies for justification to project startup.
- Prepared bid sheets and contracts for construction facilities.
- Represented the company as general contractor on project and saved approximately $4 million of the original estimates submitted by outside contractors.

Project Engineer, Gibralta Corporation, Loveland, CO
1992-96
- Planned and implemented modernization program, including installation of bloom, billet, bar, rod, and strip mills, as well as the required soaking pits and reheating furnaces.
- Directed a multi-craft maintenance force of approximately 250 craftsmen and supervisors.
- Planned and installed a maintenance program that reduced equipment downtime and substantially increased cost-per-thousand savings.

AFFILIATION
Member of American Iron and Steel Engineers Association

EDUCATION
University of Colorado at Boulder, Boulder, CO
B.S., Mechanical Engineering

✔ Conceptually grouping the bullets makes it easier to read and understand.

✔ Strong work history is listed first, education last.

CHAPTER 3

That Final Polish

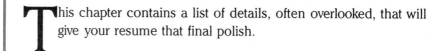

Τhis chapter contains a list of details, often overlooked, that will give your resume that final polish.

Apostrophe

A common mistake on resumes is to refer to "over five years experience in the such-and-such field." "Years" here is a type of possessive and must have an apostrophe: "five years' experience."

Capitalization

Avoid the tendency to overcapitalize. Standard editorial practice is to lowercase generic references to positions and academic courses. Specific titles may be capitalized, and, for purposes of a resume, so may college majors.

> Thus:
> **Acme Corporation**
> *Assistant Treasurer*
> Performed duties of treasurer in his absence.
>
> **Education**
> **Alma Mater University**
> *Bachelor of Arts in Accounting*
> Courses include accounting, finance, and international investment *or* Courses include Principles of Accounting, Fundamentals of Finance, and World Investment Strategies

Dates of Employment

In "1999-present" or "2000-present," "present" is lowercase. Think of it as a sentence: "Nineteen ninety-nine to present." Would you capitalize "present"?

Cum Laude

Cum laude, magna cum laude, and summa cum laude are lowercase and italic:

Bachelor of Arts in English, *summa cum laude*

Dates

In general, avoid repetition—as, for example, the "19" or "20" in dates: "1998-99" is sufficient. "1998-1999" is unnecessary, as is "1998 to 1999."

Education

"B.A. degree in . . ." is redundant. Just "B.A. in. . . ." is fine. Also, don't say "Associates degree in. . . ." or "Masters in . . . ." You may have an associate's degree or a master's degree (with apostrophe), but on a resume, you would say "Associate in [*or* of] Arts" or "Master of Arts."

Emphasis

Emphasize only what needs to be emphasized. Don't, for example, use italics or boldface for dates of employment or the city in which an employer is located. Using them for the name of an employer or your job title is fine. Similarly, in your resume heading, your name can be larger or bold, but it's unnecessary to boldface your address and telephone number. Also, blocks of capitals or italics are hard to read and are best avoided.

"Etc."

Avoid "etc." on resumes—don't expect a potential employer to imagine what else you mean. Either describe it or leave it out.

Experience

What do you call the section that describes your employment? "Career History," "Career Profile," "Employment Background," "Employment Experience," "Professional Employment," "Professional Experience," "Work Experience," "Work History"? What about just "Experience"? In addition to brevity (see Ockham's Razor, below) it

permits those without a continuous work history to legitimately include significant volunteer work. It might not be employment, but it is experience. The same applies to the other categories on the resume—for example, "Education" instead of "Educational Background."

Ockham's Razor

Ockham's (or Occam's) Razor refers to a saying by a Franciscan monk, William of Ockham (c. 1285–c. 1349): "Pluralitas non est ponenda sine necessitate," or "Entities should not be multiplied unnecessarily." This is usually applied to scientific theories, meaning that the simplest explanation is best (i.e., using the "razor" to cut away whatever is unnecessary to explain a phenomenon). In writing, the idea finds application in using the fewest number of words and the least punctuation and capitalization necessary to convey the message. More is superfluous.

This idea is the basis for the famous Rule 13 in Strunk and White's *Elements of Style:* "Omit needless words." (In recent printings, Rule 13 has inexplicably been changed to Rule 22, but it's still known to generations of students and writers—and presumably will continue to be known—as Rule 13.)

It says, "A sentence should contain no unnecessary words, a paragraph no unnecessary sentences, for the same reason that a drawing should have no unnecessary lines and a machine no unnecessary parts." This is one way writers achieve power and elegance.

Here are some examples of how Rule 13 would be applied to typical resume language.

Original	Revision
Assisted in preparation of	Assisted in preparing
Responsible for directing	Directed
Performed problem analysis and resolution activities via company help line.	Analyzed and resolved problems via help desk.
Functions performed included formatting and producing complex documents.	Formatted and produced complex documents.

APPLYING RULE 13

Note that the following examples are not just changes of format (bullets to paragraphs or vice versa) but also involve reorganizing, combining ideas, and omitting needless words for a more effective presentation.

Before

Job Placement Officer

Establish and maintain contact with various civic, cultural, and community organizations; actively participate in the development of programs designed to improve industrial and community relations through vocational training programs, OJT, and equal employment opportunities for the residents of Kensington and surrounding communities. Participate in programs, staff activities, community meetings, and conferences; prepare in-depth reports on proceedings. Establish contacts with prospective employers, union, public and private agencies, and associations to develop job opportunities for community residents. Recruit trainees from the community, and instruct them in good grooming and proper procedures for applying for a position.

After

Job Placement Officer

Establish and maintain contact with prospective employers, union, public and private agencies, and associations, to develop job opportunities for community residents. Participate in developing vocational training, on-the-job training, and equal-employment opportunities. Participate in staff activities, community meetings, and conferences; prepare in-depth reports on proceedings. Recruit trainees; instruct them in good grooming and proper procedures for applying for a position.

Before

Owner/President, Art Director/Buyer

Coordinate operations, 12-member production staff, freelance desktop publishers and illustrators. Maintain overview of works-in-progress to produce at optimum efficiency. Provide advice to personnel in designing materials to appropriately meet client needs;

Find A Computer

If you don't have access to a computer that can be used for job-hunting purposes, fear not! Places such as Kinko's Copies are open twenty-four hours and let you sign in to use a computer for about $12 per hour. This can be well worth the cost if you're typing up a quick cover letter, for example. However, if you're planning on spending a significant amount of time on the computer, you may opt to sign up to use a computer at a public library. Many libraries have a number of computers set aside for public use (including some that have Internet access). Call ahead of time to find out the library's policies.

conceptualize product; delegate staff to make decisions. Commission freelance agents by utilizing nationwide illustrator four-color manuscripts using watercolor illustrations, photography, or graphics. Act as liaison between executive personnel and staff. Budget each project; motivate artistic staff and typesetters to meet projected deadlines and remain within cost-efficient parameters. Projects include: greeting cards, care package kits, magazine fragrance inserts, cereal boxes, toy packages, coloring books (cover and contents), holographic bumper stickers, and retail store signs and logos.

After

Owner/President, Art Director/Buyer

- Coordinate operations of 12-member production staff and freelance desktop publishers and illustrators.
- Maintain overview of works-in-progress to produce at optimum efficiency.
- Provide advice to personnel in designing materials to appropriately meet client needs; conceptualize product; delegate staff to make decisions.
- Commission freelance illustrators, photographers, and graphic artists.
- Budget each project; ensure that artistic staff and typesetters meet deadlines and remain within cost parameters.

Representative projects: greeting cards, care package kits, magazine fragrance inserts, cereal boxes, toy packages, coloring books (cover and contents), holographic bumper stickers, retail store signs and logos

Remember that omitting needless words doesn't mean being sketchy about what you do.

Parentheses

Generally, avoid parentheses in a resume. Because a resume is compressed information, anything of secondary importance should be left out or rewritten to eliminate the parentheses.

Periods

On resumes, periods following elements of bulleted lists are optional. The general rule is to use periods for statements that are full sentences; otherwise not. But resumes are a hybrid form, with a telegraphic, quasi-sentence style. Therefore, either way is acceptable—but whichever way you choose, be consistent throughout the resume. With paragraphs, periods are obviously necessary.

"Responsibilities include . . ."

Starting job descriptions with "Responsibilities include . . ." or "Responsible for . . ." is usually redundant and can be eliminated. In the following example, it's also ungrammatical:

Original: Responsible for assessment, planning, implementation, and evaluation for primary-care patients.

One can assess patients and evaluate them (although what one is evaluating in this case is unclear), but one can't plan them or implement them. What is the candidate planning and implementing? What is he or she evaluating?

Besides being ungrammatical, long strings of nouns like these, though seemingly an efficient way of explaining one's responsibilities, can be hard to understand and are best avoided.

Possible revision: Assessed condition of primary-care patients. Planned and implemented services; evaluated patient outcomes.

Serial Comma

Standard editorial practice in a series of items is to use a comma after each item except the last:
Examples: Wynken, Blynken, and Nod
honor, courage, or fame

A Clear Direction

Employers like job candidates who have real interests and a clear direction. They know that if you're interested in a particular industry, company, or job, you're more likely to enjoy the position, perform well, and stay with the company.

Employers *don't* like to hear that you aren't at all discriminating—that you'll take whatever job they have available.

Slash

Avoid using a slash in place of "and" or "or"; it makes for difficult reading.

Avoid: "Planned/designed/ implemented recreational program. Evaluated/monitored new students' progress. Coached/choreographed performances. Set team goals/incentives to maximize performance."

Subheads

Following the principle of Ockham's Razor, only one form of emphasis is generally necessary in a subhead: bold, italics, or capitals. Combinations are sometimes used: bold italics or bold caps. Preferably avoid underlining, which is the typewritten designation for italics and is unnecessary on a word processor. Especially avoid it with any other form of emphasis. Also, don't use a colon after a subhead. The function of the subhead is to set off and describe what follows; the colon is unnecessary.

Generally, subheads decrease in size and weight. Rarely are more than three levels of subheads necessary. For example, one could use bold caps for the section heads (or larger bold upper- and lowercase than the subsequent head), bold upper- and lowercase for employers, and italics for job titles, with job descriptions in the roman (regular) text style.

The heads decrease in size and weight because the information decreases in importance. Therefore, the name of the company at which you were employed precedes the position you held, and the name of the university you attended precedes the degree you earned.

Summary of Qualifications

If your summary has any of the following generic statements—or anything like them—leave them out:

Over XX years' experience
Detail-oriented
Proven communications abilities
Strong interpersonal skills

Cooperative and flexible team player; equally effective working
  independently

Adapt easily to new concepts and responsibilities

Self-motivated; able to set effective priorities and implement
  decisions to achieve immediate and long-term goals and
  meet operational deadlines

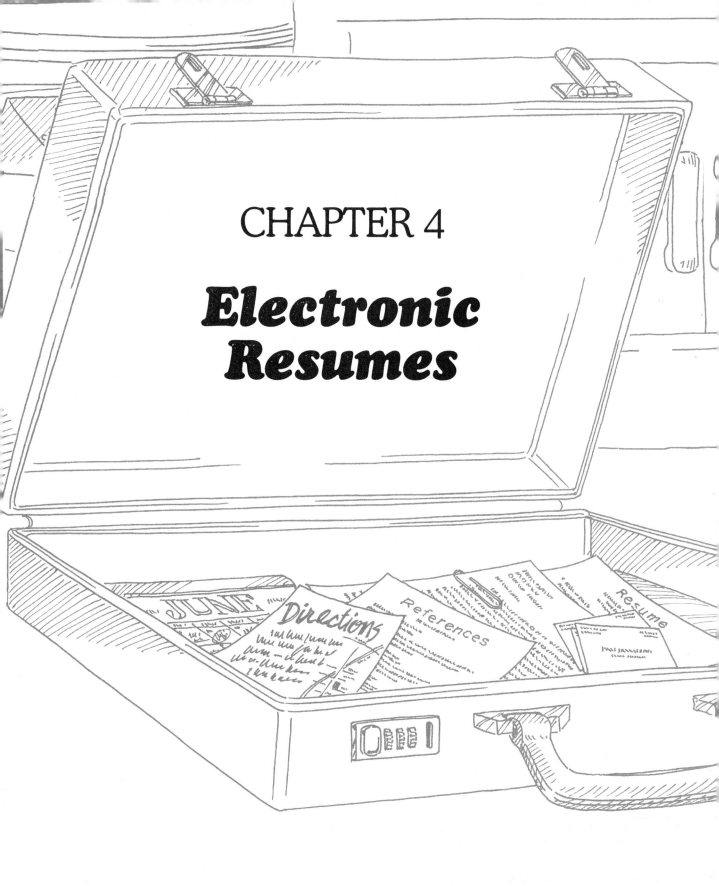

CHAPTER 4

Electronic Resumes

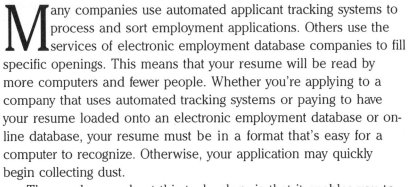

Many companies use automated applicant tracking systems to process and sort employment applications. Others use the services of electronic employment database companies to fill specific openings. This means that your resume will be read by more computers and fewer people. Whether you're applying to a company that uses automated tracking systems or paying to have your resume loaded onto an electronic employment database or on-line database, your resume must be in a format that's easy for a computer to recognize. Otherwise, your application may quickly begin collecting dust.

The good news about this technology is that it enables you to market your resume to thousands of employers quite easily. The bad news is that you must create an electronic resume in order to take advantage of the technology. An electronic resume is simply a modified version of your conventional resume.

Before you go ahead and throw out your old paper resume, be advised that not all companies stay up to speed on the latest technology. Many companies simply don't have the equipment to directly receive e-mailed resumes and search on-line databases for job candidates. Having a paper copy of your resume is still a necessity, especially since you'll need it to bring with you to all those job interviews!

Format

Keep your resume simple. The same elaborate formatting that makes your resume beautiful for the human eye to behold makes it impossible for a computer to understand.

Length

Your resume should be no longer than one page, except in unusual circumstances.

Abbreviations

Most resume scanning systems recognize a few common abbreviations, like BS, MBA, and state names, with or without periods.

Widely used acronyms for industry jargon, like A/R and A/P on an accounting resume, are also generally accepted, although it's advisable to spell out most abbreviations. If there's any question about whether an abbreviation is standard, play it safe and spell it out.

Paper

Don't bother with expensive paper. Use standard, twenty-pound, 8½- by 11-inch paper. Because your resume needs to be as sharp and legible as possible, your best bet is to use black ink on white paper.

Font

Stick to the basics; this is no time to express your creativity. Choose a nondecorative font with clear, distinct characters, like Times or Helvetica. It's more difficult for a scanner to accurately pick up decorative fonts like script. Usually the results are unintelligible letters and words.

Size

A size of 12 points is ideal. Don't go below 10 points, as type that's too small may not scan well.

Style

Most scanners will accept boldface, but if a potential employer specifically tells you to avoid it, you can substitute all capital letters. Boldface and capitals are best used only for major section headings, like "Experience" and "Education." Avoid boldface for your name, address, and telephone number. It's also best to avoid italics or underlining, since this can make the words unintelligible.

Graphics, Lines, and Shading

Avoid the temptation to use lines and graphics to liven up what is an otherwise visually uninteresting resume. A resume scanner will try to "read" graphics, lines, and shading as text, resulting in computer chaos. Also avoid nontraditional layouts, like two-column formats.

Should You Include a Cover Letter with Your Electronic Resume?

Yes. While your cover letter won't help in the initial selection process, it can distinguish you from the competition in the final rounds. If you've taken the time to craft a letter that summarizes your strongest qualifications, you'll have the edge over other contenders who skip this important step.

If you're responding to a classified ad, try to use some of the same keywords the ad mentions. And if you're sending your resume to a new networking contact, be sure to mention who referred you. Even in this anonymous electronic age, the old adage "It's not what you know but who you know" still holds true.

White Space

Don't try to compress space between letters, words, or lines to fit everything on one page—this makes it more difficult for the computer to read. Leave plenty of space between sections.

Printing

Make sure the result is letter quality. Avoid typewriters and dot matrix printers, since the quality of type they produce is inadequate for most scanners. Because your resume needs to be as sharp and legible as possible, always send an original, not a photocopy, and mail your resume rather than faxing it. For the same reason, in the unlikely event your resume is longer than one page, don't staple the pages together.

Content

The information you include in your electronic resume doesn't really differ from a traditional resume—it's simply the manner in which you present it that changes. Traditionally, resumes include action verbs, like "managed," "coordinated," or "developed." Now, employers are more likely to do keyword searches filled with nouns, like degree held or software you're familiar with. Personal traits are rarely used in keyword searches by employers, but when they are, traits like team player, creative, and problem-solving are among the most common.

Keywords

Using the right keywords or key phrases in your resume is critical. Keyword searches tend to focus on nouns. Let's say an employer searches an employment database for a sales representative with the following keyword criteria: sales representative, BS/BA, exceeded quota, cold calls, high energy, willing to travel. Even if you have the right qualifications, if you don't use these keywords on your resume, the computer will pass over your application. To complicate matters further, different employers search for different keywords.

These are usually buzzwords common to your field or industry that describe your experience, education, skills, and abilities.

Although there is no way to know for sure which keywords employers are most likely to search for, you can make educated guesses. Check help-wanted advertisements for job openings in your field. What terms do employers commonly use to describe their requirements? Job seekers in your field are another source, as are executive recruiters who specialize in your field. You'll want to use as many keywords in your resume as possible, but keep in mind that using the same keyword five times won't increase your chances of getting matched with an employer. Note, however, that if you're posting your resume to a job hunting Web site, a small number of such sites rank resumes by the number of keywords and their frequency of occurrence. Your best bet is to find out ahead of time by reading the information on the site.

Name

Your name should appear at the top of the resume, with your address, telephone number, and e-mail address immediately underneath.

Keyword Summary

This is a compendium of your qualifications, usually written in a series of succinct keyword phrases that immediately follow your name and address. Place the most important words first on the list, since the computer may be limited in the number of words it will read.

Objective

As with traditional resumes, including a job objective is advisable only in certain circumstances. (See Chapter 1 [**Resumes**].) If you choose to use a job objective, try to keep it general, so as not to limit your opportunities. After all, while the computer does the initial screening, your resume will eventually be seen by a human hiring manager. Your objective should express a general interest in a particular field or industry ("an entry-level position in advertising")

What Is HTML?

HTML (hypertext markup language) is the text formatting language used to publish information on the World Wide Web. With HTML, you can format your resume on the Web the way you did on paper, using different fonts, sizes, boldface, italics, and so on. Otherwise it would appear just as lines of unformatted text.

but should not designate a specific job title ("a position as a senior agency recruitment specialist"). Include a few keywords in the objective, to increase your chances of getting matched ("a position as a financial analyst where I can utilize my on-the-job experience and MBA").

Experience and Achievements

Your professional experience should immediately follow the key-word summary, beginning with your most recent position. (If you're a recent college graduate, list your education before your experience.) Be sure your job title, employer, location, and dates of employment are all clearly displayed. Highlight your accomplishments and key responsibilities with dashes (in place of bullets) on an electronic resume. Again, try to incorporate as many buzzwords as possible into these phrases.

Education

This section immediately follows the experience section. List your degrees, licenses, permits, certifications, relevant course work, and academic awards or honors. Be sure to clearly display the names of the schools, locations, and years of graduation. List any professional organizations or associations you're a member of; many recruiters will include such organizations when doing a keyword search.

References

Don't waste valuable space with statements like "References available upon request." Although this was standard fare for resumes of old, it won't win you any points on an electronic resume.

Personal Data

Don't include personal data, like your birthdate, marital status, or information regarding your hobbies and interests. Since it's unlikely these sections would include any keywords, they're only taking up space, and the computer will pass right over them.

Circulating Your Electronic Resume

Once you've designed a computer-friendly resume, you can circulate it in three ways. The first is to send it to a company with an in-house resume database or applicant tracking system. Whenever there's an opening, the hiring manager submits a search request, which generally includes a job description and a list of keywords. An operator searches the database to come up with viable candidates.

The second way is to send your resume to an electronic employment database service. When outside companies need candidates for a job opening, they contact the service and provide a list of qualifications (or keywords) the position requires. The service then searches the database (using a keyword search) to find suitable candidates.

The third way is to post your resume via the Internet, either by e-mail, to an on-line database service (this is the same as an electronic employment database service, except that you send your resume electronically rather than by mail), a site on the World Wide Web, a commercial on-line service (like America Online or CompuServe), or a newsgroup. Another option is to create a resume in HTML and post it to special sites on the Web that accept HTML resumes. You can even design your own home page for potential employers to visit. (For more information on using the Internet as a job search tool, see Chapter 6 [**Internet Job Search**].)

An Electronic Resume for Scanning

On page 54 is an example of an electronic resume for scanning containing no bullets, italics, or underlining. All text begins flush left, with spaces between paragraphs and sections. Boldface is usually acceptable, but if not, capital letters may be substituted.

An Electronic Request for E-mail

On page 55 is the same resume prepared for e-mail. Remember that each line must be **sixty-five characters or less.**

Cover Letters by E-mail

Omit a cover letter only if the ad to which you are responding says to. Send your cover letter in the same e-mail as your resume (preceding it, of course), and be as attentive to your grammar and spelling as with a paper cover letter. Because this way of sending information is so quick, more and more jobseekers are forgetting that the same rules apply. Sloppy cover letters via e-mail will be viewed just as poorly as sloppy work sent by regular mail.

An Electronic Resume for Scanning

Michael S. Dipenstein
27 Pageant Drive, Apartment 7
Cambridge, MA 02138
(617) 555-5555

KEYWORD SUMMARY
Accounting manager with seven years' experience in general ledger, accounts payable, and financial reporting. MBA in Management. Windows, Lotus 1-2-3, and Excel.

PROFESSIONAL EXPERIENCE
COLWELL CORPORATION, Wellesley, MA

Accounting Manager   1996–present

Manage a staff of six in general ledger and accounts payable. Responsible for the design and refinement of financial reporting package. Assist in month-end closings.

Established guidelines for month-end closing procedures, speeding up closing by five business days.

FRANKLIN AND DELANY COMPANY, Melrose, MA

Senior Accountant   1994–96

Managed accounts payable, general ledger, transaction processing, and financial reporting. Supervised staff of two.

Developed management reporting package, including variance reports and cash flow reporting.

Staff Accountant   1993–94

Managed accounts payable, including vouchering, cash disbursements, and bank reconciliation. Wrote and issued policies. Trained new employees.

EDUCATION
MBA in Management, Northeastern University, Boston, MA, 1995
BS in Accounting, Boston College, Boston, MA, 1993

ASSOCIATIONS
National Association of Accountants

An Electronic Resume for E-mail

Michael S. Dipenstein
27 Pageant Drive, Apartment 7
Cambridge, MA 02138
(617) 555-5555

KEYWORD SUMMARY
Accounting manager with seven years' experience in general ledger,
accounts payable, and financial reporting. MBA in Management.
Proficient in Windows, Lotus 1-2-3, and Excel.

PROFESSIONAL EXPERIENCE
COLWELL CORPORATION, Wellesley, MA

Accounting Manager   1996 - present

Manage a staff of six in general ledger and accounts payable.
Responsible for the design and refinement of financial reporting
package. Assist in month-end closings.

Established guidelines for month-end closing procedures, speeding up
closing by five business days.

FRANKLIN AND DELANY COMPANY, Melrose, MA

Senior Accountant   1994 - 96

Managed accounts payable, general ledger, transaction processing, and
financial reporting. Supervised staff of two.

Developed management reporting package, including variance reports and
cash flow reporting.

Staff Accountant   1993 - 94

Managed accounts payable, including vouchering, cash disbursements, and
bank reconciliation. Wrote and issued policies. Trained new employees.

EDUCATION
MBA in Management, Northeastern University, Boston, MA, 1995
BS in Accounting, Boston College, Boston, MA, 1993

ASSOCIATIONS
National Association of Accountants

Applicant Tracking Systems

As the name implies, applicant tracking systems, or in-house resume databases, are used by companies to keep track of the hordes of resumes they receive. Many companies, especially large, well-known companies, can receive two hundred resumes per week. Where once these unsolicited resumes may have headed straight for a filing cabinet or even the trash, never to be looked at again, electronic applicant tracking systems now allow employers to keep resumes in an active file.

Basically, here's how it works: a company receives your resume, either unsolicited, through a career fair, or in response to a classified advertisement. Your resume is scanned into the computer, dated, coded, and placed into the appropriate file (like administrative, financial, or technical). Other systems may simply sort resumes according to date received.

When there's a job opening, the hiring manager submits a search request to the database operator, who is usually someone in human resources or information systems. The database operator performs a keyword search to find resumes that match the criteria.

Electronic Employment Databases

An electronic employment database is simply an applicant tracking system operated by an independent commercial firm. The procedure for submitting resumes to these services varies, and most charge a nominal fee, usually $30–50. But what you get for your money is fabulous: nationwide exposure to hundreds of companies of all sizes, from Fortune 500 to smaller, rapidly expanding companies.

In many ways, an electronic resume database is similar to a traditional employment agency: you send in your resume to a service, and the service begins working to find a job for you. However, with an electronic employment "agency," you are, theoretically, in the running for every job request that comes in.

Posting Your Resume Via the Internet

To remain truly competitive, your resume needs to be in a plain-text format you can send to employers and on-line databases electronically through cyberspace.

Converting Your Resume to a Plain-Text File

An electronic resume is sparsely formatted but is filled with keywords and important facts. If you've already prepared a resume that's computer-friendly, you don't have far to go to be able to post your resume on the Internet. A plain-text resume is the next step.

Instead of a Microsoft Word, WordPerfect, or other word processing document, save your resume as a plain-text, DOS, or ASCII file. These three terms are basically interchangeable; different software will use different terms. These words describe text at its simplest, most basic level, without formatting like boldface or italics. Furthermore, an ASCII document appears on the recipient's screen as left-aligned. If you have e-mail, your messages are written and received in this format. By converting your resume to a plain-text file, you can be assured it will be readable, regardless of where you send it.

Before you attempt to create your own plain-text resume, study the resumes on the on-line databases. This will give you a good idea of what a plain-text resume looks like and will help you create your own.

Following are the basic steps for creating a plain-text resume. The particulars of the process will differ, depending on what type of computer system and software you're using:

1. Remove all formatting from your resume. This includes boldface, italics, underlining, bullets, different font sizes, lines, and any and all graphics. To highlight certain parts of your resume, like education or experience, you may use capital letters. You can also use hyphens (-) or asterisks (*) to

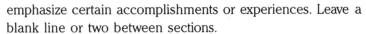

What Is ASCII?

ASCII stands for American Standard Code for Information Interchange and is pronounced *"Ask-ee."* ASCII is a code that virtually all computers can understand. It was invented to allow different types of computers to exchange information easily.

emphasize certain accomplishments or experiences. Leave a blank line or two between sections.

2. Save your resume as a plain-text file. Most word processing programs, like Word and WordPerfect, have a "Save As" feature that allows you to save files in different formats. Some of your options in Word for Windows, for instance, are saving a document as a Word document, a text-only document, or a WordPerfect document. Many programs, like Word, don't specifically give you an "ASCII" option; in these programs, choose "Text Only" or "Plain Text." In Word, plain-text files have the extension ".txt."

3. After saving your resume as a plain-text file, check the document with the text editor that most computers have. In Windows, use Notepad. Open the file to be sure your margins look right and that you don't have extra spaces between lines or letters. If parts of the text are garbled, with a group of strange characters, it most likely means you forgot to take out some formatting. A resume with a lot of formatting is likely to end up looking like hieroglyphics if it's read as a plain-text file. If this happens, go back to your original document and repeat the process.

4. Be sure all the lines contain sixty-five characters or fewer. This includes all spacing, letters, and punctuation. Often you will need to go through your entire resume line by line, counting each space, letter, punctuation, asterisk, and so forth. You may need to manually insert hard returns where the lines are longer than sixty-five characters. This may seem trivial, but it's actually extremely important. While some computers may recognize as many as seventy-five characters per line, the majority cannot recognize more than sixty-five characters.

5. Finally, e-mail your resume to yourself or a friend to test the file. Be sure it stays intact, that no extra spaces or returns are inserted during transmission, and that all text appears readable. If something doesn't look right, go back to your text editor, fix the problem, and test the resume again before e-mailing it to any companies or posting it to on-line databases.

E-mail

E-mailing your resume to potential employers is generally done in response to a help-wanted advertisement or simply as a method of direct contact. In fact, many companies now request that resumes be submitted through e-mail, rather than the U.S. mail or by fax machine. Some job listings that you find on the Internet, particularly for technical positions, include only an e-mail address for contact information; no street address or telephone number is provided. And with many companies, you can e-mail your resume directly into their in-house resume database. This eliminates the concern that it will be found unreadable by a computerized resume scanner. When e-mailing, paste your resume into the body of the message; many companies won't open an attachment because of the possibility that it may contain a computer virus.

After e-mailing your resume, wait a few days to be sure the recipient has read it. Call or e-mail the company to confirm that your resume was received intact. As with a paper resume, an e-mailed resume may do you little good unless you follow up to express your genuine interest. If you sent your resume to an individual, ask if he or she would like you to elaborate on any sections of your resume. If you sent it to a general e-mail address, call the human resources department to check the status of your application.

On-line Resume Databases

On-line resume databases are similar to electronic employment databases. Cyberspace offers three main areas for resume posting: the World Wide Web, commercial on-line services, and Usenet newsgroups. These sites range from the general *www.hotresume.com* to the specific *www.medsearch.com*. Of the three areas, you'll find the most options on the Web. Virtually all the major job-search sites on the Web, like Monster.com and E-Span, offer resume databases. One major database service, the Worldwide Resume/Talent Bank, is accessible through both the Internet and America Online. The Web

Confidentiality

Many job seekers are wary of on-line resume database services because of issues of confidentiality. When your resume is on-line, it's accessible to virtually anyone with a computer and an Internet connection. This includes personal information like your name, address, telephone number, and other details. This lack of control over who sees their resume worries many job seekers. You may receive phone calls or e-mail messages from companies, organizations, and individuals you have absolutely no interest in.

However, the biggest concern to most job seekers is, what if one of those twenty million people cruising the Internet happens to be your boss? Many services offer safeguards to ensure that this doesn't happen.

(continued on next page)

also contains dozens of other sites for resume posting, including the only sites where you can post HTML resumes.

Bulletin Board Systems (BBSs), Gopher, and Telnet aren't generally considered destinations for resume posting and are best used to find job listings or gather information on specific industries and employers. While you may post resumes to most Bulletin Board Systems, they're not an efficient way to circulate your resume. For this reason, you're better off sticking to sites on the Web and Usenet newsgroups.

Major Resume Sites on the Web

Following are just some of the major job-search sites on the Web. These listings discuss only these sites' resume posting capabilities; their job listings are discussed in Chapter 6 [**Internet Job Search**].

Unlike Usenet newsgroup databases, resume posting sites on the Web typically contain resumes from job seekers everywhere, which means that thousands of employers search the databases for potential candidates. For this reason, it's a good idea to add a line to your resume stating whether you're willing to relocate.

CareerCity *www.careercity.com* is "The Web's Big Career Site" giving job hunters access to tens of thousands of jobs via three search engines: its own CareerCity jobs database; a newsgroup job-search engine covering hundreds of newsgroups; and addresses, phone numbers, descriptions, and hot links to 27,000 major U.S. employers. You'll find access to thousands of executive search firms and employment agencies, comprehensive salary surveys for all fields, and directories of associations and other industry resources. CareerCity's easy-to-use resume database gives job seekers the opportunity to market their qualifications free to employers subscribing to the database. The site is filled with hundreds of articles on getting started, changing careers, job interviews, resumes, cover letters, and more.

CareerMart *www.careermart.com* features its "Resume Bank" which offers free resume postings to job seekers, and its "E-mail Agent" which automatically notifies you when new positions crop up. Run by BSA Advertising, the site offers links to more than four hundred major employers and some seven hundred colleges and universities. Resumes should be submitted as text files.

CareerMosaic *www.careermosaic.com* has a database called ResumeCM, which contains resumes from job seekers in all geographic areas and occupations. Besides the database on the Web, it also indexes the most popular Usenet newsgroups and automatically adds your resume to their databases. Unlike most databases, ResumeCM also allows employers to conduct a full-text search of your resume instead of searching only subject lines.

Career Shop *www.careershop.com* has a site produced by TenKey Interactive which enables you to post your resume and also e-mail it directly to employers, free. Career Shop also offers a jobs database and allows employers who register with them to search the resume database free.

CareerSite *www.careersite.com* is a free service of Virtual Resources Corporation. CareerSite's resume database allows you to submit your resume as a fully formatted document. You simply fill in some fields on-line to summarize your credentials. Information is presented to participating employers without your name and address, and your resume isn't released to a company without your consent—a great relief to job seekers concerned with confidentiality.

E-Span's JobOptions

www.joboptions.com/esp/plsql/espan_enter.espan_home is available to thousands of employers. E-Span's JobOptions Resume Database allows you to enter your resume data into a section that formats the information for you, or you may paste in your resume as a plain text file.

(continued from previous page)

The resume posting site *Monster.com,* for example, hides your personal information from employers until after they've purchased access to your resume. Some allow you to submit names of companies you'd prefer not receive your resume. Others will contact you to get your permission before forwarding your resume or employment profile to a company. Still others allow you to join the database anonymously—that is, your name, company names, education, and other identifying characteristics won't be shown to prospective employers. There are also a number of Web sites that don't offer these safeguards, so you'll want to check with your service to determine its particular policy.

A Word of Caution

Before writing a check or giving your credit card number to a company over the Internet, it's a good idea to check its reputation with the Better Business Bureau or a similar agency. While the majority of companies selling services over the Internet are reputable, remember that simply because a company has a presence on the Internet doesn't mean it's legitimate.

Monster.com *www.monster.com* has its Resume On-Line Database that allows you to paste either plain text or HTML resumes. Monster.com protects applicants by keeping their personal information, including name and address, separated from the resume. Employers can access that information only after they've purchased the resume.

CHAPTER 5

Cover Letters

Your cover letter, like your resume, is a marketing tool. Too many cover letters are merely an additional piece of paper accompanying a resume, saying "Enclosed please find my resume." Like effective advertisements, effective cover letters attract an employer's attention by highlighting the most attractive features of the product. Begin by learning how to create an effective sales pitch. As with resumes, both the format and the content of your cover letter are important.

Format

Before reading a word of your cover letter, a potential employer has already made an assessment of your organizational skills and attention to detail simply by observing its appearance. How your correspondence looks to a reader can mean the difference between serious consideration and dismissal. You can't afford to settle for a less than perfect presentation of your credentials. This chapter outlines the basic format you should follow when writing a cover letter and shows you how to put the finishing touches on a top-notch product.

The Parts of a Letter

Your cover letter may be printed on the highest-quality paper and typed on a state-of-the-art computer, but if it isn't arranged according to the proper format, you won't come across as a credible candidate. Certain guidelines apply when composing any letter.

Either of two styles may be used for cover letters: business style (sometimes called block style) or personal style. The only difference between them is that in business style, all the elements of the letter—the return address, salutation, body, and complimentary close—begin at the left margin. In personal style, the return address and complimentary close begin at the centerline of the page, and paragraphs are indented.

Return Address

Your return address should appear at the top margin, without your name, either flush left or beginning at the centerline, depending on whether you're using business style or personal style.

As a rule, avoid abbreviations in the addresses of your cover letter, although abbreviating the state is acceptable. Include your phone number if you're not using letterhead that contains it or it doesn't appear in the last paragraph of the letter. The idea is to make sure contact information is on both the letter and the resume, in case they get separated in the hiring manager's office (this happens more often than you would expect!).

Date

The date appears two lines below your return address, either flush left or centered, depending on which style you're using. Write out the date; don't abbreviate. *Example:* October 12, 2000.

Inside Address

Four lines beneath the date, give the addressee's full name. On subsequent lines, give the person's title, the company's name, and the company's address. Occasionally, the person's full title or the company's name and address will be very long and can appear awkward on the usual number of lines. In this case, you can use an extra line.

The text of the letter below the date should be centered approximately vertically on the page, so if your letter is short, you can begin the inside address six or even eight lines down. If the letter is long, two lines is acceptable.

Salutation

The salutation should be typed two lines beneath the company's address. It should begin "Dear Mr." or "Dear Ms.," followed by the individual's last name and a colon. Even if you've previously spoken with an addressee who has asked to be called by his or her first name, never use a first name in the salutation. In some cases, as when responding to "blind" advertisements, a general salutation may be necessary. In such circumstances, "Dear Sir or Madam" is appropriate, followed by a colon.

Length

Three or four short paragraphs on one page is ideal. A longer letter may not be read.

Design a Letterhead

If you have a computer, you can design a letterhead for yourself and save it in a file to use for cover letters and other correspondence. Include your name, address, telephone, and e-mail, if you have it. Experiment to find an attractive design that's different from the way this information looks on your resume. If you want typefaces other than the default fonts that come with the computer, a CD-ROM containing several thousand fonts is available in software stores for about $15. However, avoid anything too flashy for business correspondence.

Enclosure

An enclosure line is used primarily in formal or official correspondence. It's not wrong to include it in a cover letter, but it's unnecessary.

Paper Size

As with your resume, use standard 8½- by 11-inch paper. A smaller size will appear more personal than professional and is easily lost in an employer's files; a larger size will look awkward and may be discarded for not fitting with other documents.

Paper Color and Quality

The same suggestions in Chapter 1 [**Resumes**] about paper for resumes also apply to cover letters. Remember to use matching paper for both your resume, cover letter, and envelope.

Typing and Printing

Your best bet is to use a word processing program on a computer with a letter-quality printer. Handwritten letters are not acceptable. You will generally want to use the same typeface and size that you used on your resume. As discussed in Chapter 1 [**Resumes**], remember that serif typefaces are generally easier to read.

Don't try the cheap and easy ways, like photocopying the body of your letter and typing in the inside address and salutation. Such letters will not be taken seriously.

Envelope

Mail your cover letter and resume in a standard, business-sized envelope that matches your stationery. Unless your handwriting is *extremely* neat and easy to read, type your envelopes. Address your envelope, by full name and title, specifically to the contact person you identified in your cover letter.

Content
Personalize Each Letter

If you are *not* responding to a job posting that specifies a contact name, try to determine the appropriate person to whom you should address your cover letter. (In general, the more influential the person, the better.) Try to contact the head of the department in which you're interested. This will be easiest in mid-sized and small companies, where the head of the department is likely to have an active role in the initial screening. If you're applying to a larger corporation, your application will probably be screened by the human resources department. If you're instructed to direct your inquiry to this division, try to find out the name of the senior human resources manager. This may cut down on the number of hands through which your resume passes on its way to the final decision-maker. At any rate, be sure to include your contact's name and title on both your letter and the envelope. This way, even if a new person occupies the position, your letter should get through.

Mapping It Out

A cover letter need not be longer than three or four paragraphs. Two of them, the first and last, can be as short as one sentence. The idea of the cover letter is not to repeat what's in the resume. The idea is to give an overview of your capabilities and show why you're a good candidate for the job. The best way to distinguish yourself is to highlight one or two of your accomplishments or abilities. Stressing only one or two increases your chances of being remembered.

Be sure it's clear from your letter why you have an interest in the company—*so many candidates apply for jobs with no apparent knowledge of what the company does!* This conveys the message that they just want any job. Indicating an interest doesn't mean you should tell every employer you have a burning desire to work at that company, because these statements are easy to make and invariably sound insincere. Indicating how your qualifications or experience meet their requirements may be sufficient to show why you're applying.

First paragraph. State the position for which you're applying. If you're responding to an ad or listing, mention the source.

Don't Philosophize

Don't:

*"Dear Ms. Sampson:
Finding the right person for the job is often difficult, costly, and at times disappointing. However, if you are in need of a reliable individual for your management staff, I have the qualifications and dedication for the position. . . ."*

Do:

*"Dear Ms. Sampson:
I would like to apply for the position of marketing manager advertised in the Sunday Planet."*

The Comedian and the Chemist

Tone may vary somewhat according to profession: a comedian and a chemist would choose dissimilar tones. While it would be perfectly fitting for a comedian to adopt a lighthearted, familiar tone, the chemist would be best served by a more formal voice. Err on the side of caution, for there may be a lot of comedians out there, but there aren't many applying to be one.

Example: "I would like to apply for the position of research assistant advertised in the *Sunday Planet*" (or "listed on the Internet").

Second paragraph. Indicate what you could contribute to this company and show how your qualifications will benefit them. If you're responding to an ad or listing, discuss how your skills relate to the job's requirements. Don't talk about what you can't do. Remember, keep it brief! *Example:* "In addition to my strong background in mathematics, I offer significant business experience, having worked in a data processing firm, a bookstore, and a restaurant. I am sure that my courses in statistics and computer programming would prove particularly useful in the position of trainee."

Third paragraph. If possible, show how you not only meet but exceed their requirements—why you're not just an average candidate but a superior one. Mention any noteworthy accomplishments, high-profile projects, instances where you went above and beyond the call of duty, or awards you've received for your work. If you have testimonials, commendations, or evaluations that are particularly complimentary, you may want to quote a sentence from one or two of them. *Example:* "In a letter to me, Dewayne Berry, president of NICAP Inc., said, 'Your ideas were instrumental to our success with this project.' "

Fourth paragraph. Close by saying you look forward to hearing from them. If you wish, you can also thank them for their consideration. Don't ask for an interview. If they're interested, they'll call. If not, asking won't help. Don't tell them you'll call them—many ads say "No phone calls." If you haven't heard anything in one or two weeks, a call is acceptable.

Complimentary Close. The complimentary close should be two lines beneath the body of the letter, aligned with your return address and the date. Keep it simple—"Sincerely" followed by a comma, suffices. Three lines under this, type your full name as it appears on your resume. Sign above your typed name in black ink.

Don't forget to sign the letter! As silly as it sounds, people often forget this seemingly obvious detail. An oversight like this suggests you don't take care with your work. To avoid this implication if you're faxing the letter and resume directly from your computer, you can type your name directly below the complimentary close, without any intervening space. Then follow up with a hard copy of the

resume and the signed letter, with your name typed in the traditional place under the signature.

Tips for Successful Cover Letters
What Writing Style Is Appropriate?

Adopt a polite, formal style that balances your confidence in yourself with respect for the employer. Keep the style clear, objective, and persuasive rather than narrative. Don't waste space boasting instead of presenting relevant qualifications.

Example: "In addition to a Bachelor of Arts degree in Business Administration, I recently received a Master's, *cum laude*, in International Marketing from Brown University. This educational experience is supported by two years' part-time experience with J&D Products, where my marketing efforts resulted in increased annual product sales of 25 percent."

Tone: Reserved Confidence Is Always in Style

Think of how you'd sell your qualifications in a job interview. You'd probably think harder about what to say and how to say it than in an informal conversation. Above all, you'd want to sound polite, confident, and professional. Adopt a similar tone in your cover letter. It should immediately communicate confidence in your abilities. The trick is to sound enthusiastic without becoming melodramatic. Take, for example, the candidate who expressed his desire to enter the advertising field as "the single most important thing I have ever wanted in my entire twenty-three years of existence." The candidate who was actually offered the position began her letter as follows: "My extensive research into the industry, coupled with my internship and education, have confirmed my interest in pursuing an entry-level position in advertising."

Emphasize Concrete Examples

Your resume details the duties you've performed in your jobs. In contrast, your cover letter should highlight your most significant

---

Don't Be Longwinded

Don't:

"Please accept the enclosed resume as an expressed interest in contributing relevant experience to the position of Sales Representative, as advertised in the Pittsburgh Post-Gazette, *on Wednesday, April 11."*

Do:

"I would like to apply for the position of sales representative advertised in the Pittsburgh Post-Gazette.*"*

accomplishments. Instead of stating something like "My career is highlighted by several major achievements," use concrete examples:

"While Sales Manager at Shayko Chicken, I supervised a team that increased revenues by 35 percent in 18 months."

"I published four articles in *The Magical Bullet Newsletter*."

"At MUFON Corporation, I advanced from telephone fundraiser to field manager to canvassing director within two years."

List tangible, relevant skills rather than personal attributes. A sentence like "I am fluent in C+, Pascal, and COBOL" is a good substitute for a vague statement like "I am a goal-oriented, highly skilled computer programmer." Avoid using "etc."—don't expect a potential employer to imagine what else you mean. Either describe it or leave it out.

Use Powerful Language

Your language should be hard-hitting and easy to understand. Your message should be expressed using the fewest words possible. As with your resume, make your letters interesting by using action verbs like "designed," "implemented," and "increased," rather than passive verbs like "was" and "did." Use simple, common language and avoid abbreviations and slang. Change "Responsible for directing" to "Directed" if appropriate. Also steer clear of language that's too technical or jargon-heavy. The first person who reads your cover letter may not possess the same breadth of knowledge as your future boss.

Avoid Catchphrases

The same suggestions in Chapter 1 [**Resumes**] about avoiding catch phrases in resumes also apply to cover letters.

Mention Personal Preferences?

Candidates often worry if, and how, they should include salary requirements and availability to travel or relocate. Refrain from offering salary information unless the advertisement you are responding to requires it. If you must include salary requirements, give a salary range rather than a number. Another option is to simply indicate that salary concerns are negotiable.

If you're applying to an out-of-state firm, indicate a willingness to relocate; otherwise, a hiring manager may question your purpose in writing and may not take the initiative to inquire.

Proof with Care

Mistakes can be embarrassing, so proofread carefully, following the suggestions in Chapter 1 [**Resumes**] for proofreading your resume.

Cover Letter Blunders to Avoid

The following discussion focuses on examples that have been adapted from real-life cover letters. Although some of these blunders may seem obvious, they occur far more often than one might think. Needless to say, none of the inquiries that included these mistakes met with positive results.

Unrelated Career Goals

Tailor your cover letter to the position you're applying for. A hiring manager is only interested in what you can do for the company, not what you hope to accomplish for yourself. Convey a genuine interest in the position and a long-term pledge to fulfilling its duties.

Example A (wrong way): "While my true goal is to become a professional dancer, I am exploring the option of taking on proof-reading work while continuing to train for the Boston Ballet's next audition."

Example B (right way): "I am very interested in this proof-reading position, and I am confident of my ability to make a long-term contribution to your capable staff."

Comparisons and Clichés

Avoid clichés and obvious comparisons. These expressions detract from your letter's purpose: to highlight your most impressive skills and accomplishments.

Cover Letter Do's and Don'ts

Do be sure your phone number and address are on the letter, just in case it gets separated from your resume (this happens!).

Do keep the letter brief and to the point.

Do accentuate what you can offer the company, not what you hope to gain from them.

Do make sure the water-mark reads correctly.

Do be sure your letter is error free.

Do sign your letter with blue or black ink (or type your name if you're sending it electronically).

Don't just repeat information verbatim from your resume.

Don't overuse the personal pronoun "I."

Don't send a generic cover letter.

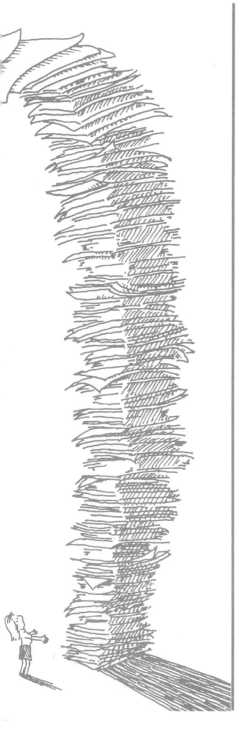

Examples of what not to do:

"My word processor runs like the wind."

"I am a people person."

"Teamwork is my middle name."

"Your company is known as the crème de la crème of accounting firms."

"I am as smart as a whip."

"Among the responses you receive for this position, I hope my qualifications make me leader of the pack."

Wasted Space

Since cover letters are generally four paragraphs long, every word of every sentence should be directly related to your purpose for writing. In other words, if you are applying for a position as a chemist, include only those skills and experiences most applicable to that field. Any other information weakens your application.

Examples of what not to do:

"As my enclosed resume reveals, I possess the technical experience and educational background to succeed as your newest civil engineer. In addition, I am a certified gymnastics instructor who has won several local competitions."

"I am writing in response to your advertisement for an accounting clerk. Currently, I am finishing an associate degree at Peacock Junior College. My courses have included medieval architecture, film theory, basic home surgery, and nutrition."

Form Letters

Mass mailings, in which you send a form letter to a large number of employers, are not recommended. This approach doesn't allow you to personalize each application. Every cover letter you write should be tailored to the position you're seeking and should demonstrate your commitment to a specific industry and familiarity with each employer. Mass mailings may indicate to a hiring manager that you're not truly interested in joining that organization.

Inappropriate Stationery

White and ivory are the only acceptable paper colors for a cover letter. Also, don't rely on graphics to "improve" your cover letter; let your qualifications speak for themselves. If you're a cat enthusiast, don't use stationery with images of favorite felines. If you're a musician, don't send a letter decorated with a border of musical notes and instruments.

"Amusing" Anecdotes

Imagine yourself in an interview setting. Since you don't know your interviewer, you wouldn't joke with him or her until you determined what demeanor was appropriate. Similarly, when writing, remain polite and professional.

Erroneous Company Information

If you were the employer, would you want to hire a candidate who confuses your company's products and services or misquotes recent activities? To avoid such errors, verify the accuracy of any company information you mention in your cover letter. On the other hand, if you haven't researched the company, don't bluff. Statements like "I know something about your company" or "I am familiar with your products" signal to an employer that you haven't done your homework.

Desperation

In your cover letter, sound determined, not desperate. While an employer appreciates enthusiasm, he or she may be turned off by a desperate plea for employment. However, a fine line often separates the two.

Examples of what not to do:

"I am desperately eager to start, as I have been out of work for six months."

"Please call today! I'll be waiting by the phone."

Next Candidate, Please

Certain formats and phrases signal an employer that you're using a form letter. Some job candidates turn this blunder into an art. In one real-life example, a candidate created a form letter with blank spaces where he penned in the employer's name and position applied for.

Another applicant who was indecisive about her field of interest created a list of possible positions in her letter. She then circled the most appropriate job description, depending on the company.

Don't Give Your Life Story

Don't:

"Six years ago, I started a career in nursing. I subsequently left to manage the division of a company and later resigned from this lucrative position to pursue my first career, nursing."

Do:

"I have several years' nursing experience and significant business management experience. I am sure that this background would make me well qualified for the Nursing Home Director position."

"I really, really need this job to pay off medical bills."

"I AM VERY BADLY IN NEED OF MONEY!"

Personal Photos

Unless you're seeking employment in modeling, acting, or other performing arts, it's inappropriate to send a photograph.

Confessed Shortcomings

Some job seekers mistakenly call attention to their weaknesses in their cover letters, hoping to ward off an employer's objections. This is a mistake, because the letter emphasizes your flaws rather than your strengths.

Examples of what not to do:

"Although I have no related experience, I remain very interested in the management consultant position."

"I may not be well qualified for this position, but it has always been my dream to work in the publishing field."

Misrepresentation

In any stage of the job-search process, never, *ever*, misrepresent yourself. In many companies, erroneous information contained in a cover letter or resume will be grounds for dismissal if the inaccuracy is discovered. Protect yourself by sticking to the facts. You're selling your skills and accomplishments in your cover letter. If you achieve something, say so, and put it in the best possible light. Don't hold back or be modest—no one else will. At the same time, don't exaggerate to the point of misrepresentation.

Examples of what not to do:

"In June, I graduated with honors from American University. In the course of my studies, I played two varsity sports while concurrently holding five jobs."

"Since beginning my career four years ago, I have won hundreds of competitions and awards and am considered by many to be the best hairstylist on the east coast."

Demanding Statements

Your cover letter should demonstrate what you can do for an employer, not what he or she can do for you. For example, instead of stating "I am looking for a unique opportunity in which I will be adequately challenged and compensated," say "I am confident I could make a significant contribution to your organization, specifically by expanding your customer base in the northwest and instituting a discount offer for new accounts." Also, since you're requesting an employer's consideration, your letter shouldn't include personal preferences or demands. Statements like "It would be an overwhelmingly smart idea for you to hire me" or "Let's meet next Wednesday at 4:00 P.M., when I will be available to discuss my candidacy further" come across as presumptuous. Job candidates' demands are rarely met with an enthusiastic response.

Missing Resume

Have you ever forgotten to enclose all the materials you refer to in your cover letter? This is a fatal oversight. No employer is going to take the time to remind you of your mistake; he or she has already moved on to the next application.

Personal Information

The same suggestions in Chapter 1 [**Resumes**] about personal information in resumes also apply to cover letters.

Choice of Pronouns

Your cover letter necessarily requires a thorough discussion of your qualifications. Although some applicants might choose the third person ("he or she") as a creative approach to presenting their qualifications, potential employers sometimes find this disconcerting. In general, using the first person ("I") is preferable.

Example A (wrong way): "Bambi Berenbeam is a highly qualified public relations executive with over seven years of relevant

Don't Be Grandiose

Don't:

"As a recent graduate of Mitzelflick University with a degree in Biology, I am currently launching my career as an environmental campaigner in hopes of reversing global warming and ozone depletion on a world-wide basis. . . ."

Do:

"I would like to apply for the position of environmental campaigner due to my strong interest in many environmental causes."

More Cover Letter Don'ts

Following are some actual real-life examples, sent by job seekers, that illustrate what NOT to write in your cover letter:

"I am excited by the prospect of growing with [BLANK SPACE] and look forward to discussing your needs."

"Marketing is in my blood, and I believe that I am genetically predetermined to enter the marketing world . . . I am writing to you about possible job openings in your company in hopes that I can fulfill my destiny there."

"As my resume indicates, I have extensive experience in pubic relations."

experience in the field. She possesses strong verbal and written communication skills, and has an extensive client base."

Example B (right way): "I am a highly qualified public relations executive with over seven years of relevant experience in the field. I possess strong verbal and written communication skills and have an extensive client base."

Tone Trouble

Tone problems are subtle and may be hard to detect. When reading your cover letter, patrol for tone problems by asking yourself, after each sentence, "Does this statement enhance my candidacy? Could a hiring manager interpret it in an unfavorable way?" Have a second reader review your letter. If the letter's wording is questionable, rewrite it. A cover letter should steer a middle course between extremely formal, which can come across as pretentious, and extremely informal, which can come across as presumptuous. Try to sound genuine, not stilted. When in doubt, err on the side of formality.

Gimmicks

Gimmicks like sending a home video or a singing telegram to replace the conventional cover letter may seem attractive. No matter how creative these ideas may sound, the majority of employers will be more impressed with a simple, well-crafted letter. In the worst-case scenario, gimmicks can even work against you, eliminating you from consideration. Examples include sending a poster-sized cover letter by courier service or a baseball hat with a note attached: "I'm throwing my hat into the ring!" Avoid such big risks; most hiring decisions are based on qualifications, not gimmicks.

Typographical Errors

It's easy to make mistakes in your letters, particularly when you're writing many in succession. But it's also easy for a hiring manager to reject any cover letter that contains errors, even those that seem minor. Don't make the mistake that one job-hunting

editor made, citing his attention to detail while misspelling his own name! Here are a few common technical mistakes to watch out for when proofreading your letter:

- Misspelling the hiring contact's name or title in the address or salutation or on the envelope.
- Forgetting to change the name of the organization you're applying to each time it appears in your application, especially in the body of the letter. For example, if you're applying to Boots and Bags, don't express enthusiasm for a position at Shoe City.
- Indicating application for one position and mentioning a different position in the body of the letter. For instance, one candidate applying for a telemarketing position included the following statement: "I possess fifteen years experience related to the marketing analyst opening." Another mistake here is that the applicant didn't use "years" as a possessive: "...fifteen years' experience...."

Messy Corrections

Your cover letter should contain *all* pertinent information. If, for any reason, you forget to communicate something to your addressee, retype the letter. Including a supplementary note, either typed or handwritten, will be viewed as unprofessional or, worse, lazy. For example, one candidate attached a "post-it" note to his cover letter, stating his willingness to travel and/or relocate. This and all other information must be included in your final draft. Also, avoid using correction fluid or penning in any corrections.

Omitted Signature

However obvious this may sound, don't forget to sign your name neatly in blue or black ink. Far too many letters have a typed name but no signature. Also, don't use a script font or a draw program on your word processor.

Details, Details . . .

Can and May

No: *I may be reached at (505) 555-5555 (days) and (505) 444-4444 (evenings).*

Better: *I can be reached at (505) 555-5555 (days) and (505) 444-4444 (evenings).*

Fused Participle

No: *I appreciate you taking the time to speak to me is an example of a fused participle and is grammatically incorrect.*

Better: *I appreciate **your** taking the time to speak to me.*

Serial Comma

Standard editorial practice in a series of items is to use a comma after each item except the last.

No: *"... lumberjack, lounge lizard and organ grinder."*

Yes: *"... lumberjack, lounge lizard, and organ grinder."*

The Internet consists of four separate areas: the World Wide Web, Usenet, Telnet, and Gopher. These areas include hundreds of thousands of job listings. Bulletin Board Systems (BBSs), which represent a part of cyberspace that doesn't fall into these areas, are also an excellent job-search resource. No surprise, then, that when most people think of electronic job searching, they think of the Internet.

The World Wide Web. The Web is the best-known area of the Internet. It has dozens of excellent electronic career centers that offer all kinds of job-search advice and information, including a growing number of large databases of job listings. The Web has by far the largest collection of job listings found on-line.

Usenet. The User's Network is comprised of more than 20,000 newsgroups, or electronic discussion groups, where people can exchange information, discuss ideas, or just chat. The nature of Usenet makes it a natural for networking—with so many different newsgroups to choose from, you're sure to find one in your field of interest. Usenet is also an outstanding resource for job listings, with over 100,000 offerings.

Telnet. Telnet is the smallest area of the Internet, and getting smaller. Telnet is a good place to look for federal job listings and other information regarding applying for a federal job. It's also useful as a way of connecting to other sites, like a Gopher server.

Gopher. Gopher is a menu-based system of organizing information on the Internet. It was also the first step in making the Internet more user-friendly, with its easy-to-manage menus and powerful search engines, Veronica and Jughead. Because it was developed at the University of Minnesota and quickly became a favorite of academics at other universities, Gopher remains a good source of academic and other specialized job listings. For example, it has one of the few on-line employment resources dedicated to the arts. However, Gopher's popularity is fading in competition with the Web and Usenet newsgroups.

The World Wide Web

The Web is fast becoming the place to look for jobs on the Internet. Dozens of career resources on the Web are devoted to job listings, with more springing up every day. Unlike Usenet newsgroups, which tend to focus on computer-related or other technical positions, the Web has listings for job hunters of all backgrounds.

Major Sites

The Web's job databases vary greatly in both the quality and quantity of job listings. Start with the all-purpose job-search sites described in Chapter 1 [**Resumes**], like CareerCity, CareerMosaic, Job Options, and the Monster Board. These are four of the largest and most popular job-search sites on the Web.

A number of listings in the major job databases overlap. The same search performed on the Monster Board and CareerSite, for example, will likely retrieve many of the same listings. Keep careful records, so you don't mistakenly send a resume to the same company twice for the same job.

It's Good to Know . . .

An understanding and knowledge of computers is the most sought-after skill in new employees. Using electronic resources to find a job demonstrates your computer savvy to an employer.

Electronic business directories, either on-line or on CD-ROM, allow you to identify companies that hire employees in your field and with your background. These databases also contain enough company information to give you an indication of whether a company is right for you.

The Internet and commercial on-line services are available twenty-four hours a day, and their national and international scope are ideal for job seekers.

JOB HUNTING SITES FOR EVERYONE

ADGUIDE'S COLLEGE RECRUITER EMPLOYMENT
SITE: *www.adguide.com*
AMERICAN JOBS: *www.americanjobs.com*
BEST JOBS USA: *www.bestjobsusa.com*
BLACKWORLD: *www.blackworld.com/careers.htm*
BUSINESS JOB FINDER:
www.cob.ohio-state.edu/dept/fin/osujobs.htm
THE CAREERBUILDER NETWORK:
www.careerbuilder.com
CAREERCITY: *www.careercity.com*
CAREER CONNECTION: *www.connectme.com*
CAREER EXCHANGE: *www.careerexchange.com*
CAREER EXPOSURE: *www.careerexposure.com*
CAREERLINK USA: *www.careerlinkusa.com*
CAREERMAGAZINE: *www.careermag.com*
CAREERMART: *www.careermart.com*
CAREERMOSAIC: *www.careermosaic.com*
CAREERPATH: *www.careerpath.com*
CAREER RESOURCE CENTER:
http://cgi.pathfinder.com/fortune/careers/index.html
CAREER SHOP: *www.careershop.com*
CAREERSITE: *www.careersite.com*
CAREERWEB: *www.careerweb.com*
CAREER WOMEN: *www.careerwomen.com*
CAREERS.WSJ.COM: *www.careers.wsj.com*
CLASSIFIEDS2000: *www.classifieds2000.com*
CLASSIFIED WAREHOUSE: *www.adone.com*
COLLEGE GRAD JOB HUNTER: *www.collegegrad.com*
CONTRACT EMPLOYMENT WEEKLY:
www.ceweekly.com
COOL WORKS: *www.coolworks.com*
E-SPAN'S JOBOPTIONS:
www.joboptions.com
4WORK: *www.4work.com*
HEADHUNTER: *www.headhunter.net*

HEART: CAREER CONNECTION: *www.career.com*
THE HELP-WANTED NETWORK:
www.help-wanted.net
HOT JOBS: *www.hotjobs.com*
INTERNET CAREER CONNECTION: *www.iccweb.com*
THE INTERNET JOB LOCATOR: *www.joblocator.com*
THE INTERNET JOB SOURCE: *www.statejobs.com*
THE INTERNET'S EMPLOYMENT RESOURCE:
www.tier21.com
JOBDIRECT: *www.jobdirect.com*
JOBEXCHANGE: *www.jobexchange.com*
JOBFIND: *www.jobfind.com*
JOBHUNT: *www.job-hunt.org*
JOBS.COM: *www.jobs.com*
JOB-SEARCH-ENGINE: *www.jobsearchengine.com*
JOBTRAK: *www.jobtrak.com*
JOBVERTISE: *www.jobvertise.com*
JOBWEB: *www.jobweb.com*
THE LATPRO PROFESSIONAL NETWORK:
www.latpro.com
MBA FREEAGENTS.COM: *www.mbafreeagents.com*
MONSTER.COM: *www.monster.com*
NET-TEMPS: *www.net-temps.com*
PASSPORTACCESS: *www.passportaccess.com*
PHILLIPS CAREER CENTER:
www.phillips.com/careercenter.htm
RECRUITING-LINKS.COM: *www.recruiting-links.com*
WESTECH VIRTUAL JOB FAIR: *www.vjf.com*

JOB OPENINGS—ASIA
ASIA NET: *www.asia-net.com*

JOB OPENINGS—AUSTRALIA
AUSTRALIAN JOB SEARCH:
http://jobsearch.deetya.gov.au

BYRON EMPLOYMENT AUSTRALIA:
http://employment.byron.com.au

JOB OPENINGS—CANADA
CANADIAN JOBS CATALOGUE: *www.kenevacorp.mb.ca*

JOB OPENINGS—EUROPE
OVERSEAS JOBS EXPRESS: *www.overseasjobs.com*

JOB OPENINGS—INDIA
CAREER INDIA: *www.careerindia.com*
JOB OPENINGS—IRELAND
THE IRISH JOBS PAGE: *www.exp.ie*

JOB OPENINGS—UNITED KINGDOM
JOBSITE GROUP: *www.jobsite.co.uk*
VACANCIES: *www.vacancies.ac.uk*
WORKWEB: *www.workweb.co.uk*

JOB OPENINGS—UNITED STATES
ALASKA JOBS CENTER:
www.ilovealaska.com/alaskajobs
AMERICA'S TV JOB NETWORK: *www.tvjobnet.com*
BOSTON.COM: *www.boston.com*
BOSTON JOB BANK: *www.bostonjobs.com*
BOSTONSEARCH: *www.bostonsearch.com*
THE CALIFORNIA JOB SOURCE:
www.statejobs.com/ca.html
CAREERBOARD: *www.careerboard.com*
CAREERGUIDE: *www.careerguide.com*
CAREERLINK: *www.careerlink.org/index.htm*
CAROLINASCAREERWEB: *www.carolinascareerweb.com*
CLASSIFIND NETWORK: *www.classifind.com*
COLORADOJOBS: *www.coloradojobs.com*
FLORIDA CAREER LINK: *www.floridacareerlink.com*
HOUSTONCHRONICLE: *www.chron.com*
JOBNET: *www.jobnet.com*
KANSAS JOB-BANK: *http://entkdhr.ink.org/kjb/index.html*

MINNESOTA JOBS: *www.minnesotajobs.com*
NEW ENGLAND OPPORTUNITY NOCS:
www.opnocs.org
NEW JERSEY ONLINE: *www.nj.com*
ONLINE COLUMBIA: *www.onlinecolumbia.com*
ORANGE COUNTY REGISTER:
www.ocregister.com/ads/classified/index.shtml
PHILADELPHIA ONLINE: *www.phillynews.com*
THE SILICON VALLEY JOB SOURCE:
www.valleyjobs.com
680CAREERS: *www.680careers.com*
STL DIRECT: *http://directory.st-louis.mo.us*
TOWNONLINE: *www.townonline.com/working*
TRIANGLE JOBS: *www.trianglejobs.com*
VIRGINIA EMPLOYMENT COMMISSION:
www.vec.state.va.us
WASHINGTON EMPLOYMENT WEB PAGES:
http://members.aol.com/gwattier/washjob.htm
WISCONSIN JOBNET: *www.dwd.state.wi.us/jobnet*

INDUSTRY-SPECIFIC JOB OPENINGS
—ACCOUNTING/BANKING/FINANCE—
ACCOUNTING & FINANCE JOBS:
www.accountingjobs.com
ACCOUNTING.COM: *www.accounting.com*
ACCOUNTING NET: *www.accountingnet.com*
AMERICAN BANKER ONLINE'S CAREERZONE:
www.americanbanker.com/careerzone
BLOOMBERG: *www.bloomberg.com*
CFO'S FEATURED JOBS:
www.cfonet.com/html/cfojobs.html
FINANCIAL, ACCOUNTING,
AND INSURANCE JOBS PAGE:
www.nationjob.com/financial
FINCAREER: *www.fincareer.com*
JOBS FOR BANKERS ONLINE: *www.bankjobs.com*
NATIONAL BANKING NETWORK:
www.banking-financejobs.com

—ADVERTISING/MARKETING/PUBLIC RELATIONS—
ADWEEK ONLINE: *www.adweek.com*
DIRECT MARKETING WORLD: *www.dmworld.com*
MARKETING JOBS: *www.marketingjobs.com*

—AEROSPACE—
AVIATION AND AEROSPACE JOBS PAGE:
   www.nationjob.com/aviation
AVIATION EMPLOYMENT:
   www.aviationemployment.com
SPACE JOBS: *www.spacejobs.com*

—ARTS AND ENTERTAINMENT—
THE INTERNET MUSIC PAGES: *www.musicpages.com*
ONLINE SPORTS:
   www.onlinesports.com/pages/CareerCenter.html

—BIOTECHNOLOGY/ SCIENTIFIC—
BIO ONLINE: *www.bio.com*
SCIENCE PROFESSIONAL NETWORK:
   www.recruitsciencemag.org

—CHARITIES AND SOCIAL SERVICES—
THE NONPROFIT TIMES ONLINE:
   www.nptimes.com/classified.html
SOCIALSERVICE: *www.socialservice.com*
SOCIAL WORK AND SOCIAL SERVICES JOBS
   ONLINE: *www.gwbweb.wustl.edu/jobs/index.html*

—COMMUNICATIONS—
   AIRWAVES MEDIA WEB:
      www.airwaves.com/job.html

THE JOBZONE:
   www.internettelephony.com/JobZone/jobzone.asp

—COMPUTERS—
COMPUTER:
   www.computer.org/computer/career/career.htm
THE COMPUTER JOBS STORE:
   www.computerjobs.com
COMPUTERWORK: *www.computerwork.com*
DICE: *www.dice.com*
DIGITAL CAT'S HUMAN RESOURCE CENTER:
   www.jobcats.com
IDEAS JOB NETWORK: *www.ideasjn.com*
1-JOBS: *www.1-jobs.com*
JOBS FOR PROGRAMMERS: *www.prgjobs.com*
JOBS.INTERNET.COM: *http://jobs.internet.com*
JOB WAREHOUSE: *www.jobwarehouse.com*
MACTALENT: *www.mactalent.com*
SELECTJOBS: *www.selectjobs.com*
TECHIES: *www.techies.com*

—EDUCATION—
ACADEMIC EMPLOYMENT NETWORK:
   www.academploy.com
ACADEMIC POSITION NETWORK: *www.apnjobs.com*
AECT PLACEMENT CENTER:
   www.aect.org/employment/employment.htm
THE CHRONICLE OF HIGHER EDUCATION/
   CAREER NETWORK: *http://chronicle.com/jobs*
DAVE'S ESL CAFE: *www.eslcafe.com*
HIGHEREDJOBS ONLINE: *www.higheredjobs.com*
JOBS IN HIGHER EDUCATION:
   www.gslis.utexas.edu/~acadres/jobs/index.html
LIBRARY & INFORMATION SCIENCE JOBSEARCH:
   www.carousel.lis.uiuc.edu/~jobs
THE PRIVATE SCHOOL EMPLOYMENT NETWORK:
   www.privateschooljobs.com
TEACHER JOBS: *www.teacherjobs.com*

—ENGINEERING—
ENGINEERJOBS: *www.engineerjobs.com*

—ENVIRONMENTAL—
ECOLOGIC:
  www.rpi.edu/dept/union/pugwash/ecojobs.htm
ENVIRONMENTAL JOBS SEARCH PAGE!:
  http://ourworld.compuserve.com/homepages/
  ubikk/env4.htm
WATER ENVIRONMENT WEB: *www.wef.org*

—GOVERNMENT—
CORPORATE GRAY ONLINE: *www.greentogray.com*
FEDERAL JOBS CENTRAL: *www.fedjobs.com*
FEDERAL JOBS DIGEST: *www.jobsfed.com*
FEDWORLD FEDERAL JOB ANNOUNCEMENT
  SEARCH: *www.fedworld.gov/jobs/jobsearch.html*
THE POLICE OFFICERS INTERNET DIRECTORY:
  www.officer.com/jobs.htm

—HEALTH CARE—
HEALTH CAREER WEB: *www.healthcareerweb.com*
HEALTH CARE JOBS ONLINE: *www.hcjobsonline.com*
HEALTH CARE RECRUITMENT ONLINE:
  www.healthcarerecruitment.com
MEDHUNTERS: *www.medhunters.com*
MEDICAL-ADMART: *www.medical-admart.com*
MEDICAL DEVICE LINK: *www.devicelink.com/career*
MEDZILLA: *www.medzilla.com*
NURSING SPECTRUM CAREER FITNESS ONLINE:
  www.nursingspectrum.com
PHYSICIANS EMPLOYMENT: *www.physemp.com*
SALUDOS HISPANIS WEB CAREER CENTER:
  www.saludos.com/cguide/hcguide.html

—HOTELS AND RESTAURANTS—
ESCOFFIER ONLINE:
  www.escoffier.com/nonscape/employ.shtml

HUMAN RESOURCES/ RECRUITING
HR WORLD: *www.hrworld.com*
JOBS 4 HR: *www.jobs4hr.com*

—INSURANCE—
THE INSURANCE CAREER CENTER:
  www.connectyou.com/talent
INSURANCE NATIONAL SEARCH:
  www.insurancerecruiters.com/insjobs/jobs.htm

—LEGAL—
LAW NEWS NETWORK: *www.lawjobs.com*
THE LEGAL EMPLOYMENT SEARCH SITE:
  www.legalemploy.com
RIGHT OF WAY EMPLOYMENT JOBLINE:
  www.rightofway.com/jobline.html

—MINING/GAS/PETROLEUM—
OIL-LINK: *www.oillink.com*

—PRINTING AND PUBLISHING—
JOBLINK FOR JOURNALISTS:
  http://ajr.newslink.org/newjoblink.html
JOBS IN JOURNALISM:
  http://eb.journ.latech.edu/jobs.html

—TRANSPORTATION—
INTERNATIONAL SEAFRERS EXCHANGE:
  www.jobxchange.com/xisetoc.com
1-800-DRIVERS:
  http://204.32.45.41/final/seek.htm

—RETAIL—
RETAIL JOBNET: *www.retailjobnet.com*

—UTILITIES—
POWER: *www.powermag.com*

Meta-List

This is a "list of lists" found on the Web, with links to sites and other Internet resources on a particular subject, like job hunting. These lists are good time-savers—they generally include a short description or review of the site or service, so you won't waste time visiting irrelevant or low-quality sites. To access a particular site, you need only click on the site name.

Meta-Lists

Also, check out some job-related meta-lists, which contain links to other on-line career resources. The Career Resource Center *www.careers.org* contains thousands of links, broken down into categories like financial services or computers and engineering. Other meta-lists to consult include Stanford University's JobHunt *www.job-hunt.org* and Purdue University's Center for Career Opportunities Sites for Job Seekers and Employers *www.purdue.edu/student/jobsites.htm*. The Riley Guide *www.dbm.com/jobguide* is another superb source of job-related resources on the Web.

Keyword Search

Another way to find job listings on the Web is to perform a keyword search in a search engine like Yahoo! or Lycos. Try using keywords like "employment opportunities," "job listings," or "positions available." Finally, a company's Web page is often an excellent source for job listings.

Commercial On-line Services

These services, which charge users to access their resources, are more recognizable by their brand names: America Online, CompuServe, Microsoft Network, and Prodigy. All these services provide users with full access to the Internet and the vast employment resources available there. America Online (AOL) and CompuServe are the two largest services and, not surprisingly, have the most resources to offer job seekers.

America Online is considered by many to have the strongest and largest collection of job listings available through a commercial on-line service. CompuServe has dozens of high-quality professional discussion groups that are ideal for networking, as well as a number of searchable business databases that offer in-depth information on tens of thousands of companies. Microsoft has worked to get into the game through acquisitions and partnerships with various Internet software companies, and Prodigy also has several quality resources worth checking out. The smaller services—like Delphi and

Genie—lack the quantity of resources presently found on AOL or CompuServe.

The following overview indicates the strengths and weaknesses of each service. To find out how to sign up with a service, visit the Web address listed.

America Online *www.aol.com* is the largest commercial on-line service, with more than 17 million households. America Online is well known for its wide range of home and leisure activities for the entire family. Since the creation of the on-line Career Center in 1989, AOL has been the leader among commercial on-line services in the resources it offers job seekers. AOL's employment databases contain thousands of job listings, all of which use the same fairly simple search engine. These listings can be accessed with the keyword "Career Center." For on-line newspapers, click on "Local Resources"; for federal opportunities, click on "Find a Job," then select a relevant site from the WorkPlace site.

CompuServe *www.compuserve.com* was purchased by America Online in 1998, yet it remains a separate and distinct service. A large portion of CompuServe's two and a half million subscribers are businesses, which is a good indication of the service's orientation. CompuServe has by far the best collection of business resources on-line, including dozens of business-related databases. Job listings are not the primary reason most job seekers like CompuServe. CompuServe's strengths lie in its research capabilities and professional forums—over nine hundred special groups for people of like ideas and interests to gather and exchange information.

The Microsoft Network *http://home.microsoft.com* has certainly drawn lots of new subscribers due to the popularity of Microsoft's Windows 95 and 98 operating systems. MSN Members will want to check out its Career Forum, which features a wealth of job search and career advice, tutorials, and information. Specialized forums include those devoted to nursing and theater professions.

In addition to these major services, the following two services are worth mentioning here—although keep in mind that they were once somewhat more prominent than they are today.

On-line Strategies

Know what you want to accomplish before you go on-line. Have an agenda prepared, complete with keywords to search for, or the names and addresses of sites you want to visit. This will save you time and money, because you won't be fumbling around on-line for the right keyword or address. Also, having a plan will lessen the chances that you'll get sidetracked into a discussion group.

On the Web, use search engines like Yahoo!, Excite, and Alta Vista to help you find what you need.

(continued on next page)

Delphi *www.delphi.com* allows free access to its many forums. Searching the "Business/Finance" forums will lead you to a number of career-related forums, though few have job listings. These forums are best used for networking, finding the occasional job lead, or staying up-to-date on discussions in different fields.

Prodigy *www.prodigy.com* was best known in the past as the favorite on-line service of families with young children, mainly because of its educational resources and games. Today, Prodigy's greatest asset is the easy Internet access it provides for its subscribers. Users can easily switch between Prodigy's services, the Web, Usenet newsgroups, and Gopher. Plus, Prodigy's main menu even contains some hypertext links to Prodigy-sponsored Web sites. *Note:* Prodigy offers *Prodigy Classic*, which provides a wide variety of member services, and *Prodigy Internet*, which is distinguished primarily by its faster and more complete access to the Internet, via partnership with Microsoft's Internet Explorer. Prodigy's Career Channel is a good example of the service's ability to incorporate the World Wide Web into a traditional on-line service.

Usenet Newsgroups

Usenet newsgroups are one of the oldest and most misunderstood areas of the Internet. What was once the exclusive territory of this country's brain trust—academics, scientists, and top government officials—has developed into one of the most popular means of exchanging information on the Internet. At the same time, many new users are scared off by what they perceive as an intimidating Usenet culture. But by ignoring the discussion groups on Usenet, you could miss out on hundreds of potential job opportunities.

Getting Started

Usenet newsgroups are accessible either through your Internet carrier or commercial on-line services. In America Online, try keyword: Newsgroups. If you have a regular Internet connection, you'll need the help of a newsreader, like Trumpet Newsreader, to organize the thousands of available newsgroups and allow you to read and post messages. Many Web browsers, like Netscape Navigator,

have a built-in newsreader. Netscape's newsreader is called Netscape News. If you can't find a newsreader on your system, call your Internet provider and ask where to find one.

Once you're in Usenet, read the messages in the newsgroups news.newusers.questions and news.announce.newusers. You'll find answers to the most commonly asked questions regarding Usenet, or you can post your own questions about Usenet. You can also find information like a history of the Internet, rules for posting messages, and hints about the Usenet writing style.

This Is a Test

After reviewing the basics of Usenet, post a test message to the newsgroups alt.test or misc.tests. This test allows you to check whether your newsreader is configured properly. If you can't post test messages, ask your Internet carrier or commercial service provider for assistance. If your test goes off without a hitch, you're all set.

A Few Basic Facts

Before you begin posting messages to dozens of newsgroups on the Web, you need to know a few basic facts about Usenet. Different hierarchies and newsgroups have different tones to their discussions. In general, *alt.* newsgroups are more casual, while the *comp.* and *sci.* newsgroups are more formal and factual. And *talk.* newsgroups discuss serious subjects in a serious manner. It's important to take the time—at least one week—to get a feel for a newsgroup. This can usually be done simply by reading a few days' worth of messages. Doing this should decrease your chances of posting an inappropriate message.

Bulletin Board Systems

Bulletin Board Systems are an often overlooked on-line resource for job listings. These days, it seems everyone is more interested in the Web and services like CareerMosaic. But job-related bulletin boards can contain up to 10,000 job listings, and Bulletin Board Systems are much easier to connect to than the Web is.

(continued from previous page)

Try going on-line during off-peak hours, either early morning or late night. Services experience less traffic at these times, so it can be much easier to get through. And be sure you're dialing into a local phone number, to save money on your phone bill.

Don't rely on one particular area of the on-line world for all your job information. The Web is glamorous, but don't forget those old reliables like Usenet newsgroups and Bulletin Board Systems, as well as off-line options like joblines and directories. After you spend some time exploring, you'll probably discover that certain resources work best for you. Narrow your efforts to those areas.

Tech and Fed Jobs on BBS

Job seekers interested in finding technical positions or jobs in federal, state, or local governments should take special note of the number of BBSs dedicated to those areas.

Basically, a BBS is a computer set up with special software that you access by using a telephone line and the communications software on your computer. BBSs were created as a way for people to exchange information and discuss ideas, much like a Usenet newsgroup. Usenet newsgroups, unlike BBSs, require Internet access.

The biggest problem with BBSs is the difficulty in searching for particular boards. To dial up a BBS, you need to have the phone number beforehand for the specific board you want to access. Unlike the Web, you can't connect to a general BBS and do a search for specific BBSs by name or keyword. If you have access to the Web, try a search engine like Yahoo! or a commercial on-line service like America Online to find bulletin boards in your area. Another good resource is the BBS Corner at *http://www.thedirectory.org/diamond/bbslists.htm*

After connecting to a new BBS, you'll be required to register to use the services. This helps to discourage casual users from tying up the phone lines. Since most BBSs have a limited number of phone lines (some may have only four or five), the system operators, or sysops, limit the number of minutes users can spend on the system in one day. The systems listed here allow a maximum of one hour per day.

BBSs of job listings are quickly becoming a thing of the past. The most reliable sites are maintained by the federal government and are also available on the Web.

Exec-PC (414-789-4210)—This is an enormous BBS, with thousands of files available for download, including job listings nationwide. Also contains local access numbers for users dialing long-distance.

Federal Job Opportunities Board (FJOB) (912-757-3125 or by Internet telnet: *telnet://jobentry.opm.gov*)—Sponsored by the U.S. Office of Personnel Management, this BBS contains federal job listings and other employment information.

OPM Mainstreet (202-606-4800)—Includes federal job listings from the Office of Personnel Management as well as access to other federal job BBSs and employment-related mailing lists and Usenet newsgroups.

Networking On-line

While some may think that top executives and industry insiders are the only people to benefit from networking, that is not the case. The development of specialized on-line discussion groups has made it easier for all job seekers to meet and interact with other professionals in the same field or industry.

Job seekers should look at three main areas as potential networking resources: Usenet newsgroups, mailing lists, and special interest groups on commercial on-line services. Gopher, Telnet, and the Web don't lend themselves well to networking, since they weren't designed for two-way communication. Newsgroups, mailing lists, and SIGs, on the other hand, were designed expressly for the purpose of disseminating and receiving information. The dozens of career-related discussion groups available cover fields like accounting, education, journalism, and microbiology.

Also keep an eye out for Web sites of industry organizations and associations. While they don't have the ability to accept posted messages, field-specific Web sites are still a good way to stay current with the latest developments in a field.

Don't expect to be besieged with job offers and contact names simply because you logged on to a professional discussion group and posted a message full of intelligence and insight. Networking on-line is a slow process, since in the on-line world, as in real life, relationships don't form overnight. It may be months before any job leads materialize. That's why it's advisable to maintain a continual presence in appropriate discussion groups, even when you're happily employed, since the opportunity of a lifetime may turn up when it's least expected.

Networking on Usenet Newsgroups

Newsgroups are a terrific place for networking, with discussion groups to suit almost every interest. They also tend to have the harshest rules of netiquette, in part because their participants are more technologically savvy than the on-line world as a whole. At the same time, their users are helpful to those who have taken the time to learn the rules.

The Meter Is Running

Remember that while these services are free, you'll be charged the cost of a regular long-distance call while connected to the BBS. Try calling during off hours to minimize your phone bill.

Advantages of On-line Networking

Discussion group participants often include human resources representatives and hiring managers, who lend their expertise by discussing the qualities they look for in employees. Many recruiters report visiting field-specific discussion groups to look for potential job candidates.

Participating in on-line discussion groups brings far greater exposure than, for instance, going to a meeting of a local industry group. A discussion group's audience is most often nationwide and may even include participants from around the world.

Monitoring discussion groups makes it easy to determine what skills and experiences employers are looking for. It's also a good way to find out which companies are hiring and what the hot topics are in the field.

The following are some that you should know about:

alt.journalism.moderated—Moderated discussion group for journalists

bionet.women-in-bio—Discusses issues relevant to women in the field of biology

bionet.microbiology—Discussion of issues related to microbiology

hepnet.jobs—Discussion of issues relating to high-energy nuclear physics

k12.chat.teacher—Discussion group for teachers, from kindergarten to 12th grade

misc.business.consulting—Discusses the consulting business

misc.education—General discussion of the educational system

misc.jobs.contract—Discussion of both short- and long-term contract labor

misc.jobs.misc—General issues of employment and careers

misc.legal—Discussion group for lawyers and other legal professionals

misc.writing—Discussion group for writers of all types

sci.med—Discussion group for those interested in science and medicine

sci.med.pharmacy—Discusses the pharmaceutical field

sci.research.careers—Discusses the various careers relating to scientific research

Networking with Mailing Lists

Like newsgroups, mailing lists, also known as list-serves or e-mail discussion groups, allow users to post and read messages that contain threads of discussions on various topics. What sets mailing lists apart from newsgroups is that instead of users logging in to a specific group and posting and reading messages on-line, subscribers both receive new messages and post messages to the group via e-mail. Many users like mailing lists because it's possible to monitor discussion groups simply by checking one's e-mail.

To subscribe to a mailing list, send an e-mail to the list's system administrator. The administrator makes sure all messages are sent to subscribers and moderates the content, ensuring that postings are relevant to the topic. Like other discussion groups, each

The Importance of Netiquette

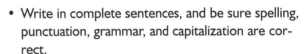

"Netiquette" is a combination of the words "network" (or Internet) and "etiquette," and refers to the widely accepted do's and don'ts for on-line discussion groups. It is essential that new users, or "newbies," be familiar with the netiquette of a group before joining the discussion; otherwise, they may get "flamed" (criticized and ridiculed by established group members).

The easiest way to avoid getting flamed is to spend time observing and reading the group's posted messages before joining the discussion. Each discussion group, especially those on Usenet, have a particular tone and rules. "Lurking" (reading messages but not posting your own) will give you a good sense of the group's personality. This is also a good way to ensure that a group fits your interests.

When you're ready to join the discussion, don't simply post a general message along the lines of "Hi, I'm new here and just wanted to drop in and say hello!" Post a message asking for specific advice or introduce an original thought or comment to the discussion. A boring, generic posting with headers like "Help!" or "Hire Me!" will be ignored at best and will get you flamed at worst. If you do get flamed—something bound to happen to every new user once or twice—just ignore it. Unless you violated a sacred rule of netiquette, someone was probably just having a bad day.

Following are some other basic rules of netiquette, as well as some general guidelines for professional discussion groups:

- Write in complete sentences, and be sure spelling, punctuation, grammar, and capitalization are correct.
- Don't type messages in capital letters, because that's the on-line equivalent of SHOUTING.
- Don't use "emoticons," like :) [happy face] or : ([frown] or common abbreviations like BTW (by the way) or IMHO (in my humble opinion), which are commonly used in recreational discussion groups. These types of cutesy shorthand are out of place in a professional discussion group. For more information, visit the following sites:

  www.utopiasw.demon.co.uk/emoticon.htm
  www.ultranet.com/support/netiquette/
  emoticons.shtml

- Understand the appropriate times to post or e-mail a reply to a particular message. Many new and experienced users alike are often unsure of when to direct an e-mail to the message's author and when a reply should be posted to the group. In general, post a reply if your message is something the group as a whole could appreciate and learn from, but use e-mail if your comment concerns only the poster. This is important because no one wants to participate in a discussion that is little more than a dialogue between two or three people.
- Use your best manners. Respect and be tolerant of others' ideas and opinions.

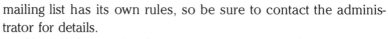

mailing list has its own rules, so be sure to contact the administrator for details.

Tens of thousands of mailing lists cover subjects like arts, business, health, politics, and religion. To find the ones that match your
interests, consult one of the following on-line directories. Each
directory contains contact information, like the system administrator's e-mail address, for over 50,000 mailing lists.

Liszt: The Mailing List Directory *www.liszt.com* claims to
be the largest directory of mailing lists, and it just may be, with
84,792 lists available for searching. The site also allows you to
search by keywords.

Publicly Accessible Mailing Lists *www.neosoft.com/*
internet/paml contains hundreds of subject classifications and is
searchable by name or subject. Check under "jobs" or "employment"
for job-related mailing lists, but check out lists in your field as well.
This list is also posted to the Usenet newsgroups news.lists and
news.answers around the end of each month.

CHAPTER 7

Interviewing

At last, you've reached the long-sought goal. All your efforts spent writing the resume and cover letter, answering job listings, networking, and researching companies have paid off—you've been called for an interview! As with these previous steps, certain techniques will increase your chances of success. Follow these techniques to maximize your chances of landing the job.

Know the Company

As each interview is arranged, begin your in-depth research. You should arrive at an interview knowing the company upside down and inside out. You need to know the company's products, types of customers, subsidiaries, parent company, principal locations, rank in the industry, sales and profit trends, type of ownership, size, current plans, and much more. By this time, you've probably narrowed your job search to one industry. Even if you haven't, you should still be familiar with common industry terms, the trends in the firm's industry, the firm's principal competitors and their relative performance, and the direction in which the industry leaders are headed.

Dig into every resource you can! Surf the Internet. Read the company literature, the trade press, the business press. If possible, speak to someone at the firm before the interview, or if not, speak to someone at a competing firm. The more time you spend, the better. Even if you feel extremely pressed for time, set aside several hours for pre-interview research.

Attire

How important is proper attire for a job interview? Buying a complete wardrobe, donning new shoes, and having your hair styled every morning aren't enough to guarantee you a career position as an investment banker. On the other hand, if you can't find a clean, conservative suit or won't take the time to wash your hair, you're wasting your time by interviewing at all.

Men applying for any professional position should wear a suit, preferably in a conservative color like navy or charcoal gray. It's easy to get away with wearing the same dark suit to consecutive interviews at the same company; just wear a different shirt and tie for each interview.

Women should also wear a businesslike suit. Professionalism still dictates a suit with a skirt, rather than slacks, as proper interview garb for women. This is usually true even at companies where pants are acceptable attire for female employees.

The final selection of candidates for a job opening won't be determined by dress, but inappropriate dress can quickly eliminate a first-round candidate. So while you shouldn't spend a fortune on a new wardrobe, be sure your clothes are adequate. The key is to dress at least as formally and conservatively as the position requires, or slightly more so.

Grooming

Personal grooming is as important as finding appropriate clothes for a job interview. Careful grooming indicates both a sense of thoroughness and self-confidence. Women should not wear excessive makeup, and both men and women should refrain from wearing perfume or cologne. (It only takes a small spritz to leave an allergic interviewer with a fit of sneezing and a bad impression of your meeting.) Men should be freshly shaven, even if the interview is late in the day.

What to Bring

Everyone needs a watch, a pen, and a notepad. Finally, a briefcase or a leatherbound folder (containing extra, unfolded copies of your resume) will help complete the look of professionalism.

Sometimes the interviewer will be running behind schedule. Don't be upset—be sympathetic. Recruiters are often under pressure to interview a lot of candidates to quickly fill a demanding position. Come to your interview with good reading material to keep yourself occupied and relaxed.

The Crucial First Few Moments

The beginning of the interview is the most important, because it determines the tone. Do you smile when you meet? Do you establish enough eye contact, but not too much? Do you walk into the office with a self-assured and confident stride? Do you shake hands firmly? Do you make small talk easily, without being garrulous, or do you act formal and reserved, as though under attack? It's human nature to judge people by that first impression, so make sure it's a good one.

Do you wait for the recruiter to invite you to sit down before doing so? Alternatively, if the recruiter forgets to invite you to take a seat, do you awkwardly ask if you may be seated, as though to remind the recruiter of a lapse in etiquette? Or do you gracefully help yourself to a seat? As you can see, much of the first impression you make at an interview will be dramatically affected by how relaxed and confident you feel. This is why it's important to practice for each interview.

Avoid the Negative

Try not to be negative about anything during the interview, particularly any past employer or previous job. Even if you detest your current or former job or manager, don't make disparaging comments. The interviewer may construe this as a sign of a potential attitude problem and not consider you a strong candidate.

Take some time to really think about how you'll convey your work history. Present "bad experiences" as "learning experiences." Instead of saying "I hated my position as a salesperson because I had to bother people on the phone," say "I realized cold-calling wasn't my strong suit. Though I love working with people, I decided my talents would be best used in a more face-to-face atmosphere." Always find some sort of lesson from previous jobs, as they all have one.

Money: Don't Ask

It's usually best to avoid talking finances until you receive the offer. Otherwise you'll look like you care more about money than putting your skills to work for the company. Your goals at an interview are simple: 1) to prove to the recruiter that you're well-suited to the job

as you understand it, and 2) to make sure you feel comfortable with the prospect of actually doing the job and working in the environment the company offers. Even if you're unable to determine the salary range beforehand, don't ask about it during the first interview. You can always ask later. Above all, don't ask about fringe benefits until you've been offered a position. (Then be sure to get all the details.)

If you're pressed about salary requirements during an interview and you feel you must name a figure, give a salary range instead of your most recent salary. Naming a salary range gives you a chance to hook onto a figure that's also in the range the company has in mind. In fact, many companies base their offers on sliding salary scales. Therefore, if you name a range of, say, $25,000–30,000, it may be that the company was considering a range of $22,000–28,000. In this case, you'll be more likely to receive an offer in the mid-to-upper end of your range. Of course, your experience and qualifications also play a part here. If you're just starting out and have little experience, the recruiter may be more likely to stick to the lower end of the scale.

Handling Impossible Questions

One of the biggest fears candidates harbor about job interviews is the unknown question for which they have no answer. To make matters worse, some recruiters may ask a question knowing full well you can't answer it. They don't usually ask such questions because they enjoy seeing you squirm—they want to judge how you might respond to pressure or tension on the job. If you're asked a tough question you can't answer, think about it for a few seconds. Then, with a confident smile and without apology, simply say "I don't know" or "I can't answer that question."

You'll find some of the toughest of these questions later in the chapter, under "Zingers."

After the Interview

You've made it through the toughest part—but now what? First, breathe a sigh of relief! Then record the name and title of the person you interviewed with, as well as the names and titles of anyone else you may have met. Ideally, you'll have collected their business cards. Don't forget to write down what the next agreed-upon step will be. Will the recruiter contact you? How soon?

Don't Forget to Write

Write a follow-up letter immediately afterward, while the interview is still fresh in the interviewer's mind. Not only is this a thank-you, it also gives you the chance to provide the interviewer with any details you may have forgotten (as long as they can be added tactfully). If you lost any points during the interview, this letter can help you regain your footing. Be polite and make sure to stress your continued interest and competence to fill the position. Just don't forget to proofread it thoroughly. If you're unsure of the spelling of the interviewer's name, call the receptionist and ask.

Handling Rejection

Rejection is inevitable, and it's bound to happen to you, just as it happens to all other job seekers. The key is to be prepared for it and not take it personally.

One way you can turn rejection around is by contacting each person who sends you a rejection letter. Thank your contact for considering you for the position and request that he or she keep you in mind for future openings. If you feel comfortable about it, you may want to ask the person for suggestions to help you improve your chances of getting a job in that industry or for the names of people who might be looking for someone with your skills—something like "Do you have any suggestions about whom else I might contact?"

Two cautions are in order: First, don't ask employers to tell you why they didn't hire you. Not only will this place a recruiter in an awkward position, you'll probably get a negative reaction. Second, keep in mind that if you contact employers solely for impartial feedback, not everyone will be willing to talk to you.

Zingers!

Following are some of the most challenging questions you'll ever face. If you're able to answer these questions, you'll be prepared to handle just about anything the recruiter comes up with.

Tell me about yourself.

I'm a production assistant with a B.A. in communications and three years of solid broadcasting and public-relations experience. I have extensive experience developing and researching topics, prein-terviewing guests, and producing on-location videotapings. I have a tremendous amount of energy and love to be challenged. I'm constantly trying to take on additional responsibilities and learn new things. I've been watching your station for some time now, and I've been impressed with your innovative approach and your fast growth. I'd like to be a part of that winning team.

This is a perfect opportunity to "sell" your qualifications to the interviewer. Develop the sales messages that you want to convey, and condense them into a summary you can use in situations like this. Briefly describe your experience, skills, accomplishments, goals, and personal qualities. Explain your interest in the company and how you plan on making a contribution. If you're a recent college graduate, be sure to discuss your educational qualifications as well, emphasizing the classes you took that are relevant to the position.

What is your biggest weakness?

I admit to being a bit of a perfectionist. I take a great deal of pride in my work and am committed to producing the highest-quality work I can. Sometimes if I'm not careful, though, I can go a bit overboard. I've learned that it's not always possible or even practical to try to perfect your work—sometimes you have to decide what's important and ignore the rest to be productive. It's a question of trade-offs. I also pay a lot of attention to pacing my work, so I don't get too caught up in perfecting every detail.

If Your Skills Aren't Appropriate . . .

If it looks as though your skills and background don't match the position the interviewer was hoping to fill, ask him or her if another division or subsidiary could perhaps profit from your talents.

This is a great example of what's known as a negative question. Negative questions are a favorite among interviewers, because they're effective at uncovering problems or weaknesses. The key to answering negative questions is to give them a positive spin. For this particular question, your best bet is to admit to a weakness that isn't catastrophic, inconsistent, or currently disruptive to your chosen professional field, and emphasize how you've overcome or minimized it. Whatever you do, don't answer this question with a cop-out like "I can't think of any" or, even worse, "I don't really have any major weaknesses." This kind of response is likely to eliminate you from contention.

Tell me about a project in which you were disappointed with your personal performance.

In my last job for a manufacturing company, I had to analyze all the supplier bids and present recommendations to the vice president of logistics. Because the supplier bids weren't in a uniform format, my analysis often consisted of comparing dissimilar items. This caused some confusion in my final report, and by the time I'd reworked it and presented it to the vice president, we'd lost the critical time we needed to improve our approval process for these bids. In hindsight, I should have taken a simpler approach to the problem and not tried to make it so complex or all-inclusive. Ever since, I've paid more attention to making recommendations in a timely manner.

Describe roadblocks and what you've done to try to get around them. How have your skills come into play? In hindsight, what could you have done differently? What lessons have you learned?

What aspects of your work are most often criticized?

I remember in my first job as marketing assistant, I spent endless hours analyzing a particular problem. I came up with a revised marketing plan that was extremely well received. Unfortunately, when it came time to present the plan to top management, I hadn't prepared the fine points of the presentation—overheads and slides—and the proposal was turned down. I'd failed to make clear the savings that would result from the plan. I spent the next two weeks working on my presentation. On my second try management approved it, and my recommendations were carried out to everyone's satisfaction.

This question is similar to the question on weaknesses. Try to give an example from a job early on in your career. Discuss what you did to overcome the situation and to improve your work. You could also discuss how the failure has inspired you to pay more careful attention to detail in all your work.

Why did you stay in your last job so long?

I was in my last job over seven years. During that time, I completed an advanced technical degree at an evening university and also had two six-month assignments in which I was loaned out to different departments. As a result, I acquired some additional skills that normally aren't associated with that job. Therefore, I think I've made good progress and am ready to accept the next challenge.

The interviewer may be curious about your interest in personal improvement, tackling new assignments, and so on. He or she may also be concerned about whether you have a tendency to get too comfortable with the status quo. Demonstrate how you've developed job responsibilities in meaningful new ways.

Would you be willing to relocate to another city?

I'd prefer to be based here, but it's certainly a possibility I'd be willing to consider.

You may, even in some first interviews, be asked questions that seem to elicit a tremendous commitment on your behalf, like this one. Although such questions may be unfair during an initial job interview, you may well conclude that you have nothing to gain and everything to lose with a negative response. If you're asked such a question unexpectedly during an initial job interview, simply say something like

Skirt versus Pants for Women

For those women who are still convinced that pants are acceptable interview attire, listen to the words of one career counselor from a prestigious New England college: "I had a student who told me that since she knew women in her industry often wore pants to work, she was going to wear pants to her interviews. Almost every recruiter commented that her pants were 'too casual' and even referred to her as 'the one with the pants.' The funny thing was that one of the recruiters who commented on her pants had been wearing jeans!"

"That's certainly a possibility" or "I'm willing to consider that." Later, if you receive an offer, you can find out the specific conditions and then decide if you wish to accept the position. Remember, at the job-offer stage you have the most negotiating power, and the employer may be willing to accommodate your needs. If that isn't the case, you might wish to explain that upon reflection, you've decided you can't (for instance) relocate, but you'd like to be considered for other positions that might open up in the future.

Why should I hire you?

I offer over five years of expertise in management, including electronic assembly for a major computer manufacturer and injection-molding operations for a prominent plastics company. Because I have the ability to adjust and learn new skills quickly, I've often been called upon to start new operations. I'm confident, on the basis of my skills and experience, that I can help improve production by leading a team effort directed at achieving your company's goals.

You'll usually encounter this question toward the end of a job interview; how you answer it can make or break your candidacy. Instead of reiterating your resume, emphasize only a few of your strongest qualifications and relate them to the position in question.

What would you do if I told you I thought you were giving a very poor interview today?

Well, the first thing I'd do is ask you if there was any part of the interview you thought I mishandled. After that, I'd think back and try to remember if there had been any faulty communication on my part. Then I'd try to review possible problems I had understanding your questions, and I'd ask for clarification if I needed it. Finally, if we had time, I'd try to respond more fully and appropriately to the problem areas you identified for me.

Interviewers like to ask stress questions like these to see how well you hold up under pressure. Your best bet is to stay calm, relaxed, and don't allow your confidence to be shaken.

Sometimes recruiters ask seemingly impossible questions just to see how you'll respond. No matter how you may feel at the time, being subjected to a ridiculous question like this one is probably a good sign. If you're asked a tough question that you can't answer, think about it for a few seconds. Then, with a confident smile, simply say something like "I don't know, but if you hire me, I'll sure find out for you."

Illegal Questions

Illegal interview questions probe into your private life or personal background. Federal law forbids employers from discriminating against any person on the basis of sex, age, race, national origin, or religion. For instance, an interviewer may not ask you about your age or your date of birth. However, she or he may ask you if you're over eighteen years of age. If you're asked an illegal question at a job interview, keep in mind that many employers simply don't know what's legal and illegal.

One strategy in such cases is to try to discover the concerns behind the question and then address them. For instance, an employer who asks about your plans to have children may be concerned that you won't be able to fulfill the travel requirements of the position. Try to get to the heart of the issue by saying something like "I'm not quite sure I understand." If you can determine the interviewer's concerns, you can allay them with a reply like "I'm very interested in developing my career. Travel is definitely not a problem for me—in fact, I enjoy it tremendously."

Alternatively, you may choose to answer the question or to gracefully point out that the question is illegal and decline to respond. Avoid reacting in a hostile fashion— remember that you can always decide later to decline a job offer.

Any of the following responses is an acceptable way to handle these situations. Choose the response that's most comfortable for you, keeping in mind that adhering to your principles may cost you the job.

Bring a Good Book

The Corporate Controller at one large company makes everyone wait for at least one hour before he will interview them. He feels his time is more valuable than anyone else's. This is where you have to ask yourself: "How much do I really want this job—especially if I have to report to this person?"

What religion do you practice?

Answer 1: I make it a point not to mix my personal beliefs with my work, if that's what you mean. I assure you that I value my career too much for that.

Answer 2: I'm not quite sure I understand what you're getting at. Would you please explain to me how this issue is relevant to the position?

Answer 3: That question makes me uncomfortable. I'd really rather not answer it.

How old are you?

Answer 1: I'm in my fifties and have over thirty years of experience in this industry. My area of expertise is in . . .

Answer 2: I'm not quite sure I understand what you're getting at. Would you please explain to me how this issue is relevant to the position?

Answer 3: That question makes me uncomfortable. I'd really rather not answer it.

Are you married?

Answer 1: No.

Answer 2: Yes, I am. But I keep my family life separate from my work life so that I can put all my effort into my job. I'm flexible when it comes to travel and late hours, as my references can confirm.

Answer 3: I'm not quite sure I understand what you're getting at. Would you please explain to me how this issue is relevant to the position?

Answer 4: That question makes me uncomfortable. I'd really rather not answer it.

Do you have children?

Answer 1: No.

Answer 2: Yes, I do. But I keep my family life separate from my work life so that I can put all my effort into my job. I'm flexible when it comes to travel and late hours, as my references can confirm.

Answer 3: I'm not quite sure I understand what you're getting at. Would you please explain to me how this issue is relevant to the position?

Answer 4: That question makes me uncomfortable. I'd really rather not answer it.

Do you plan to have children?

Answer 1: No.

Answer 2: It's certainly a consideration, but if I do, it won't be for some time. I want to do the best job I can for this company and have no plans to leave just as I begin to make meaningful contributions.

Answer 3: I can't answer that right now. But if I ever do decide to have children, I wouldn't let it detract from my work. Becoming a parent is important, but my career is certainly important to me, too. I plan on putting all of my efforts into this job and this company.

Answer 4: I'm not quite sure I understand what you're getting at. Would you please explain to me how this issue is relevant to the position?

Answer 5: That question makes me uncomfortable. I'd really rather not answer it.

For Students and Recent Graduates

Being So Positive That It Hurts

Many inexperienced job candidates kill their chances for a job by making negative comments during an interview. A college student or recent grad should never make a negative statement about a former boss or teacher—even if it's completely true and fully justified. If the recruiter asks why you had an unsatisfactory grade in a particular course, don't say "The professor graded me unfairly" or "I didn't get along with the professor."

A recruiter would rather hire someone who gets and deserves an unsatisfactory grade in a course than someone who either doesn't get along with people or shifts blame to others. On the other hand, you can greatly increase your chances of getting any job by projecting a positive, upbeat attitude. This is one of the best ways to stand out from the competition. You can project this image by smiling from time to time during the interview; by responding to interview questions with enthusiasm; by demonstrating excitement about your past accomplishments; and by showing optimism about the prospect of starting your career.

Commonly Asked Questions

Whether you're graduating from high school or college, those of you with little or no work history face the same dilemma: it's tough to get a job without experience, and it seems impossible to gain experience without getting hired. But, as you'll see, there are ways to get around this problem—by emphasizing your strengths and educational achievements.

The following responses to interview questions are listed as examples to show you how questions should be handled. They should not be used as the basis of "canned" or scripted answers. Adapt these responses for your own circumstances, but remember that, especially for college students or recent grads, how an answer is given can be more important than what's said. Be positive, project confidence, smile and make eye contact with the interviewer, listen carefully, and go with the flow!

About School Grades

It's likely that if you've made it to the interview stage, you fulfill the basic criteria for the position, including the education requirements. The recruiter is probably trying to judge here how well the candidate handles adversity. It's important not to get defensive or to place blame. Instead, try to put a positive spin on the question—for example, by concentrating on what you learned and the extra effort you put in rather than on the grades you received.

Why are your grades so erratic?

I never hesitated to sign up for a course just because it had a reputation for being difficult. In fact, my American History professor, whose course I enjoyed tremendously, is notorious for giving out only one "A" for each class. You may have noticed that while my major is English, I did take four courses in physics, because I thought they were important to round out my education, and I enjoyed the challenge they presented. Almost everyone else in these courses was a physics major.

About Academics

What course did you find most challenging?

Initially, I was completely overwhelmed by the introductory chemistry course I took last year. No matter how hard I studied, I seemed to be getting nowhere. I failed the first three quizzes. So I tried a new approach. Instead of just studying by myself, I had a friend—a chemistry major—help me with my studies. I also began to get help after class from the professor from time to time. And I found that more time spent in the lab was critical. I ended up with a B+ in the course, and I felt I achieved a solid understanding of the material. More than that, I learned that tackling a new field of study sometimes requires a new approach, not just hard work, and that the help of others can be crucial!

The interviewer will want to see how well you respond to difficult situations. Demonstrate that you won't fold in the face of difficulty and that you're willing to put in the extra effort to meet a challenge.

Why did you decide to major in history?

It was a difficult choice, because I was also attracted to government, international relations, and economics. But the study of history allowed me to combine all three, especially since I focused on

economic history. I also found several of the professors in the department exceptionally knowledgeable and stimulating.

Show that you have solid, logical reasons for choosing your major. If you can't defend your choice of major, the interviewer will wonder how much thought you've put into choosing a career. You should also be sure that your reasons for choosing your major are compatible with your career choice. For instance, if you're applying for a position as a banker, don't say you were an English major because you love literature and writing.

About Extracurricular Activities

You seem to have participated a little bit in a lot of different extracurricular activities. Didn't any of them really hold your interest?

I've always felt it was important to have a well-rounded education, and I looked at extracurricular activities as an important part of that education. That's why I participated in many different activities—to broaden my experience and meet new people. I did particularly enjoy the drama club and the cycling team, but I made a conscious effort not to spend too much time on them and to try new and different activities.

About Lack of Work Experience

I see that while you returned to your hometown each summer, you worked at different companies. Why didn't you work the same job two summers in a row?

My career goal is to get a job in business after graduation. Because I attend a liberal arts college, I can't take any courses in business. So even though I was invited back to each summer job I held, I thought I could develop more experience by working in different positions. Although I didn't list high school jobs on my resume, I did work for almost three years at the same grocery store chain.

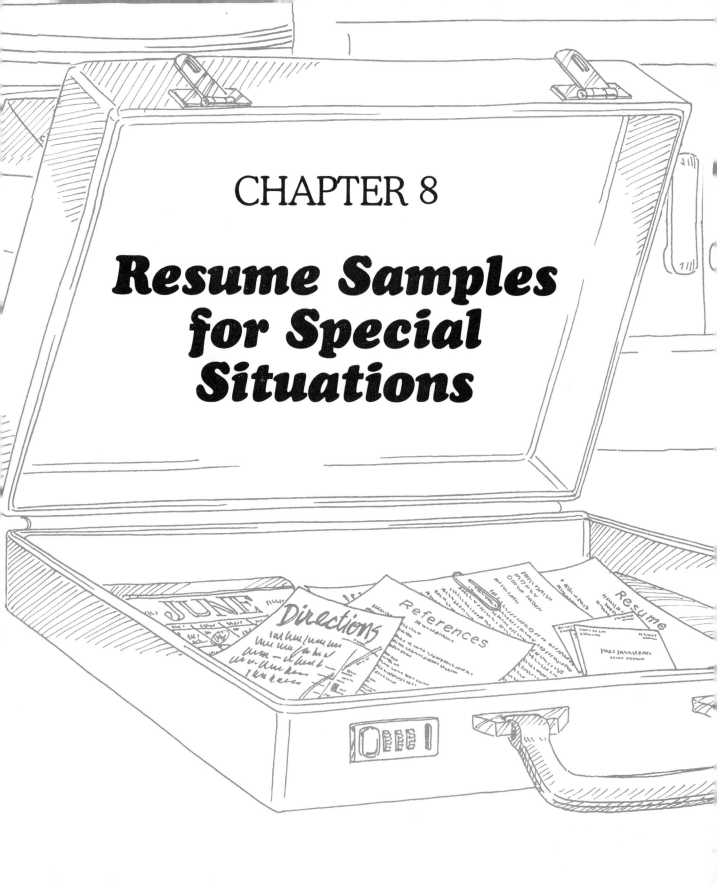

CHAPTER 8

Resume Samples for Special Situations

50-PLUS JOB CANDIDATE (Management)

CHRIS SMITH
178 Green Street
Huntington, WV 25702
(304) 555-5555

SUMMARY OF QUALIFICATIONS
Accomplished career counselor in the educational field
Extensive experience in management, including hiring and training
Good background in customer relations and human resources

EXPERIENCE
The Westview Schools, Huntington, WV
Career Counselor
1985-present
- Contact and interview potential candidates for business courses.
- Describe school programs and provide literature.
- Administer aptitude tests; advise prospective students as to their best courses to pursue.
- Organize welcoming ceremony and orientation meetings for new students each semester.
- Track completion and job-placement statistics.

Greenbriar Corporation, Huntington, WV
General Manager
1976-85
Greenbriar Corporation is a manufacturer of stamped metal parts.
- Selected, set up, equipped, and staffed new facilities. Supervised plant maintenance.
- Hired, trained, and supervised 18 skilled production personnel, 4 executives, and 16 support staff.
- Established incentive plans and quality, production, and cost controls.
- Supervised payroll, billing, credit and collection, purchasing, and finance for this $24 million company.

EDUCATION
Northeastern University, Boston, MA
Bachelor of Science in Business Administration
Concentration: Industrial Relations and Accounting

Chris Smith
178 Green Street
St. Louis, MO 63130
(314) 555-5555

EXPERIENCE
MARCA INFRARED DEVICES, St. Louis, MO
Manufacturers of infrared sensing and detecting devices.

Administrator 1998-present

Personnel
- Maintain engineering personnel status and monitor performance to plan.
- Automated weekly labor reports to calculate staffing levels and labor effectiveness.
- Train staff in library functions involving documentation ordering and CD-ROM usage.

Capital Expenditures
- Automated capital equipment planning cycle. Act as capital expenditure liaison for all of engineering.
- Perform year-end closeout on engineering purchase orders.

Budget Support
- Automated calculation of vacation dollars for engineering budget planning.
- Track contractor and consultant requisitions.

Documentation Control Clerk 1997-98
- Tracked and maintained changes to engineering documentation.
- Trained personnel in status accounting function and audit performance.

Documentation Specialist 1994-97
- Tracked and maintained changes to manufacturing and engineering documentation.
- Generated parts lists and was initial user of computerized bills of materials.
- Directed changes in material requirements to material and production control departments.

Configuration Management Analyst 1992-94
- Tracked and maintained changes to engineering documentation.
- Chaired Configuration Review Board.
- Presented configuration status reports at customer reviews.

Inside Sales Coordinator 1991-92
- Served as first customer contact.
- Directed customer calls and customer service.
- Maintained literature files and processed incoming orders.

EDUCATION
B.S. in Biology, Washington University

Chris Smith
178 Green Street
Upper Montclair, NJ 07043
(201) 555-5555

EXPERIENCE

MONTCLAIR MEMORIAL HOSPITAL, Montclair, NJ   1994-97
R.N. Staff Nurse
Addictions Treatment Program
Provide patient care on 40-bed mental health unit, administering medication, Emergency
Room consulting, collaborating with health-care providers.
- Assess and evaluate patients in substance abuse crises. Conduct post-crisis interview and
  provide counseling.
- Assess medical complications.
- Collaborate with treatment team to implement inpatient and aftercare plans.
- Verify and pre-certify insurance providers.
- Lead and co-lead educational groups for patients and their families.

Staff Nurse/Psychiatric Addiction Emergency Service   1991-94
- Assessed addicted and psychiatric patients to determine severity of illness and level of
  care needed.
- Collaborated with health-care providers and medical team.

MONMOUTH COLLEGE/NURSING PROGRAM, West Long Branch, NJ   1989-91
Instructor/Medical Assisting Techniques
- Instructed students in the arts and skills of office medical procedures.
- Organized and planned curriculum, tested and graded students in written and practical
  methods.

CITY OF NEWARK SCHOOL DEPARTMENT, Newark, NJ   1987-89
Substitute School Nurse
- Administered first aid for students in K-12.
- Performed eye and ear testing. Provided counseling and health instruction.

LICENSE
Registered Nurse: Registration Number 10468

EDUCATION
JERSEY CITY HOSPITAL SCHOOL OF NURSING, Jersey City, NJ

CAREER CHANGER (Public Relations)

CHRIS SMITH
178 Green Street
Juneau, AK 99801
(907) 555-5555
csmith@netmail.com

SUMMARY
- Over 3 years' experience in public relations
- Proven ability to plan and supervise major special events
- Knowledge of all aspects of media relations
- Skilled educator and public speaker

EXPERIENCE
1998-present   ALASKANS FOR A CLEANER WORLD,
Juneau, AK
Public Relations Coordinator (part-time)
- Handle all aspects of media relations.
- Plan and supervise special events. Organized first annual "Breath of Life" walk-a-thon, raising over $15,000.
- Educate public about environmental issues, including speaking at local schools.

1997-present   MT. JUNEAU MEDICAL CENTER,
Juneau, AK
Coordinator, Department of Neurosurgery
- Promote department; oversee public relations.
- Coordinate communications for medical and nonmedical activities within department.
- Serve as liaison between administrations of two hospitals, physicians, and nurses.
- Educate in-house staff, patients, and families on techniques, equipment, and related subjects.

PRESENTATIONS AND LECTURES
Have given over 25 presentations and lectures to various schools, hospitals, in-house staff, and professional associations.

COMPUTER SKILLS
Windows, WordPerfect, Lotus 1-2-3, Excel

EDUCATION
UNIVERSITY OF ALASKA, Anchorage, AK
Bachelor of Science in Nursing

CHRIS SMITH
178 Green Street
Cheyenne, WY 82009
(307) 555-5555

SUMMARY
Award-winning country-style cook
Knowledge of commercial food preparation and service
Experience in quantity cooking

EXPERIENCE
Lion's Club Carnival, Cheyenne, WY
1994-present
Cook
Staff concession booths at annual carnival; prepare and serve such items as fried dough, sweet sausage, pizza, and caramel apples. Maintain a receipt record of profits for event administrators.

St. Bernadette's Parish, Cheyenne, WY
1996-present
Bake Sale Coordinator
Coordinate annual bake sale; provide approximately 10% of bakery items sold.

Payne Community Center, Cheyenne, WY
1999-present
Instructor
Conduct informal weekly cooking classes.

Jameson Homeless Shelter, Cheyenne, WY
1999-present
Weekday Server
Serve 200 lunches per day. Act as liaison between homeless guests and national food distributor, securing special requests and unanimously favored items.

AWARDS
First prize in national fruit-based pie competition
$100 *Reader's Digest* prize for best pot roast recipe

EDUCATION
Cheyenne Community College, Cheyenne, WY
Associate in Home Economics

FORMER SMALL-BUSINESS OWNER (Desktop Publishing) SEEKING STAFF POSITION

CHRIS SMITH
178 Green Street
Clarksville, TN 37044
(615) 555-5555
csmith@netmail.com

SUMMARY OF QUALIFICATIONS
- More than 15 years' of art director/buyer and graphics/design production experience in the publishing field; extensive knowledge of type and mechanical preparation, budgeting, and scheduling.
- Excellent interpersonal, communication, and managerial skills; adept at coordinating and motivating creative artists to peak efficiency.
- Self-motivated; able to set effective priorities and meet impossible deadlines.

EXPERIENCE
1993-99   NO CONTEST GRAPHICS, Nashville, TN
Owner/President, Art Director/Buyer
- Coordinate operations of 12-member production staff and freelancers.
- Maintain overview of works-in-progress to produce at optimum efficiency.
- Provide advice to personnel in designing materials to appropriately meet client needs; conceptualize product; delegate staff to make decisions.
- Commission freelance illustrators, photographers, and graphic artists.
- Budget each project; ensure that artistic staff and typesetters meet deadlines and remain within cost parameters.

Representative projects: greeting cards, care package kits, magazine fragrance inserts, cereal boxes, toy packages, coloring books (cover and contents), holographic bumper stickers, retail store signs and logos

1991-1993   NEW JERSEY LITHOGRAPH, Newark, NJ
Head of Typesetting and Design Department
Supervised staff in design and execution of print materials for commercial printer.

1989-91   FREELANCE DESIGNER
Designed brochures, posters, booklets, ads, and direct-mail pieces for various clients.

EDUCATION
CENTENARY COLLEGE, Hackettstown, NJ
A.S. in Technical Illustration

ART INSTITUTE OF NEWARK, Newark, NJ
Certified in Graphic Design

FREELANCER (Writer and Editor)

CHRIS SMITH
178 Green Street
Richmond, VA 23294
(804) 555-5555
csmith@netmail.com

EXPERIENCE

Freelance Writer   1997-present
Projects include:
Teaching the Gifted Child (7-12), Ben Curtis and Company
Writing (handbooks, 7-9), Tallvia Kincaide, Inc.
Ancient Civilizations (textbook, 12), Jean K. Simmons Press
Studies in Literature (9-12), Jean K. Simmons Press

Create original manuscripts for student textbooks; annotate teacher's editions. Materials include teaching apparatus; questions for responding, analyzing, and interpreting; thinking, writing, language, and vocabulary exercises and worksheets; multi-page writing workshops; end-of-unit features for writing and language skills; and collaborative learning activities.

Design prototypes for textbook and ancillary features. Conduct multicultural literature searches.

Jean K. Simmons Press, Washburn, NH

Senior Editor, Secondary English   1992–97
Acted as project supervisor for teacher's editions of a composition and grammar program, levels 6-9. Edited manuscript for *Writing is Fun,* levels 7 and 8. Wrote manuscript for *Writing is Fun,* levels 9-12, including instruction, model paragraphs, and assignments. Developed content and approach for units on critical thinking and word processor use.

Educational Press, Orangeville, MA

Editor, Secondary English   1990–92
Acted as project supervisor for teacher's editions and teacher's resource masters of vocabulary program, levels 9-12. Edited manuscript for four levels of pupil books for vocabulary program. Wrote exercises, reading comprehension passages, and activities to support instruction. Conducted writing workshops for teachers as follow-up to sales.

EDUCATION
Clark University, Worcester, MA   *Master of Arts in Education*
Boston College, Chestnut Hill, MA   *Bachelor of Arts in English*

CHRIS SMITH
178 Green Street
Sumter, SC 29150
(803) 555-5555

Summary of Qualifications
More than 7 years' writing and editing experience
Adept at managing multiple responsibilities simultaneously
Experienced at delegating authority and motivating others, to ensure efficiency and productivity

Work Experience
Editor-in-Chief, *Renegade* magazine, Sumter, SC   1996-99
Selected submissions, edited and wrote headlines for submissions and columns, laid out pages, recruited columnists, trained associates. Frequently performed copyediting and research.

Associate Editor, *Modern Daze,* New York, NY   1990-94
Wrote articles for both the magazine and its associated newsletter, *Disembodied Voices.* Edited features and department articles. Read and critiqued assigned articles from contributing editors.

Copyeditor, *Heathcliff's Garden,* Boston, MA   1986-88
Edited news stories, wrote headlines, assisted with layout of page. Occasionally solicited advertising and helped with distribution.

Other Experience
Writer, professional musician

Computer Skills
Operating Systems   DOS, Windows 2000, Macintosh
Writing/publishing   Word, WordPerfect, PageMaker
Business   Lotus 1-2-3

Military
Army Corporal (honorable discharge)

Education
Le Student Roma, Rome, Italy
Intensive study of Italian language and culture

University of Richmond, Richmond, VA
Bachelor of Arts in English

MILITARY BACKGROUND (Intelligence Specialist)

CHRIS SMITH
178 Green Street
Appleton, WI 54912
(414) 555-5555

Experience
UNITED STATES NAVY
Intelligence Specialist   1995-99
Served as intelligence analyst in photographic interpretation for FIRST at NAS Boston and Fleet Intelligence Center Pacific. Participated in intelligence operations on month-long active duty assignments. Edited and compiled contingency briefs for fleet surface ships at Commander Naval Surface Force, Miami.

Intelligence Specialist   1991-95
Served as intelligence assistant at Commander Naval Surface Force, U.S. Pacific Fleet, Miami. Edited and compiled point papers on foreign navies. Briefed shipboard intelligence officers on intelligence collection effort.

Performed various other functions, including standing watch, serving as classified control custodian, and clerical and editorial duties. Performed administrative duties in Special Security Office at Fleet Intelligence Center Pacific, Los Angeles, CA.

Education
Marquette University, Milwaukee, WI   B.A. in Soviet Politics
Hamburg, St. Petersburg, Moscow, Paris   5-week study of Soviet languages

Military Training
National Imagery Interpretation Rating Scale School   Miami, FL
Shipboard Intelligence School   Miami, FL
Intelligence Specialists "A" School   Bangor, ME
Basic Training   Maui, HI

Languages
Fluent in German, French, Russian

Honors and Awards
Two Naval Certificates of Achievement

Clearance
Top Secret

NO CLEAR CAREER PATH (Human Resources)

CHRIS SMITH
178 Green Street
Wise, VA 24293
(703) 555-5555

OBJECTIVE
A position in Human Resources

SUMMARY OF QUALIFICATIONS
- Developed interpersonal skills; excellent mediation abilities; supervisory experience
- Extensive experience in training; able to explain procedures and achieve significant results in a brief time

EXPERIENCE
1997-present   BENNIE WARD'S STYLE SHINDIG, Winchester, VA
Sales Associate
Provide customer assistance and advise on selections. Develop ongoing customer relationships, enhancing future sales. Assist with promotions and special seasonal sales. Handle cash transactions. Acknowledged as one of top salespeople; consistently meet or exceed sales goals.

1990-present   ARMY NATIONAL GUARD, Richmond, VA
Assistant Section Coordinator, Sergeant/ E-5
Coordinate training of soldiers and work assignments. Maintain personnel records. Complete performance evaluations and recommend awards. Create schedules, oversee adherence to rules, assist in directing operations.

1994-97   MARTELL BLUE SECURITY SERVICES, Salem, MA
Shift Supervisor
Handled employee ID checks; secured building; ensured other site call-ins. Worked independently on onsite assignments.

COMPUTER SKILLS
Word, Lotus 1-2-3

EDUCATION
RICHMOND JUNIOR COLLEGE, Richmond VA
Associate in Management Science
Major: Business Administration

Chris Smith
178 Grunstrasse
Berlin, Germany
011-49-30-555-5555
csmith@strix.com.de

EXPERIENCE

WELBRUN STATE UNIVERSITY, European Region, Berlin, Germany   1998-present
Field Administrator/Manager
- Serve as liaison at military-based college, resolving military-civilian, faculty-student clashes. Requires ability to maneuver politically, observing military priorities.
- Supervise all office activities.
- Coordinate with Education Service Officer, Education Center staff, and faculty in planning educational programs for community.
- Assist students in course registration and planning academic and vocational needs.
- Process registration forms and financial reports.

UNIVERSITY OF MASSACHUSETTS, European Sect, Paris, France   1996-98
Field Registrar
- Managed office to plan and implement educational program for military community.
- Initiated innovative marketing policy and personal outreach program; increased student enrollment from 250 per year to 700.
- Prepared and processed registration forms and financial packets.
- Organized student tours and field trips.

ISLEFORT, Paris, France   1994-96
Retail Manager
- Supervised retail store complex operations, including theater, barbershop, temporary concessions, and pickup point. Tripled sales.
- Monitored retail store renovation, inventory, fixed assets, and cash/receipts.
- Interviewed, hired, trained, and cross-trained personnel.

THE GUIMBLEY SCHOOL, Lancaster, England   1992-94
Administrative Assistant
- Supervised and implemented clearance updating for 2,000 personnel files, to improve faculty academic qualifications.
- Transcribed edited reports and correspondence; oversaw publication of reports and catalogs.

EDUCATION

WELBRUN STATE UNIVERSITY, European Region, Berlin, Germany
M.P.A., Public Administration, Cognate: Counseling,

UNIVERSITY OF MASSACHUSETTS, European Division, Paris, France
B.A., Business Management, *cum laude*

CHRIS SMITH
178 Green Street
Arkadelphia, AK 71923
(501) 555-5555

EXPERIENCE
ARKANSAS PUBLIC SCHOOL SYSTEM

Principal 1985-98
RODHAM ELEMENTARY SCHOOL Arkadelphia, AR
Oversaw all school operations. Supervised and evaluated teachers and teaching assistants. Developed curriculum for mainstream and special-needs children. Chaired monthly staff meetings, oriented new administrative and teaching staff. Interacted with parents and school board for educational program development.

- Oversaw introduction of computer labs and instruction. Obtained donations from hardware and software manufacturers.
- Introduced new methods of teaching based on recent published research, using visual, auditory, tactile, and kinesthetic techniques.
- Wrote grant proposals to fund remedial teaching.
- Remained consistently within budget.

HOPE CLINTON JUNIOR HIGH SCHOOL Arkadelphia, AR
Principal 1979-85
In addition to same duties as above, established program to strengthen instruction in "3 Rs," languages, and arts. From 1981, students exceeded state norms and previous school record on standardized testing, GPA, and number of students continuing to college.

NOAH JUNIOR HIGH SCHOOL Arkadelphia, AR
Teaching Assistant Principal 1976-79
- Served as acting principal and directed operational processes.
- Assisted and supervised teaching staff.
- Interfaced with parents and teachers for educational program development.

EDUCATION
JOHN BROWN UNIVERSITY, Siloam Springs, AK
Master of Arts in Education
Bachelor of Arts in History

CERTIFICATION
Arkansas Teacher Certification

SHORT EMPLOYMENT HISTORY (Legal Assistant)

CHRIS SMITH
178 Green Street
Fairfax, VA 22030
(703) 555-5555

EXPERIENCE
Legal Assistant
Parnell & Swaggert
Fairfax, VA   1997-present
- Correspond via courier, telephone, letter, and facsimile with clients, attorneys, secretaries of state, U.S. Department of State, and foreign associates in matters of intellectual property law, primarily trademarks.
- Meet with clients regarding applications for and registration of trademarks.
- Duties also include compiling information from other Parnell & Swaggert branches, paying company's debit notes, and billing clients.

Legislative Intern
Office of Senator John Fisher
Washington, D.C.   Summer 1997
Handled legislative correspondence involving case work. Assisted Labor and Human Resources Committee, Judiciary Subcommittee, and Fund for a Democratic Majority. Projects included research, writing, and covering hearings.

Legislative Aide
Office of Senator Arthur Florio
Washington, D.C.   Summer 1996
Answered communications from constituents

COMPUTER SKILLS
Word, WordPerfect, Lotus 1-2-3

EDUCATION
George Mason University, Fairfax
BA, Law and Society

HONORS & AWARDS
- Oxford Honor Scholar
- Who's Who Among Students
- Student Government Award

Chris Smith
178 Green Street
Myrtle Beach, SC 29577
(803) 555-5555

OBJECTIVE

To apply skills attained through experience in supervision of parking facilities to the position of assistant manager of parking facilities.

SUMMARY

- Proven abilities have resulted in rapid advancement to a supervisory position
- Familiar with all functions of maintaining a smooth-running parking facility
- Sworn deputy sheriff, Birchwood County

EXPERIENCE

PORT AUTHORITY ROLLINS AIRPORT, Lexington, SC
1998–present   **Supervisor of Parking Facility**
Assign duties, administer work schedules and payroll. Oversee collection of money. Attend to snow removal. Resolve all problems. Maintain public relations and customer service. Represent Port Authority at scheduled court appearances.

1998–present   **President of Local Chapter of NAGE**
Represent all cashiers and attendants. Settle all problems pertaining to parking facilities. Negotiate contracts.

1996–98   **Assistant Supervisor/Cashier**
Assisted supervisor. Collected all parking fees. Achieved high standard of customer relations.

1993–96   **Attendant**
Patrolled parking facility, maintained cleanliness standards. Assisted customers.

EDUCATION

Jefferson High School, Myrtle Beach, SC

CHAPTER 9

Resume Samples for Students

ACCOUNTING MAJOR

Chris Smith
178 Green Street
Auburn, WA 28764
(206) 555-5555
csmith@netmail.com

EDUCATION
B.S. in Accounting, 1999
University of Washington, Seattle, WA
- Founder of Student Credit Union, run solely by and for students.
- Treasurer of Senior Class Council.
- Member of Women's Rugby Team.

EXPERIENCE

Sunnybrae Street Bank   Auburn, WA
Portfolio Accountant   1999-present
Determine cash available for daily security investment on $4.0 billion portfolio. Ensure timely settlement on fixed-income and equity trades. Calculate and post amortization of long-term fixed income holdings. Compute net asset value of funds on a monthly basis. Calculate interest accruals on fixed-income securities.

Gentle Warrior Marketing   Vancouver, WA
Marketing Intern   Summer 1998
Created project timelines, drafted budget estimates; created copy, edited, proofread, supervised production.

Rainy Day Business Machines   Bellevue, WA
Marketing Support Assistant   Summer 1997
Assisted marketing reps in making sales calls. Participated on sales team supporting account executives.
Maintained a PC help line for customer questions.

University of Washington Coffeehouse   Seattle, WA
Bar Director   1996-99
Managed student-run concession for college community. Supervised daily operation with a staff of 30+ employees. Operated with a budget of $175,000 a year. Directed numerous capital improvement projects.

COMPUTER SKILLS
Word, Lotus 1-2-3, WordPerfect, PageMaker, Excel

Chris Smith
178 Green Street
Elsah, IL 62028
(708) 555-5555

EDUCATION
NORTHWESTERN UNIVERSITY SCHOOL OF PUBLIC HEALTH, Evanston, IL
Part-time studies toward Master of Public Health. Degree to be awarded May 2000.

NORTHWESTERN UNIVERSITY, Evanston, IL 1997
B.S., Business Administration/Marketing.
Member, Alpha Beta Gamma and National Business Honor Society.
Certificate of Award for Outstanding Business Administration Graduates.

LARSON COLLEGE, Malibu, CA 1990
A.A., Merchandising
Emphasis on Communication and Public Presentation
Certificate in Professional Modeling

EXPERIENCE
RED SAVIOR INSURANCE, Elsah, IL
1995-present   Information Consultant
- Assist Department Supervisor as required with responsibility for work assignments, quality control, and resolving problems. Trained on all contracts and systems.
- Educate public on applicable BC/BS policies, guidelines, and procedures.
- Resolve complaints and disputes in billing or contract specifications.
- Research and write customer requests for appeal; present findings.

Achievements
- Identified existing problems and provided research data to ombudsman, contributing to revision of applicable underwriting policy.
- Selected to assist the Consumer Relations Department with inquiries from the media and third-party inquiries from the Division of Insurance.
- PACE 5 Awards (Public Acknowledgment for Conscientious Effort).

1993-95   Senior Information Representative
- Assisted in training and orienting new information representatives.
- Interacted directly with Research on legal cases for Law Department.
- Selected to attend training program on new computer system with subsequent responsibility to train coworkers.
- Responded to inquiries, identified and researched subscriber problems.
- Drafted series of form letters to accompany payments to participating medical providers.

COLLEGE STUDENT APPLYING FOR AN INTERNSHIP

CHRIS SMITH

School Address:
178 Green Street
Skidell, LA 70458
(504) 555-5555

Permanent Address:
23 Blue Street
New Orleans, LA 70128
(504) 555-5555

OBJECTIVE
A summer internship in the book-publishing industry.

SUMMARY OF QUALIFICATIONS
- Copyediting: Two years' experience copyediting monthly church newsletter using *Chicago Manual of Style*
- Proofreading: Familiar with proofreading symbols
- Prolific writer; voracious reader

EDUCATION
TULANE UNIVERSITY, New Orleans, LA. **Bachelor of Arts in English and American Literature** with a concentration in film. Degree to be awarded May 1999. Dean's list. GPA in major: B+

EMPLOYMENT
THE NEW ORLEANS PEOPLE FIRST PROGRAM, Skidell, LA   1997-present
Adult Literacy Tutor
Travel to various prisons, nursing homes, boardinghouses, and learning centers. Tutor residents in elements of spelling, grammar, and parts of speech. Issue progress reports, bestow awards.

TULANE UNIVERSITY, New Orleans, LA   1996 - present
Manager, film series
Booked and publicized weekly films, arranged for projectionist and ticket taker, maintained accounts, paid bills.

TULANE MAILROOM, New Orleans, LA   Spring 1995
Mail sorter
Routed mail to appropriate departments and individual mailboxes (incoming); sorted mail by zip code (outgoing).

SKILLS
Computer: Word, Excel, QuarkXPress
Language: Intermediate-level French, American Sign Language

Chris Smith
178 Green Street
Goshen, IN 46526
(219) 555-5555
csmith@netmail.com

EDUCATION
United States Naval Academy, Annapolis, MD
B.S. Computer Science, 1999
Curriculum emphasized analytical and technical skills for identifying, studying, and solving informational problems in business organizations.

COMPUTER SKILLS
- Programming in C++, Java, and BASIC
- Hardware-oriented courses: Microprocessors
- Software-oriented courses: Programming in BASIC, Operating Systems, File Structures, DATA Structures, Database Techniques, and Software Engineering
- Analysis and Design courses: Systems Analysis, Systems Design, and Programming Languages

EXPERIENCE
Summers 1998-99
The Let It Rise Restaurant, Goshen, IN
Waited tables, acted as host; developed good personal relation skills. Received deliveries and supplies and distributed them throughout the restaurant. Managed inventory.

Summer 1997
The Squeaky Cleaners, Goshen, IN
Shift supervisor responsible for staff of six. Handled and tallied cash receipts. Oversaw pickup and drop-off of clothing.

COLLEGIATE
United States Naval Academy is the nation's oldest private military college, which places demands upon its students beyond academic curriculum. The Academy develops leadership and organizational skills through a disciplined environment.

Charter Member of the Association for Computing Machinery (ACM)

Member of the USNA Division 1 Crew Team

ENGLISH MAJOR

Chris Smith
178 Green Street
Columbia, MO 65201
(314) 555-5555

OBJECTIVE
A position in the publishing field.

SUMMARY OF QUALIFICATIONS
- Four years' publishing experience.
- Proven writing skills; authored hundreds of pages of fiction and nonfiction in the past three years.
- Excellent communication abilities; lectured to a wide variety of audiences in a museum setting.

EDUCATION
DOWLING COLLEGE, Oakdale, NY
B.A., English, *magna cum laude,* 1999

SKILLS
Computer: Word, Excel, QuarkXpress, PageMaker
Languages: Bilingual in English and Spanish; some knowledge of French

COLLEGE ACTIVITIES
Plume, Literary Magazine   Fall 1995-Spring 1999
Editor (from Spring 1997), Production and Business Coordinator
Composed magazine budget and arranged specifications with printers.

Freelance Writer   Spring 1996-Spring 1999
Published book and movie reviews, essays, and stories in campus publications.

WORK EXPERIENCE
The Damien House Museum, Oakdale, NY   Spring 1999
Museum Assistant
Interpreted exhibits for visitors. Prepared and delivered short talks on historical subjects.
Participated in organizing creative educational programs.

Bindings Bookstore, Oakdale, NY   Fall 1997
Sales Clerk/Floor Person
Maintained stock; helped customers make selections; registered sales.

Chris Smith
178 Green Street
Georgetown, TX 78676
(517) 555-5555
csmith@netmail.com

OBJECTIVE
A position in Finance

SUMMARY OF QUALIFICATIONS
- College major, relevant coursework, and tutoring experience in finance, economics, and accounting.
- Strong analytical and numerical abilities.
- Excellent sales and closing skills.
- Calm under pressure; meet deadlines; strong on follow-up.

SKILLS
Computer: Word, Excel, Lotus 1-2-3
Language: Bilingual in French

EDUCATION
SOUTHWESTERN UNIVERSITY, Georgetown, NY
Bachelor of Science in Finance, 2000
Major GPA: 3.55/4.0

EXPERIENCE

THE TURKEY TROUGH, Alpine, TX 1999-present
Assistant to Manager/Server and Bartender
- Provided customer service; balanced nightly receipts.
- Shift supervisor for staff of eight.

SOUTHWESTERN UNIVERSITY, Georgetown, TX 1997-99
Teaching Assistant/Tutor in Finance, Economics, Accounting
Tutored students and assisted professor in Corporate Finance course.

BENOIT ASSOCIATES, Austin, TX 1995-97
- Payroll and Daily Journal Bookkeeper
- Administered bookkeeping, cash intake and reconciliation, and order placement.
- Verified balanced invoices.

NURSING MAJOR

Chris Smith
178 Green Street
Bennington, VT 05201
(802) 555-5555

SUMMARY OF QUALIFICATIONS
- Nine years' experience in a medical or health-care setting.
- RN completion in 1999; BSN anticipated 2000.
- Certified phlebotomist.
- Demonstrated composure under pressure.
- Flexible, decisive, patient.
- Intuitive; enjoy patients and work well with them.

EDUCATION
VERMONT SCHOOL OF NURSING, Montpelier, VT
R.N. Diploma expected December 1999.
Received Bailey Howe Award for Outstanding Students in Nursing, 1997.

EMPLOYMENT
1997-present   TRINITY HOSPITAL, Burlington, VT per diem/16-24 hours
Intensive Care Aide/Surgical Floor Aide—Floater
Assist with burn dressings and trauma patients. Provide postsurgical care assistance with vital signs, ADLs, insertion of Foley catheters, dressing changes. Monitor IV fluids and blood sugar; collect specimens.

1995-97   VERMONT GENERAL HOSPITAL, Bennington, VT
Undergraduate Nursing Assistant—Phlebotomist
Monitored all aspects of patient care: vital signs, ADLs, IVs, collected specimens. Input and output records.

1994-95   NEW AGE PUBLISHERS, Killington, VT
Graphic Designer
Designed newspaper and high-quality magazine ad work.

COMPUTER SKILLS
Word, WordPerfect, Lotus 1-2-3, and various hospital-related databases

CHRIS SMITH
178 Green Street
Ypsilanti, MI 48198
(313) 555-5555

EDUCATION
Eastern Michigan University, Ypsilanti, MI
Bachelor of Science, Occupational Therapy, 1999
Dean's list four consecutive semesters.

CLINICAL AFFILIATIONS
LEARNING PREP SCHOOL, Ypsilanti, MI   1998-present
Assistant Occupational Therapist
- Work with students having developmental delays, mental retardation, and related learning disabilities.
- Perform interventions, including gross and fine motor therapy, visual-perceptual-motor therapy, vocational training, and neurodevelopmental technique in individual therapy.
- Oversaw community outings. Supervised visual-perceptual-motor group and pre-vocational and vocational work centers.

SPAULDING REHABILITATION HOSPITAL   Summer 1997
Assistant Occupational Therapist
- Caseload included patients with cardiac and pulmonary disorders, lower limb amputations, stroke, brain injury, and reflex-sympathetic dystrophy.
- Performed interventions, including neurodevelopmental technique, joint mobilization, deep friction massage, computer-assisted cognitive therapy, community mobility, home program planning, home evaluations, and evaluations in all related areas.

MORING PSYCHIATRIC HOSPITAL   Summer 1996
Occupational Therapy Internship
- Worked with adolescent, adult, and geriatric patients with affective, chronic thought process, social, and personality disorders, as well as substance abuse disorders.
- Supervised general activities period.
- Administered initial evaluations, vocational readiness evaluations, and leisure-planning evaluations.
- Undertook student project: Occupational Therapy in Psychiatry.

PROFESSIONAL ASSOCIATIONS
Michigan Occupational Therapy Association
American Occupational Therapy Association.

PHYSICAL THERAPY MAJOR

CHRIS SMITH

School:	Home:
178 Green Street	23 Blue Street
East Lansing, MI 48824	Rockland, MA 02370
(517) 555-5555	(617) 444-4444

EDUCATION
MICHIGAN STATE UNIVERSITY, East Lansing, MI
Bachelor of Science in Physical Therapy, expected 2000

ACCOMPLISHMENTS/AWARDS
- Dean's List, two semesters
- Student-Athlete of the Year, 1999
- Michigan State University Varsity Hockey, 1996-present; Captain, 1998-present

EXPERIENCE
1997-present   MICHIGAN STATE UNIVERSITY, East Lansing, MI
Athletics Instructor
> Lead numerous outdoor physical activities. Assist and teach undergraduates.
> Organize coed intramural sports for the entire campus, including scheduling,
> arranging for field and court time, and awarding prizes on a limited budget.

RELATED EXPERIENCE
Summers 1996-98   EAST LANSING DAY CAMPS, East Lansing, MI
Activities Coordinator
> Organized and guided inner-city youth in recreational activities, new games, arts and
> crafts. Responsible for group of eight 10-year-olds.

Summer 1995   ROCKLAND PARKS COMMISSION, Rockland, MA
Activities Supervisor
> Participated in weekend field days. Organized sports and recreational activities for
> groups of children ranging in age from six to fifteen.

1993-95   ROCKLAND SKATING RINK, Rockland, MA
Skate Guard/Instructor
> Assisted patrons with equipment. Taught people of all ages skating basics.

Chris Smith
178 Green Street
Mossyrock, WA 98564
(509) 555-5555
csmith@netmail.com

EDUCATION
WHITWORTH COLLEGE, Spokane, WA
Master of Science in Mass Communications, 1999
WALLA WALLA COLLEGE, College Place, WA
Bachelor of Arts in Communications and Theater, 1997

PROFESSIONAL BACKGROUND
LOCKWOOD ENGINEERING, Ravensdale, WA   1997-present
Editor/Writer, Worldwide Business Development Division
- Prepare bid proposals for government, industrial, and utility contracts, including engineering and construction.
- Interpret client RFP requirements; determine applicability of proposal response to RFP.
- Write and edit proposals; coordinate production, organize and maintain up-to-date dummy book through several revision cycles.
- Act as liaison between proposal/marketing engineer and graphic arts, word processing, and production departments.

GLACIER PEAK, INC., Nahcotta, WA   1995-97
Assistant to the Director, Publications Department
- Researched, wrote, and supervised production of employee orientation brochures.
- Edited and proofread most intracompany published materials. Special projects included establishing corporate slide library and preparing quarterly budget forecasts and analyses.

RUSTLEAF PAGING SERVICES, INC., Deerpark, WA   1993-95
Assistant to the Manager, Computer Resources Department
- Developed computerized report program to track personnel productivity and department project and task management.
- Monitored customer accounting, including answering inquiries and preparing service reports.

COMPUTER SKILLS
Operating systems	Windows, UNIX, Macintosh
Writing/publishing	Word, WordPerfect
Business	Excel, Lotus 1-2-3, INFORMIX

Chris Smith
178 Green Street
Jamaica, NY 11451
(718) 555-5555

WORK HISTORY

1998-present   Governess
MR. AND MRS. KURT URBANE
15 Goldstone Road, Jamaica, NY
- Provide full-time care for a 6-year-old girl.
- Duties include dressing, tutoring, chauffeuring, running errands, housework, cooking, and seeing to the child's needs and well-being.
- Live-in position.

1997   Governess
MR. AND MRS. PAUL McMAHON
145 Nicole Lane, Kutztown, PA
- Provided care for three children: an infant, a 3-year-old girl, and a 5-year-old boy.
- Live-in position.

1993-97   Babysitter
MR. AND MRS. STEVE McGYVER
333 Sunshine Court, Loveland, CO
- Provided care for an infant girl and toddler twin brothers.

SKILLS

- Valid driver's license; perfect driving record
- CPR/first aid certified
- Skiing, reading, horseback riding, traveling, swimming

EDUCATION

Boulder High, Boulder, CO

Chris Smith

178 Green Street
Goodwell, OK 73939
(405) 555-5555

EDUCATION

UNIVERSITY OF MIAMI, Coral Gables, FL
MBA with concentration in Finance, 1998
COLLEGE OF THE HOLY CROSS, Worcester, MA
Bachelor of Science in Economics/Finance, 1993

EXPERIENCE

NAOT, INC., Goodwell, OK   1997-present
Accountant
- Prepare payroll, general ledger, daily cash, accounts payable and receivable, monthly financial statements, and general ledger reconciliations.
- Act as project manager for ongoing upgrade to accounting database.
- Provide cost proposals on government and commercial accounts.
- Execute billing on Timberline software for company projects and maintain Timberline system.

O'CONNOR, RAISTY & ROSS, Oklahoma City, OK   1993-95
Contract Billing Administrator
Worked for BBN Systems & Technologies.
- Interpreted billing provisions of government and commercial contracts, maintained interactive billing systems, prepared accounts receivable and sales adjustments.
- Maintained MIS database and reconciled mailing list to invoice register.

THE MUTUAL CORP., Shawnee, OK   1992-93
ABI-Boston Coordinator
- Designed procedures to implement new Automated Brokerage Interface.
- Supervised transformation from manual to computerized operation, trained personnel.
- Maintained system software and daily records.
- Researched and reconciled complex international transactions.

COMPUTER SKILLS

Word, Excel, Lotus 1-2-3, Timberline, dBase

SOME COLLEGE BUT NO DEGREE (Accounting)

CHRIS SMITH
178 Green Street
Dahlonega, CA 31597
(404) 555-5555

SUMMARY OF QUALIFICATIONS
- Eight years' experience and broad-based knowledge of the accounting field.
- Proficient with Lotus 1-2-3; general ledger, accounts receivable and payable, auditing and cash flow functions.
- Strong numerical and administrative abilities.
- Experience training incoming personnel.

EXPERIENCE
1999-present   SAVANNA COMPTROLLER'S OFFICE, Dahlonega, CA
Accounting Assistant
- Monitor funding and financial reporting associated with various federal sponsors.
- Perform internal cost audits of terminated research contracts and grants.
- Coordinate audit and cash flow functions between CAO and other university departments.
- Create financial reports, monthly and quarterly reports, required governmental reports, and correspondence.

1996-99   NOSTRADAMUS CORPORATION, Dahlonega, CA
Accounting Assistant
- Held complete responsibility for receivables and payables.
- Computerized financial reports and auditing.
- Served as telephone and personal contact in customer service and in resolving problems with purchasing department.
- Maintained computer master files and related input data.

EDUCATION
CREIGHTON UNIVERSITY, Omaha, NE
> Coursework in accounting, statistics, corporate finance, business law, and computers

COMPUTER SKILLS
> Lotus 1-2-3, Excel, Word, WordPerfect, Access, dBase

TRANSFER STUDENT

Chris Smith

178 Green Street
Rochester, NY 14623
(716) 555-5555

EDUCATION

Cornell University, Ithaca, NY
B.S. in Earth Science, 1999
Massachusetts Institute of Technology, Cambridge, MA, 1997
Coursework in biology, chemistry, and environmental science

EXPERIENCE

Cornell University, Ithaca, NY

Intern, Biobased Materials Center, Forest Products Department   1998-99

Developed an understanding of the materials science aspects of polysaccharide (cellulose, hemicellulose, chitin) regeneration in the form of hydrogen beads. This research focused on examining relationships between the nature of the polysaccharide (chemistry, molecular weight, viscosity) and important hydrogen parameters, like gel structure, morphology, bead pore size, flow characteristics, mechanical strength, and reactivity.

Assistant, Wood Chemistry Laboratory, Forest Products Department   1997

Assisted professor on chemical modification of lignin with propylene oxide for the synthesis of urethanes and thermoplastic elastomers. Performed the synthesis and full characterization (chemical, thermal, mechanical, and morphological) of multiphase block copolymers containing lignin and either polycaprolactone, cellulose propionate, or polystyrene as the hard segments.

American Center of Technology (ACT), Boston, MA   1996
Assistant

Developed projects on alternative energy from biomass residues, mainly sugar cane bagasse.

SKILLS

Languages: Fluent in English and German, proficient in Spanish, working knowledge of Dutch

AFFILIATION

American Chemical Society, member since 199

CHAPTER 10

Resume Samples for Common Jobs

ACCOUNT EXECUTIVE

CHRIS SMITH
178 Green Street
Wise, VA 24293
(703) 555-5555
csmith@netmail.com

EXPERIENCE

WCVT-TV (NLC-Channel 3), Wise, VA
Account Executive/Sales Department   1999-present
- Established and maintained new and existing corporate accounts, representing more than $1.5 million in new clients.
- Initiated and developed marketing strategies and target grids for the second-ranked TV station in fifth-largest market for effective sales programs and promotions.
- Aided potential clients in developing effective marketing strategies and programs.

Associate Director/Stage Manager   1998-99
- Production Department stage manager for noon, five o'clock, and News at Ten newscasts, all public-affairs programs, editorials, and news cut-ins.
- Assembled sets and operated Chyron machine.

Production Intern   1997
- Wrote hard news and feature stories; scheduled and interviewed guests.
- Researched materials and packaged tapes for production.
- Operated TelePrompTer.

UNIVERSITY OF VIRGINIA, Charlottesville, VA
Producer, Television and Radio Station WNUV-Channel 62   1996-97
- Researched materials for mini-documentary.
- Scheduled and interviewed guests for roundtable discussions.
- Wrote and edited scripts and edited master tape.

Production Assistant   1995-96
- Acted as camera technician, stage manager, and Chyron operator.
- Assembled lighting and audio equipment.

EDUCATION

RANDOLPH-MACON WOMAN'S COLLEGE, Lynchburg, VA
B.A., Communications/Mass Media, *magna cum laude,* 1998
Concentration: Economics and Afro-American Studies

HONORS AND AFFILIATIONS

Recipient, Virginia Chapter, National Association of TV Arts and Sciences Award.
National Association of Women Journalists.
National Association of Media Workers.

CHRIS SMITH
178 Green Street
Billings, MT 59105
(406) 555-5555

EMPLOYMENT HISTORY
ROSS PECOE, INC., Billings, MT
A $20 million publicly held company that develops, manufactures, and markets proprietary x-ray systems
Financial Analyst/Accountant 1998-present
- Assist controller in preparing financial statements and SEC reports.
- Prepare budgets and projections; prepare monthly budget-to-actual reports and distribute to managers.
- Review work of staff accountant and approve journal transactions for data entry.
- Manage accounting duties of a venture-capital-funded start-up organization, Beta Technologies, including financial reporting and coordinating annual audit with external auditors.
- Assisted in consolidation of three European subsidiaries.

Accountant 1996-98
- Assisted with monthly closings and financial reporting.
- Worked directly with controller to prepare primary and secondary public stock offerings.
- Implemented Solomon general ledger accounting package. Installed and set up modules, developed procedures for new system, and trained staff.

1994-96
STEADFAST CORPORATION, Cherry Creek, MT
A venture-capital-funded software development firm
Staff Accountant
- Monitored cash and accounts receivable.
- Assisted in general ledger close, including foreign currency translation of foreign subsidiaries.
- Trained new employees to administer the accounts payable and order entry functions.

EDUCATION
Bronte College, Newcastle, ME
Master of Science in Accountancy; expected completion May 2001
Carroll College, Helena, MT
Bachelor of Arts in Business Management

COMPUTER SKILLS
Excel, Lotus 1-2-3, Ask ManMan General Ledger

ACCOUNTING CLERK

CHRIS SMITH
178 Green Street
Brimfield, MA 01010
(413) 555-5555

EXPERIENCE
1999-present   APPLEDYNE CORP., Brimfield, MA
Accounting Assistant
- Maintain computerized accounts payables and receivables. Verify accuracy of purchase orders and invoices.
- Implemented a user-friendly billing system to improve relations with clients.
- Established an employee check-cashing center.
- Received written commendation from Appledyne president John Pacs.

1998-99   TERRIO LYCRA CORP., Amherst, MA
Accounts Receivable/Payable Clerk
- Maintained computerized accounts receivable and payable.
- Handled outgoing communications.
- Generated and mailed accounts payable checks.

1996-98   MAYFLOWER DATING SERVICE, Manomet, MA
Accounting Clerk/Assistant to Vice President of Finance
- Generated income statements, balance sheets, general ledger, checks and reports.
- Entered payable vouchers.
- Received and deposited monthly rent checks.

COMPUTER SKILLS
Word, Excel, Lotus 1-2-3

EDUCATION
JASPER COLLEGE, Nashua, NH
B.S., Mathematics
GPA 3.0

ACCOUNTS PAYABLE CLERK (General)

CHRIS SMITH
178 Green Street
Newark, NJ 07102
(201) 555-5555

EXPERIENCE

1998-present   BETTY LOU'S LINGERIE, Newark, NJ
Accounts Payable/Payroll Department
- Light typing, filing, and other general office duties.
- Key in bills on computer and print checks for 6 offices.
- Assist in payroll preparation by calculating time sheets and performing related duties.

1995-98   DYNAMO DANCE SUPPLIES, Teaneck, NJ
Accounts Payable
- Set up invoices to match purchase orders for input into computers.
- Added up invoices to match check amounts.
- Performed filing, mail sorting, and general office duties.
- Assisted in general ledger monthly closings.

1993-95   LEDA AND THE SWAN PETSITTERS, New Brunswick, NJ
General Office Support
- Acted as cashier, light typist, bank depositor, and keypunch operator.
- Handled filing and accounts payable/receivable.
- Interacted extensively with customers.

COMPUTERS
WordPerfect, Lotus 1-2-3

EDUCATION
DIRK JUNIOR COLLEGE, Camden, NJ
Courses in Accounting, Typing, and Data Processing

ACCOUNTS RECEIVABLE CLERK

CHRIS SMITH
178 Green Street
Newark, NJ 07107
(201) 555-5555

EXPERIENCE
THE FULLER COMPANY, Newark, NJ   1997-present
Assistant Manager—Accounts Receivable
In addition to traditional accounting functions, performed the following:
- Posted receivables to electronic spreadsheet. Posted month-end journal entries on MILLENNIUM system.
- Documented "proofed" checks and monies for deposit. Coordinated with other departments to resolve problems with checks that failed to clear.
- Maintained $10,000 petty cash fund and $15,000 American Express Travelers' Checks account.
- Researched interdepartmental queries and provided results to requester.

Financial Associate—Accounts Payable
- Audited documents, including expense reports, invoices, and check requests for payment.
- Generated disbursement instructions for accounts.
- Assigned and maintained on-line vendor identification files.
- Developed and maintained 1099 tax information on vendors.
- Assisted in establishing and validating travel reimbursement programs.

B. PARR AND ASSOCIATES, West Orange, NJ   1995-97
Bookkeeper
- Performed all accounting functions: journal entries, accounts payable and receivable, petty cash, deposits, bank reconciliations, and trial balances.
- Calculated payroll deductions and processed payroll.
- Executed monthly, quarterly, and year-end payroll and sales-tax forms.
- Performed phone collection of overdue accounts, decreasing over-30-day payables by 11%.

HACKENSACK HOME FURNISHINGS, Hackensack, NJ   1992-95
Manager/Bookkeeper
- Brought new company to full operational status.
- Supervised inventory, orders, sales, rent-to-own contracts, and part-time employees.
- Performed all bookkeeping, banking, sales, payroll taxes, and bank reconciliations.

EDUCATION
Kean College of New Jersey, Union, N.J.
A.S. in Accounting

ACTOR/ACTRESS

CHRIS SMITH
178 Green Street
Seattle, WA 98103
(206) 555-5555

Hair: Blonde   D.O.B.: 7/20/75   Eyes: Hazel
Height: 5'8"   Sex: Female   Weight: 135 lbs

EXPERIENCE
1999   WHITEWATER COMMUNITY THEATER, Seattle, WA
Mrs. Babson, *Lights, Camera, Action*

SUMMER ARTS THEATER, Seattle, WA
Karen Arnold, *Life in the Slow Lane*

NIGHT OWL THEATER, Seattle, WA
Candice Lloyd, *World's End*

1998
ST. MARY'S CONGREGATION, Black Diamond, WA
Director, Assorted children's plays

REGGAE FEST, Jamaica
Actor/Director, Several "Festival" performances during this annual national celebration

CHARLES STREET THEATER, Black Diamond, WA
Therese Dupuis, *The Deal*

EDUCATION
1999-present   ACTING UP DRAMA WORKSHOP, Seattle, WA
Advanced Acting, Acting for Stage and Television, Ritual and Performance

Related performances:
* Carolyn Christian, *Many Moons*
* Sarah Downs, *Two for Lunch*
* Maryanne Walsh, *Computer Geeks*
* Lisa, *Cranberry with a Twist*

1997
EMERSON COLLEGE, Boston, MA
Bachelor of Fine Arts, Acting

LANGUAGE
Bilingual in Italian and English

AD COPYWRITER (Direct Mail)

CHRIS SMITH
178 Green Street
South Paris, ME 04281
(207) 555-5555

PROFILE
A professional writer with demonstrated expertise in promotional concept, design, and copy. Proven ability to market a product or company to best advantage.

EXPERIENCE
A. MARTIN ART CATALOGUES, Bangor, ME
Direct Mail Copywriter, 1999-present
Implement direct mail and all other in-print marketing and advertising campaigns for leading modern art catalogue service. Establish direct-mail schedules for all products and coordinate activities with field sales and telemarketing. Write and track brochures, catalogues, letters, and ads. Oversee outside freelance design and printing.

SEDOTE DESIGN, Newark, NJ
Senior Writer, 1997-99
Wrote and edited direct-mail brochures, letters, catalogues, and ads for a leading textbook publisher. Interacted with marketing and product-development staffs to produce effective promotional material. Planned and executed writing and production schedules. Supervised staff of copywriters, and managed activities of designers, photographers, and printers. Promoted from position of *advertising copywriter*.

G. EDMUND SUKKIENIK PUBLISHING, South Paris, ME
Marketing Writer, 1995-97
Wrote copy for direct-mail catalogues and promotions. Worked closely with marketing and creative staffs on press releases, space ads, posters, card decks, and dealer promotions.

NORTHERN LIGHTS ASSOCIATION, Northfield, MN
Public Relations Assistant, 1994-95
Coordinated media relations and arranged promotional events. Wrote press releases, press kits, and newsletters.

EDUCATION
CARLETON COLLEGE, Northfield, MN
B.A. in Communications, *summa cum laude*
Concentration: English; Minor: Journalism

ADMINISTRATIVE ASSISTANT (Investments)

CHRIS SMITH
178 Green Street
Albany, NY 12208
(518) 555-5555
csmith@netmail.com

EXPERIENCE

1998-present   LOYALTY INVESTMENTS, Albany, NY
Administrative Assistant

Provide administrative support for new business development group; assist CFO with special projects. Ensure smooth workflow; facilitate effectiveness of 14 sales consultants. Direct incoming calls; initiate new client application process, maintain applicant record database. Aided in streamlining application process. Assisted in design and implementation of computer automation system. Oversee office equipment maintenance.

1996-98   THE GYMNASTIC SCHOOL, Albany, NY
Instructor

Planned and implemented recreational program for 70 gymnasts at various skill levels. Evaluated new students' progress; maintained records. Choreographed competitive performances; motivated gymnastics team of 20. Set team goals and incentives to maximize performance levels.

1993-96   GROVER FINANCE, Buffalo, NY
Telemarketing Sales Representative

Secured new business using customer inquiries and mass mailing responses; provided product line information to prospective clients. Initiated loan application and qualifying processes. Maintained daily call records and monthly sales breakdown. Acquired comprehensive product line knowledge and ability to quickly assess customer needs and assemble appropriate financial packages.

EDUCATION

Hofstra University, Hempstead, NY
Bachelor of Arts, English
Concentration: Business; Dean's List, GPA 3.3

COMPUTER SKILLS

Word, WordPerfect, Lotus 1-2-3, Act!

ADVERTISING ASSISTANT

CHRIS SMITH
178 Green Street
Buckeye, WV 24924
(304) 555-5555
csmith@netmail.com

SUMMARY
- Bachelor of Arts in Advertising; basic knowledge of mass marketing and communications; consumer oriented; computer literate.
- Three years of full- and part-time employment experience in positions of supervisory responsibility.
- Excellent verbal and written communications skills; experienced in personnel relations, brochure and documentary film production; high aptitude for acquiring new business technologies.

EDUCATION
Bachelor of Arts, University of Massachusetts, Amherst, MA, 1997
Major: Advertising
- Core GPA 3.48/4.0; Dean's List of Distinguished Students
- Relevant courses include Organizational Communication; Interpersonal Communication; Advanced Mass Media; Advanced Video; Consumer Motivation; Advertising; Writing for Film, Radio, and T.V.; Graphic Design
- Assisted in production of an independent documentary film, *Now I Lay Me Down to Sleep,* about homelessness. Acted as script advisor, cameraperson, and sound assistant.

EMPLOYMENT EXPERIENCE
Fanfare, Inc.   1996-99
Assistant Manager   Northampton, MA
- Provided support services for the operations manager, including determination of costs and analysis of old and current accounts.
- Oversaw distribution of warehouse inventory to branch offices.
- Scheduled and dispatched truck fleet.
- Documented billing and posting of union labor.
- Devised daily cut sheets.

COMPUTER SKILLS
Word, Lotus 1-2-3, QuarkXPress, Photoshop

AIRCRAFT MECHANIC

CHRIS SMITH
178 Green Street
Northfield, MN 55057
(507) 555-5555

EDUCATION

NORTHFIELD COMMUNITY COLLEGE, Northfield, Minnesota
Currently attending Applied Science degree program in Aeronautics;
expected graduation May 2000.

UNITED STATES AIR FORCE AIRCRAFT MAINTENANCE SCHOOL
Grisham Air Force Base, Indiana
Graduated 170-hour program—KC/RC/EC-135, Periodic
    December 1998
Graduated 110-hour program—KC/RC/EC-135, Able Chief
    May 1998

UNITED STATES AIR FORCE AIRCRAFT MAINTENANCE SCHOOL
Sheppard Air Force Base, Texas
Graduated 150-hour program in Tactical/Airlift Bombardment
    December 1997

AIRCRAFT MAINTENANCE COURSE
Lubbock Air Force Base, Texas
Graduated 120-hour program
    September 1996

EXPERIENCE

Trained in maintenance, servicing, and troubleshooting on all areas of
KC/RC/EC-135 aircraft, from wingtips to landing gear, nose to tail, interior
and exterior, including removals and replacements of component parts,
repairs, lubrications, refueling, and flight-line launching and recoveries.

Perform inspections of J57-59 Turbo Jet Engines, plus troubleshooting of
component parts. Certified in aircraft towing, aircraft power and battery
connections and disconnections, engine cowl removal and installation.

RELATED INFORMATION

Received honorable discharge.

AIRCRAFT PILOT

CHRIS SMITH
178 Green Street
Glendale, AZ 85306
(602) 555-5555

FLIGHT TIME

Total Time: 6500	Jet Engine: 900	Pilot in Command: 3800
Turbine: 5200	Second in Command: 2600	Instrument: 350

QUALIFICATIONS
AIRLINE TRANSPORT PILOT
* Airplane Multi-Engine Land
* BAE 3100 Type
* FAA Class I Medical
* Flight Engineer-Basic-Turbojet written
* SF-340 Type

EDUCATION

EMORY-RIDDLE AERONAUTICAL UNIVERSITY Daytona Beach, FL
Professional Pilot 1986-87

MISSISSIPPI STATE UNIVERSITY Starkville, MS
Business Administration 1978-80

SAINT LOUIS UNIVERSITY St. Louis, MO
Business Administration/Physical Education 1975-76

EMPLOYMENT

SOUTHWEST AIRLINES Phoenix, AZ
First Officer 1996-99
DC-9

NORTHEAST AIRLINES Portland, ME
Captain 1992-95
Saab-Fairchild 340

VANTAGE ENTERPRISES, INC. Wayne, NE
Line Pilot 1990-92

IPHAGENA INDUSTRIES Wayne, NE
Line Pilot 1989-90

APPLICATIONS PROGRAMMER (General)

CHRIS SMITH

178 Green Street
Los Altos, CA 91335
(415) 555-5555
csmith@netmail.com

COMPUTER SKILLS
Operating systems: DOS, Windows, Macintosh, UNIX
Programming: C++, Java, Pascal, COBOL, Visual Basic
Writing/publishing: Word, WordPerfect, QuarkXPress, FrameMaker
Financial: Excel, Lotus 1-2-3
Database: Access, Oracle, dBase, Act!
On-line help: RoboHELP

EXPERIENCE

Harley Morrison Associates   1997-present
Los Altos, CA
Systems Engineer

Design and Testing
- Designed and implemented real-time "Build-to-Order" manufacturing test systems to meet
  new marketing strategies and reduce overhead costs. Designed network-based applications
  for manufacturing process control and test-data collection, improving product quality and
  manufacturing efficiency.
- Adapted manufacturing test process to new computer technologies and customer specifications. Evaluated test procedures and documentation.

Support and Training
- Supplied technical support to facilities in California, Virginia, and Beijing. Isolated com-
  puter system failures to component level.
- Trained and supervised 10 foreign and domestic test engineers and technicians.

Richard Rondoni Business Machines   1990-97
Reseda, CA
Co-Op Engineer
- Designed and maintained computer-based electronic test hardware. Developed hardware-
  control software and computer interface circuitry.
- Correlated production data using dBASE. Published failure and analysis reports.

EDUCATION
University of California at Santa Barbara
Bachelor of Science in Electrical Engineering

ARCHITECT

CHRIS SMITH
178 Green Street
East Brunswick, NJ 08816
(908) 555-5555

SUMMARY
Over seven years in architecture and facility management (FM) related industries, with emphasis in Computer Design Base (CDB), education, and communication.

EXPERIENCE
CDB INC., East Brunswick, NJ   1998-present
Architect
- Provide industry consultation and implementation expertise in architecture and FM, computer-aided design (CAD) and database management software packages on PC.
- Provide demonstration, presentations, and technical support for pre- and post-sales activity.
- Act as subject matter expert for future software enhancements and requirements.
- Perform lead role in various joint studies teaming with IBM and other major corporations in evaluating CDB software for architecture.

CITY OF PITTSBURGH, Pittsburgh, PA   1994-98
Building Inspector
Worked in both the public and private sectors. Applied knowledge of local government agency procedures (e.g., obtaining permits, variances, interfacing with the Building, Planning, and Engineering Departments). Projects included:
- Commercial and industrial interior spaces
- Small commercial and low-rise buildings
- Large customer and multi-family residential housing
- Creating architectural renderings and presentation graphics

PROFESSIONAL REGISTRATIONS
Licensed architect—State of New Jersey, C100468

EDUCATION
University of Pennsylvania, Philadelphia, PA
Master of Architecture, 1994

Massachusetts Institute of Technology, Cambridge, MA
Bachelor of Science in Architecture, 1992

COMPUTER SKILLS
Word, Lotus 1-2-3, CAD-CAM

ART INSTRUCTOR

CHRIS SMITH
178 Green Street
Gary, IN 46408
(219) 555-5555

AREAS OF EXPERTISE

Art

Education

Teaching/Training

Crafts Instruction

Program Coordination

Curriculum Development

EXPERIENCE

Gary Regional School District   Gary, IN

Art Instructor   1986-present

Develop curriculum; teach aesthetics, art history, and art appreciation. Oversee studio work; manage supply inventory and $10,000 budget. Implemented curriculum with classes for gifted art students.

Gary Parks and Recreational Association   Gary, IN

Arts and Crafts Program Director/Instructor   1994-98

Created and led arts and crafts programs, including sewing, weaving, knitting, 3-dimensional work, sculpting, clay, paris craft, jewelry, enameling, painting, and drawing. Managed department budget; selected, purchased, and distributed supplies; supervised and directed arts aides in various duties. Produced annual arts show, with competition winners traveling to compete in national show in Washington, DC. Commended for exceptional Arts & Crafts display, 1996. Arranged school tours with Parks and Recreation members.

Indiana Educational Program   Gary, IN

Basic Skills Teacher   1990-94

Tutored individuals in reading, math, and oral language skills. Assessed students' accomplishments and prepared educational plans based on life and career skills. Directed and supervised teaching aides.

LICENSES AND CERTIFICATES

State of Indiana Elementary Education Certificate
Elementary and Secondary Education Certificate in Art

EDUCATION

Indiana University,   Bloomington, IN

Bachelor of Fine Arts in Art Education, *cum laude*

ASSISTANT EDITOR

CHRIS SMITH
178 Green Street
Philadelphia, PA 19103
(215) 555-5555

EXPERIENCE
1997-present   MUNSON MUSEUM, Philadelphia, PA
Assistant Editor, Publications Department
Editorial
- Copyedit and proofread scholarly archaeological monographs and museum catalogues.
- Prepare and organize artwork for reproduction; supervise pasteup; review and approve proofs.
- Recommend and supervise freelance artists. Manage a staff assistant.
- Serve as Rights and Permissions Editor.

Reprints
- Manage inventory control of entire publications stock. Identify titles to be reprinted. Make necessary editorial changes; obtain estimates; contract typesetting, printing, and binding services.

Promotional
- Promote materials at conferences. Select appropriate titles and contract with a combined exhibit group.

1992-97   VILLANOVA UNIVERSITY, OFFICE OF INTERNATIONAL
                              PROGRAMS FOR AGRICULTURE, Villanova, PA
Assistant to the Director
- Edited and typed grant proposals, research papers, and reports.
- Coordinated preparation and distribution of an international newsletter.
- Served as contact between federal agencies and university departments for sponsored foreign students.
- Coordinated arrangements for visitors, seminars, conferences, and overseas and domestic travel.

1990-92
Project Administrator
- Controlled export trade of endangered floral species within Pennsylvania for U.S. Fish and Wildlife Scientific Authority.

SKILLS
Computer: Word, WordPerfect, Lotus 1-2-3
Other: Proficient in Spanish and French

EDUCATION
SWARTHMORE COLLEGE, Swarthmore, PA
Bachelor of Arts in English

CHRIS SMITH
178 Green Street
Vienna, VA 22180
(703) 555-5555

EXPERIENCE

VIRGINIA GENERAL HOSPITAL, Suffolk, VA
Assistant Personnel Officer, 1999-present
- Recruited and trained administrative and clerical staffs, ancillary and works department staffs, professional and technical staffs.
- Signed employees to contracts.
- Advised staff on conditions of employment, entitlements, maternity leave.
- Revised, expanded, and managed induction program.
- Evaluated personnel.
- Conducted disciplinary and grievance interviews.
- Supervised personnel assistant, personnel clerk, and secretary.

SOUTHERN CHARM STORES, Roanoke, VA
Assistant Staff Manager, 1995-99
- Recruited and selected employees.
- Developed staff in various job descriptions.
- Administered wages, salary, and worker's compensation.
- Performed inductions.
- Supervised personnel clerk.
- Served as interim Staff Manager at Raleigh store.

ALLSTAR INSURANCE, Blacksburg, VA
Human Resources Assistant, 1993-95
- Present company policies and procedures to new employees.
- File workmen's compensation claims.
- Provide general office support.

EDUCATION

YALE UNIVERSITY, New Haven, CT
Bachelor of Science in Sociology

COOK COLLEGE, Los Angeles, CA
Personnel Management Exams

ASSISTANT STORE MANAGER

CHRIS SMITH
178 Green Street
Mantua, NJ 08051
(609) 555-5555

EXPERIENCE

Assistant Store Manager   1997-present
LORAX SUPERMARKETS   Woodbury, NJ
- Control and administer financial transactions in high-volume retail environment. Control cash flow and expenses, perform internal audits, protect corporate assets, and establish seasonal budgets.
- Manage schedule and procedure of over 175 personnel. Directly supervise customer services, lottery sales, display merchandising, maintenance, sanitation, and employee training. Set goals and adjust departmental budgets by sales projection.
- Received awards for best cash variance and payroll percentage.

Deli Supervisor   1995-97
LORAX SUPERMARKETS   Woodbury, NJ
- Scheduled and supervised staff of nine.
- Trained new employees in safety procedures.
- Responsible for customer service, cleanliness of area, keeping inventory stocked, and operating department within budget.
- Received Employee of the Month award twice.

Deli Clerk   1992-95
LORAX SUPERMARKETS   Trenton, NJ

COMPUTER SKILLS

WordPerfect, FileMaker Pro, Lotus 1-2-3

EDUCATION

STOCKTON STATE COLLEGE   Pomona, NJ
Bachelor of Science in Business Management

VOLUNTEER

Reader Program at Children's Hospital, Red Cross Blood Donor, Youth Tutor Program

ASSOCIATE EDITOR

Chris Smith
178 Green Street
Little Rock, AR 72204
(501) 555-5555
csmith@netmail.com

WORK EXPERIENCE

THE SOUTHWEST TRAVEL REPORT   Little Rock, AR
Associate Editor   1999-present
Assign and manage contributing writers, coordinate art and production elements. Reported and wrote stories for prototype issue.

THE JENSEN COMPANY   Little Rock, AR
Associate Editor   1997-99
Reported and wrote features for five departments for three trade magazines covering the meeting, convention, and incentive travel industries. Assisted in developing story and art ideas and in copyediting and proofreading.

DEYLAH PUBLISHING   Little Rock, AR
Assistant Editor   1996-97
Researched and wrote items for annual fact books and their weekly supplemental updates covering communications industry.

WHERE TO EAT   Little Rock, AR
Contributing Editor   1993-96
Wrote articles for monthly restaurant trade newspaper.

CONWAY ARTS JOURNAL   Conway, AR
Administrative Assistant   1993
Assisted business and marketing directors in direct-mail projects, classified advertising, and fulfillment of book and subscription orders.

Editorial Intern   1992
Reported and wrote articles and columns for twice-monthly newspaper for the arts and entertainment industry. Position also involved research, fact checking, and production support.

EDUCATION
Hendrix College, Conway, AR
B.A. in English and Political Science

PROFESSIONAL AFFILIATIONS
Member, Society of Professional Journalists

CHRIS SMITH
178 Green Street
Baltimore, MD 21202
(301) 555-5555

EXPERIENCE

1999-present
BANK OF BALTIMORE Baltimore, MD
Teller
- Process account transactions, reconcile and deposit daily funds.
- Inform customers of bank products, refer public to designated personnel, provide account status data, and handle busy phone.
- Orient, train, supervise, and delegate tasks for new hires.
- Serve as team leader for Christmas Clothing Campaign for homeless.
- Helped organized extended hours institution.

1998-99
MEYER, GREEN AND FAZIO Princess Anne, MD
Office Assistant
- Collected, sorted, and distributed incoming mail. Processed outgoing mail.

1997-98
TANNENBAUM SOCIETY Washington, DC
Sales Associate
- Serviced customers, reconciled cash drawer.
- Created effective product displays.

1995-96
KENT AND LANE ASSOCIATES Richmond, VA
Office Assistant
- Produced correspondence, responded to public inquiries, monitored and maintained confidential records.

EDUCATION
GENEVA COLLEGE, Annapolis, MD
Associate in Business/Travel

COMPUTERS
WordPerfect, Lotus 1-2-3, SABRE, Access

BENEFITS COORDINATOR

CHRIS SMITH
178 Green Street
Nordland, WA 98358
(509) 555-5555

EXPERIENCE
Jennings One-Stop Stores, Inc., Seattle, WA

Union benefits coordinator assistant supervisor—payroll 1999-present
- Maintain and update changes to the union benefits contract run for propriety, i.e., Pension/Health and Welfare reports. Mail benefit checks to union offices.
- Handle weekly balancing of employee master file from 450 stores and verify information before entering data into keypunch system.
- Research and resolve errors and warning messages that appeared on the MSA edit.
- Edit the telxon field payroll transmissions.
- Reconcile checks to the unclaimed wages account.
- Assist department supervisor in day-to-day operations; supervise staff of 30; handle special projects as assigned.

Lease administrator 1998-99
- Assisted in preparing monthly percentage rent accruals. Prepared quarterly gross sales reconciliation to the general ledger. Prepared gross sales figures. Updated regular price files for stores with advance price reductions.
- Analyzed and paid common-area maintenance bills. Updated and maintained automatic payment run for theatre rents and payments as per lease agreements.
- Logged and filed lease agreements, amendments, and other documents in the lease files. Reviewed and prepared lease summaries.

Marketing research assistant 1997-98
- Gathered technical computer-related material for various Jennings publications.
- Procured information, determined accuracy, and performed continuous updating, while meeting deadlines.
- Chosen to train new employees in comprehensive aspects of computer trends throughout the United States.

EDUCATION
University of Maine, Orono, ME
Bachelor of Arts in Economics
Concentration: Business/Finance/Communications

BILLING CLERK

CHRIS SMITH
178 Green Street
Derry, NH 03038
(603) 555-5555

SUMMARY OF QUALIFICATIONS
- Experience in office supervision and prioritizing and coordinating workflow
- Knowledge of billing functions and collecting delinquent accounts
- Skilled at resolving customer problems and complaints
- Familiar with utility, insurance, and credit environments

EXPERIENCE
REGIONAL WATER QUALITY CONTROL AUTHORITY, Derry, NH
Senior Customer Service/Billing Clerk   1998-present
- Process all invoices and collect delinquent accounts.
- Compile and prepare monthly cash-flow reports.
- Process semiannual sewer bills, calculating interest and penalty charges.
- Answer customer inquiries, problems, and complaints, composing correspondence.
- Act as supervisor when needed, prioritizing and coordinating office workflow.

THE PRAGMATIC INSURANCE COMPANY, Manchester, MA
Administrative Technician—Service Bureau, Group Administration   1994-98
- Processed and billed clients choosing COBRA (benefits continuation).
- Provided customer service, researched accounts, and informed clients of their monthly rate and payment.
- Processed and deposited monthly payments. Created and maintained monthly delinquent rosters.

COMMERCIAL REPORTS & TITLE AGENCY, Nashua, NH
Office Manager   1990-94
- Interviewed, hired, trained, and supervised office employees.
- Traveled throughout New Hampshire completing title searches and credit reports and supervising field staff.
- Assisted clients with mortgage or title insurance questions.

SKILLS
Word, Lotus 1-2-3

EDUCATION
Pennsbury High School, Levittown, PA   Diploma

CHRIS SMITH
178 Green Street
Miami, FL 33054
(305) 555-5555

EXPERIENCE
The Pearl Co.   Miami, FL
Limited Partnerships Accounting and Administration
BILLING SUPERVISOR   1998-present
Created and implemented billing system for reimbursing departmental salaries, rent, and out-of-pocket expenses. Initiated computerized accounts receivable spreadsheet system. Researched and projected yearly management fees and cash distributions. Supervised daily invoice preparation and monthly bank statement reconciliation.

CONTROL ACCOUNTANT   1996-98
nciliation of transfer agent and shareholder records for Mutual Fund
daily posting and reconciliation of demand deposit accounts and settle-
re and dollar positions. Reconciled and reported net changes in Fund

Miami, FL
R   1995
hipments of coin and currency, handling large cash orders from banks
out currency transaction reports. Distributed and collected monies from

LER   1993-94
customer checks. Verified signature of business and individual cus-
and certified checks. Trained new tellers. Assisted supervisor with
es.

Winter Park, FL

Administration

Boca Raton, FL

Lotus 1-2-3

p, Protectograph machine, and Regiscope

BOOKKEEPER (Agency)

CHRIS SMITH
178 Green Street
Albuquerque, NM 87140
(505) 555-5555

SUMMARY OF QUALIFICATIONS
- More than 18 years' experience in accounting and bookkeeping.
- Able negotiator and liaison, dealing with professionals, clients, and staff.
- Accurate, organized, aware of importance of meeting deadlines and maintaining smooth workflow.

EXPERIENCE
CHUTES AND LADDERS DAYCARE CENTER, Albuquerque, NM

Agency Bookkeeper   1998-present
Handle cash disbursement, verify vendor invoices, generate weekly checks. Administer general ledger and fund coding for agency accounts. Record transactions; maintain checkbook and up-to-date bank balances. Prepare and post disbursements and monthly invoices to state and municipal contractors.

Voucher Bookkeeper   1997-98
Processed current and outstanding requests for reimbursement for over 300 providers (3,000 payments). Dealt with underpayment/overpayment and rate changes; verified adjustment requests against payment history. Issued and recorded advance-payment checks. Ensured immediate update of computerized fiscal files and accounts payable to meet rigid deadline. Assisted providers; verified payments for auditors. Oversaw part-time staff.

Assistant Bookkeeper   1995-97
Supervised current and outstanding invoice payment approval, computerized data input, invoice verification, posting to ledger and dispatching checks.

SAWYER REALTY TRUST, Las Cruces, NM   1991-95
Part-Time Bookkeeper
Recorded rent payments, paid banks and vendors, reconciled bank statements.

EDUCATION
NEWBURY JUNIOR COLLEGE, Boston, MA
Associate in Accounting

MONTREAL UNIVERSITY, DIVISION OF CONTINUING EDUCATION, Montreal, Canada
Bachelor of Arts in Teaching/Education (equivalent)

BOOKKEEPING CLERK

CHRIS SMITH
178 Green Street
Eden Prairie, MN 55347
(902) 555-5555

PROFESSIONAL EXPERIENCE
ASSOCIATES, INC., Eden Prairie, MN
Bookkeeping Clerk, 1997-present
- Monitor general ledger and investors' monthly reports.
- Oversee accounts receivable and accounts payable staff to ensure accuracy.
- Monitor payroll taxes for accuracy and on-time payment.
- Manage multiple accounts for real estate developer with commercial and residential properties in several states.

MORNINGSIDE CO., Hopkins, MN
Bookkeeping Clerk, 1995-97
- Supervised general ledger through trial balance, as well as accounts payable, payroll, and payroll tax returns.
- Converted bookkeeping procedures from one-write system to in-house computer system.
- Coordinated department's workflow.

Accounts Receivable Clerk, 1994-95

HAWTHORNE MEDICAL CENTER, Howard Lake, MN
Secretary, Cardiac Care Unit, 1992-94
- Scheduled patients for appointments and tests.
- Answered phones, resolved problems.
- Transcribed doctors' orders, ordered supplies.
- Maintained patient records, set up charts.

EXCELSIOR CORPORATION, Mankato, MN
Secretary to Vice President, 1990-92
- Performed office duties, such as monitoring personnel files, scheduling, and paying operating expenses.

Receptionist, 1989-90
- Answered phones, scheduled travel, acted as liaison between management and staff.

EDUCATION
SOUTHWEST STATE UNIVERSITY, Marshall, MN
Accounting courses

BRANCH MANAGER (Temporary Services)

CHRIS SMITH
178 Green Street
Oxnard, CA 93033
(805) 555-5555

EXPERIENCE
BRANCH MANAGER
Bangtail Temps, Oxnard, CA
1998-present
Supervise all aspects of a $5.5 million dollar temporary services branch, including outside sales and inside support staffs, recruiting and referring temporary employees, and selecting and training new sales representatives. Within four months, established 10 new corporate clients, resulting in $150,000 in new revenue.

BRANCH MANAGER
NETA Temporary Services, Inc., San Mateo, CA
1996-98
After branch consolidation and reorganization by NETA, assumed responsibility for budget planning and administration, developing new business, and retaining accounts.

Obtained new accounts to replace lost business and maintain profitability. Used sales expertise, account management, and proven sales techniques and strategies to develop an 80% new client base.

MAJOR ACCOUNT MANAGER
Transon Electronics, Inc., Torrance, CA
1986-96
Marketed direct-mail pieces to major corporations, direct-response agencies, and dealers. Used application selling process and innovative approaches to consistently achieve and exceed sales objectives. Skills in cold calling, lead development, and appointment generation resulted in promotion from Account Representative to Major Account Manager within six months.

EDUCATION
Transon Electronics Sales Training Program

Rice University, Houston, TX
Bachelor of Fine Arts in Theatre Arts

BUDGET DIRECTOR

CHRIS SMITH
178 Green Street
Chicago, IL 60604
(312) 555-5555

PROFESSIONAL EXPERIENCE

ILLINOIS TREASURY DEPARTMENT, Chicago, IL   1999-present
Assistant to the Treasurer
- Administer budget, payroll, and personnel for a 322-person staff and $17 million budget. Assist with opening and closing of monthly and yearly budgets and payroll.
- Act as liaison with accountants and Budget Bureau.
- Pay Treasury bills; ensure payroll coverage. Determine emergency allotment needs.
- Negotiate contract work; assist with public relations.

CRAVEN TRANSPORT, Midway Airport, Chicago, IL   1994-99
Budget Director
- Set up and implemented $7 million budget and payroll for main branch and subsidiaries.
- Negotiated contracts with air freight agencies.
- Assumed duties of Purchasing Manager.

NANETTE CONSTRUCTION, Elsah, IL   1992-94
Budget Director
- Created original budget for new company; ensured appropriation of monies for payroll.
- Trained shift supervisors on the new budget and financial system.
- Approved or rejected all purchase orders.

ABC LIFE INSURANCE, Chicago, IL   1988-92
Budget Analyst
- Assist management in preparation of $700 million budget.
- Conduct training classes on the financial system for upper-level management.
- Generate financial analysis reports for executives.

EDUCATION
Western Illinois University, Macomb, IL
Major: Business Management

BUILDING INSPECTOR

CHRIS SMITH
178 Green Street
Prichard, AZ 36610
(205) 555-5555

SUMMARY OF QUALIFICATIONS
- More than 15 years' experience, ranging from carpenter apprentice to general contractor and project superintendent in military, custom, and general construction.
- Sound knowledge of state building codes and the inspection of all construction projects.
- Capable of enforcing full range of building codes and working with all construction and mechanical trades on codes, including electrical and plumbing regulations.

EXPERIENCE
PERMANENT LOCAL BUILDING INSPECTOR, Prichard, AL   1998-present
As Local Inspector:
- Inspect Mobile District residential, commercial, and industrial buildings during and after construction, to ensure that components such as footings, floor framing, completed framing, chimneys, and stairways meet provisions of building, grading, zoning, and safety laws.
- Interact with construction and mechanical trades and architects and engineers to assure adherence to improved plans, specifications, and standards.
- Prepare reports concerning violations not corrected, interpret legal requirements, and recommend compliance procedures to contractors, craft workers, and owners.
- Maintain inspection records and prepare reports for use by administrative or judicial authorities.

As Acting Building Commissioner:
- During the absence of the Building Commissioner, assume full responsibility for administering and enforcing state building codes as well as all state rules and regulations involving construction in Mobile.

GENERAL CONTRACTOR
Prichard Construction, Pritchard, AL   1988-97
- Built custom homes for clients insisting on high degree of skill, quality workmanship, and ability to complete projects to schedule and budget.
- Negotiated all subcontracts. Supervised up to 25 carpenters and laborers.

EDUCATION
Mobile Junior College, Mobile, AL
Associate of Industrial Arts.
Completed apprenticeship with John Skrensky.
Journeyman Carpenter, Mobile, AL.

CASE WORKER/LEGAL ADVOCATE

CHRIS SMITH
178 Green Street
East Troy, WI
(414) 555-5555

EXPERIENCE
1999-present
Case Worker/Legal Advocate
The Women's Safe Place   East Troy, WI
- Night manager at shelter for abused women and their children. Monitor 24-hour hotline and authorize admitting residents on an emergency basis.
- Provide support and access to legal resources to women in crisis situations. Advocate for women before judges in family court proceedings. Assist women in completing temporary restraining orders. Act as Coalition observer during domestic violence legal cases and report outcomes to staff.
- Organize, prepare, and present seminars to high school students on domestic violence and lead discussions to raise awareness. Assist associate director in planning public relations and fundraising events.

1996-98
Associate Editor/Program Coordinator
Baby's Breath Press   Madison, WI
- Developed, wrote, and edited articles for monthly business-management newsletter. Combined multiple sources of information and organized pertinent facts for a business-oriented audience. Developed and wrote articles with outside authors involving case studies on management development within their organizations. Performed all work under strict deadlines.
- Assisted editorial department in planning content of newsletter by selecting topics for publication. Worked with the 50 people who presented at the annual conference by assisting them with their presentations.

1995-98
Writer, *The Republic*   Madison, WI
- Researched a variety of sources incorporating various philosophies and wrote articles on women's issues for a quarterly literary magazine in Madison.

EDUCATION
Beloit College   Beloit, WI
Bachelor of Arts in Sociology, 1996
Courses include Poverty and Crisis, Gerontology, and Women in Society. Independent study topic: "The Feminization of Poverty in the United States."
Elected to Phi Beta Kappa

CHRIS SMITH
178 Green Street
Dillon, MT 59725
(406) 555-5555

EDUCATION
BURDAN COLLEGE, Missoula, MT
- Candidate for B.A. in Criminal Justice, expected 2000.
- President of Christiansen Hall; manage budget of $800.

EXPERIENCE
YOUR STORE, Dillon, MT   1999-present
Cashier
- Provide customer and personnel assistance.
- Handle cash intake, inventory control, and light maintenance.
- Train and schedule new employees.
- Instituted store recycling program benefiting the Dillon Homeless Shelter.

RONDELL IMAGE, Helena, MT   1998-99
Data/File Clerk
- Assisted sales staff.
- Performed general office tasks, including data entry, typing, and filing invoices.

TARPY PERSONNEL SERVICES, Bozeman, MT   1997-98
General Clerk
- Handled shipping and receiving
- Filed invoices.

TELESTAR MARKETING, Great Falls, MT   1995-97
Telephone Interviewer
- Conducted telephone surveys dealing with general public and preselected client groups in selected demographic areas.
- Consistently placed within top 10 percent for number of surveys administered.
- Received Associate of the Month award twice and Outstanding Service Certificate.

CATERER

CHRIS SMITH
178 Green Street
Las Vegas, NV
(505) 555-5555 (Work)
(505) 444-4444 (Home)

ACCOMPLISHMENTS
- Named "Best & Brightest New Business Owner" by The Entrepreneurial Expo, 1999.
- Coordinated and implemented CCC Employee Training Program, voted "Most Effective" by the Restaurant Association of New Mexico.
- Catered The Governor's Dinner, 2000.

PROFESSIONAL EXPERIENCE
1999-present   CHRISTINE'S CATERING COMPANY, Las Vegas, NV
Owner/Manager
- Manage operations and service, handling $40,000/week sales.
- Organize weekly work schedules for staff of 25.
- Resolve staff and client problems.
- Create innovative incentive programs to motivate staff and improve customer service.

1995-99   CAMPUS CATERERS, Hobbs, NV
Banquet Supervisor
- Coordinated banquets for up to 450 guests.
- Organized dining area.
- Trained new employees.
- Supervised staff of 30.

1988-89   THE OASIS COUNTRY CLUB, Las Vegas, NV
Server
- Handled cash and credit card transactions.
- Resolved customer complaints.
- Trained new bus and wait staff.

EDUCATION
COLLEGE OF THE SOUTHWEST, Hobbs, NV
Bachelor of Science in Management, 1999

AFFILIATIONS
Southwest Restaurant Association
The National Caterers' Guild

CERTIFIED PUBLIC ACCOUNTANT (CPA)

CHRIS SMITH, CPA
178 Green Street
Houston, TX 77029
(713) 555-5555
csmith@netmail.com

EXPERIENCE

1998-present   **Mastermind Engineering**, Houston, TX
Accounting Manager
- File SEC reporting and disclosure forms.
- Manage general ledger closing and maintenance.
- Supervise and review all areas of accounting and finance.
- Administer 401(k) pension plan.
- Implement accounting/payroll/manufacturing software.

1992-97   **Dunphy & Reilly, Inc.**, Houston, TX
Senior Internal Auditor
- Conducted operational and financial audits of manufacturing subsidiaries.
- Designed and implemented audit programs to test the efficiency of all aspects of accounting controls.
- Trained and supervised staff auditors in all aspects of the audit engagement.
- Advised corporate management regarding acquisition and corporate development.

1990-92   **Churchill North**, Houston, TX
Supervising Senior Accountant
- Supervised, planned, and budgeted audit engagements.
- Prepared financial statements and tax filings.
- Recruited, trained, supervised, and evaluated staff accountants.

CERTIFICATION
CPA, State of Texas

COMPUTER SKILLS
Word, Excel, Lotus 1-2-3

EDUCATION
UNIVERSITY OF TEXAS   Houston, TX
Bachelor of Science, Accountancy
Associate in Science, Management

CHEF (Assistant)

CHRIS SMITH
178 Green Street
Boston, MA 02116
(617) 555-5555

EXPERIENCE

1998-present   THE WILLARD HOTEL, Boston, MA
Assistant Pastry Chef
- Work directly with the executive pastry chef. Monitor the mixing, baking, and finishing of cakes, pastries, and a full range of bakery products on a daily basis. Fulfill special orders for banquets, functions, and the hotel restaurant. Schedule and manage personnel. Supervise a staff of four.

1998, part-time   CATERING BY C. SMITH, Everett, MA
Pastry Cook
- Worked concurrently with above position, helping out during the busy season on a half-time basis, with baking and finishing of breads and pastries.

1996-97   THE BANNEN INN, Bangor, ME
Rounds Cook
- Cooked dishes to order as needed. Streamlined workflow, acted as management liaison, scheduled shifts, provided inventory control, and resolved related problems.

1995-96   LE HOTEL DE VIVRE, Bangor, ME
Pastry Cook
- Assisted the manager with all phases of shop management. Mixed, baked, and decorated cakes. Serviced accounts. Provided inventory control.

1993-95   KIKI COUNTRY CLUB, Boston, MA
Saute and Broiler Cook
- Performed prep work, handled stations, cooked food.

EDUCATION

AMERICAN PASTRY ARTS CENTER   Medford, MA
Course in Chocolates and Candy
- Understudy of Sid Cherney

GOURMET INSTITUTE OF AMERICA   Boston, MA
A.O.S.
- Earned Certificates in Food and Management Sanitation

CHEF (Executive)

CHRIS SMITH
178 Green Street
Montego Bay, Jamaica
(876) 555-5555

EXPERIENCE

1999-present   TORPEDO CLUB, Montego Bay, Jamaica
Executive Chef—Sand Dollar Restaurant
265-seat restaurant—two seatings for dinner, all-inclusive concept. Supervise head chef, sous
chef, pastry chef, butcher, and 53 additional staff. Trained all staff with exception of pastry
and head chefs. Run complete party system with 15 sections, including breakfast, lunch,
garde manger, vegetables, roasts and sauces, soups, pastry staff, butchering, kitchen clerks,
buffet runners, and sanitation section. Plan menu.

1997-99   THE SIN SHACK, South Negril Pt., Jamaica
First Sous Chef
Responsible for overall running of two kitchens. Oversaw kitchen and 38 additional staff.
Seating 175 on a la carte menu.

1996-97   THE BARNYARD, Mandaville, Jamaica
Head Chef
Hired and trained all staff to provide 30 entrees and 175 a la carte dinners per night. Reported
directly to executive chef.

1994-96   CLUB CURPCO—HOTEL BRIGADOON, Lucea, Jamaica
Sous Chef
Directly responsible to head chef. Complete charge of 52-member brigade. Assisted with
menu planning. Responsible for cost and quality control, production, and food cost.

EDUCATION

Jamaica Community College, Mandaville, Jamaica
Food and Beverage Management

Jamaica Hospitality Center, Lucea, Jamaica
Dessert Finesse

COACH

CHRIS SMITH
178 Green Street
Orono, ME 04473
(207) 555-5555

EXPERIENCE

University of Maine, Orono, Maine   1999-present
Assistant Varsity Hockey Coach
- Goaltender coach.
- Lead drills and practice.
- Coach individual team members in shooting, passing, and goaltending.
- Set up playing strategies.
- Scout opposing teams in preparation for games.
- Recruit potential student athletes.

Saint Joseph's College, North Windham, Maine   1998-99
Assistant Varsity Hockey Coach
Same responsibilities as in current position.

State Hockey School of Maine, Augusta, Maine   1994-97
Hockey Instructor, summer program

Maxfield All-American Hockey School, Orono, Maine   1993
Hockey Instructor

National Sports Camp of America at University of Maine, Orono, Maine   1992
Hockey Counselor and Instructor

EDUCATION
University of Maine, Orono, Maine
M.S. in Human Movement, Health, and Leisure, 1997
B.S. in Human Movement, Health, and Leisure, 1991

HONORS AND AWARDS
- Captain, NCAA Division I Champions, 1991
- Starting Varsity Hockey Goaltender, 1988-91
- All-East, 1988
- All-Star Goaltender, Bangor Tournament, 1988
- Outstanding Goaltender, Portland Tournament, 1988

COMEDIAN

CHRIS SMITH
178 Green Street
Miami, FL 33199
(305) 555-5555

PROFILE
Charismatic, crazy, creative, daring, dastardly, hilarious, hyper, hysterical, and of course zany!

PERSONAL
D.O.B.: 9/5/71	Height: 6'1"	Hair: Brown
Weight: 165 lbs	Eyes: Blue	Sex: Male

LAST SEEN
MIAMI
Comedians At Large	Beachside Comedy Review
Miami Moon	Laughter Unlimited
Carlisle's Lounge	Give It Up

CHICAGO
Wind It Down	The Funny Farm
Comedy Central	

DETROIT
Let It Slide	Can You Stand It?
Barry's Bar & Grill	The Haverill House

SAN FRANCISCO
Wild Child	The Funny Bone
Check It Out	Tickle My Fancy

ORLANDO
Church Street Station	The Mad Hatter
Mickey's	

TELEVISION
LOSIN' IT
• Co-producer of local cable program, showcasing a variety of standup performers

COMEDIANS FOR HIRE
• Numerous standup appearances

KNOWN ASSOCIATES
The American Comedians Association

COMPUTER OPERATOR

CHRIS SMITH
178 Green Street
Belleville, IL 62221
(618) 555-5555
csmith@netmail.com

SKILLS
Computer
Operating systems: DOS, Windows, Macintosh
Programming: C++, Java, Lotus Notes
Writing/publishing: Word, QuarkXPress
Financial: Excel, Lotus 1-2-3

Languages
Fluent in Spanish and German

EXPERIENCE
Mayfair Products, Inc., Kent, OH
Computer Operator, summers, 1997, 1998, 1999
- Had sole responsibility for operating computer systems, entering data, and compiling records in 1999. Assisted with operation in 1997.
- Supervised and processed accounts receivable, billing, and invoices.
- Processed backup at the end of the day.
- Provided general office assistance.

Agamemnon Electroplating, Kent, OH
Computer Operator, summer 1996
- Assisted in operating the computer systems.
- Served as assistant to the office manager.

EDUCATION
Kent State University, Kent, OH
Bachelor of Arts in Economics, 1993
Courses include extensive computer programming. Other courses include Financial and Administrative, Accounting, and Corporate Finance. Economics courses include Human Resources, Law and Economics, Statistics, and Monetary Theory.

ACTIVITIES AND HONORS
Third Place in the Kent Financial and Administrative Accounting Achievement Awards. Dean's List (6 semesters).

CHRIS SMITH, CPA
178 Green Street
Richmond, VA 23225
(804) 555-5555

EXPERIENCE

KENDALL MANAGEMENT GROUP, Richmond, VA   1998-present
Controller
Initiate and maintain general ledgers for three closely held corporations. Process payroll and accounts payable and receivable. Verify and authorize invoices. Establish and approve credit lines for clients and suppliers. Compile and audit monthly, quarterly, and yearly cash disbursement and financial reports. Prepare budget and cost reports.

B.T. JOHNSON, C.P.A., Richmond, VA   1995-98
Staff Accountant
Prepared individual, corporate, and fiduciary income and estate tax returns. Generated compilations and financial statement audits. Researched tax issues.

ASHLAND AUTHORITY, Ashland, VA   1992-95
Assistant Terminal Agent
Supervised 10 ticket agents. Implemented Accounting Department policies. Assisted in conversion of sales reporting to Lotus 1-2-3.

SKILLS

Computer: Word, Lotus 1-2-3, Quicken
Languages: Spanish, French

EDUCATION

Passed CPA Examination, 1995

UNIVERSITY OF VIRGINIA, Charlottesville, VA
Certificate in Accountancy with high honors

UNIVERSITY OF MADRID
Graduate School of Spanish Literature, two semesters

UNIVERSITY OF RICHMOND, Richmond, VA
Bachelor of Arts, Modern Languages

COPY EDITOR

CHRIS SMITH
178 Green Street
Columbia, MO 65201
(314) 555-5555

EXPERIENCE
UNIVERSITY OF MISSOURI, Columbia, MO
Managing Editor, *The Circle*   1999-2000
Copyedit and supervise the writing, formatting, and layout of a biweekly college newspaper.
Monitor and order supplies. Compile and submit monthly payroll.

Assistant Editor, Book Editing Internship   1999
Copyedited multicultural college English teaching text (forthcoming). Conducted correspondence with authors. Fact-checked references. Suggested editorial changes.

Teaching Assistant and Writing Center Tutor, English Department   1998
Assist instructor in leading class discussion for freshman composition course. Advise class
groups on papers. Grade freshman composition papers. Tutor individual students in any curriculum.

Writer, *Science World Newsletter*   1997-98
Write feature articles for biennial college newsletter spotlighting UM faculty and student
activities and accomplishments. Conduct interviews and research as basis for articles.

THE ART JOURNAL
Assistant Editor, Internship   1997
Aided in submission selection. Managed correspondence. Copyedit articles and collaborated
on editorial changes with editor. Fact-checked references. Wrote contributor section.

COMPUTER SKILLS
Word, WordPerfect, QuarkXPress, PageMaker

EDUCATION
University of Missouri, Columbia, MO
B.A. candidate, English Literature, expected 2000
Cumulative GPA: 3.1/4.0; Major: 3.4/4.0

CORRECTIONAL OFFICER

CHRIS SMITH

178 Green Street
Sabattus, ME 04280
(207) 555-5555

EXPERIENCE

1999-present MAINE STATE PRISON, Lewiston, ME
Correctional Officer
Monitor 50 prisoners. Conduct population counts, cell checks, and searches. Oversee dinner and yard duty. Supervise prisoner visitation. Issue money orders for prisoners. Prepare and file incident reports. Assignments have included escorting special prisoners and serving as outside hospital guard.

1998 BIDDEFORD POLICE DEPARTMENT, Biddeford, ME
Part-time Police Officer
Protected property and persons of Biddeford. Responded to burglar alarms and citizen complaints. Performed routine patrol, issued criminal arrest citations, and testified in court.

1997 SOUTH PORTLAND POLICE DEPARTMENT, South Portland, ME
Part-time Police Officer
Same duties as above.

1994-96 FIRST FEDERAL SAVINGS BANK, Cape Elizabeth, ME
Security Guard
Ensured safety and security of customers, bank employees, and bank assets.

VOLUNTEER

Volunteer Firefighter, Cape Elizabeth Fire Co.

CERTIFICATIONS

- NRA, shotgun and firearms; Monadnock PR 24; VASCAR plus
- CPR, First Aid

EDUCATION

BANGOR POLICE ACADEMY, Bangor, ME
Act 120 Certificate with 90% average

CORRESPONDENT

CHRIS SMITH
178 Green Street
Swannanoa, NC 28778
(704) 555-5555
csmith@netmail.com

EXPERIENCE

1998-present   *Le Record du Jour*
French Daily Newspaper
- Write stories and features on local affairs for the Cultural and National sections.
- Travel extensively throughout France.
- Broke story on Sorbonne smuggling, resulting in the recovery of six pieces of priceless art stolen from the Louvre.
- Received six Globe journalism awards for international reporting.

1991-97   *Tokyo Record*
Japanese Daily Newspaper, English Edition (second largest in country)
- Wrote stories and features on social and political issues.
- Covered government proceedings on trade, foreign policy, and business.

WRITING

Author of fiction and poetry (novel is pending publication)

SKILLS

Computer: WordPerfect, Lotus 1-2-3
Languages: Fluent in French and Spanish
Other: 35mm photography

EDUCATION

WAKE FOREST UNIVERSITY, Winston, NC
Master of Arts in Print Journalism

SHEFFIELD UNIVERSITY, Sheffield, U.K.
Degrees in History and Literature

PRINCETON UNIVERSITY, Princeton, NJ
Summer Program in Anthropology

COSMETOLOGIST

CHRIS SMITH
178 Green Street
Marion, IN 46952
(317) 555-5555

EXPERIENCE

1998-present   LATITIA GREEN ACADEMY, Marion, IN
Instructor
- Provide instruction to all levels in cosmetology theory and practical applications.
- Develop lesson plans in all subjects; administer tests; give demonstrations.
- Motivate and counsel 20-student classes; evaluate tests and performances.

1995-present   LE SALON DESIREE, Lafayette, IN
Owner/Operator
- Hairdresser/Cosmetologist, performing all relevant functions.
- Promote business and maintain good customer relations.

1991-95   DYE HEALTHY SALON, Muncie, IN
Hairdresser
- Performed hairdressing, manicuring, skin care, hairstyling, and coloring.

1990-91   BORELLI MORTALIO SALON, Lisbon, Portugal
Hairdresser
- Provided hairdressing, skin care, facials, permanents, and hair coloring.

1988-90   ZACHARY DRAKE'S SHOP, Lisbon, Portugal
Hairdresser
- Serviced customers with hairdressing, manicuring, skin care, facials.

EDUCATION

WINIFRED ACADEMY, Muncie, IN
Completed Cosmetology coursework. Received License #1 (#1372)

BONNIE LASS BEAUTY ACADEMY, Lisbon, Portugal
Completed one-year course in Cosmetology

LANGUAGES

Bilingual in English and Portuguese

COUNSELOR (Mental Health)

Chris Smith
178 Green Street
Atlanta, GA 30314
(404) 555-5555

SUMMARY OF QUALIFICATIONS
- Skilled at developing treatment plans for various populations within social service arenas; coordinating special-service networks; collaborating with health-service professionals to establish procedural guidelines; and placing individuals.
- Experienced at providing recommendations for programming and curriculum.
- Proficient in recruiting prospective parents for adoption, conducting home studies, assigning children, and following up.
- Completed training with the Department of Social Services.

EXPERIENCE
1999-present   *Residential Counselor*
MENTAL HEALTH SERVICES OF ATLANTA   Atlanta, GA
- Collaborate with health-service professionals to development treatment plans for emotionally disturbed adolescents.
- Assist clients in developing survival skills to aid transition from residential to independent living.
- Coordinate service networks for academic, psychological, and social assistance.

1998-99   *Agency Recruitment Specialist*
TYLER ADOPTION AGENCY   Atlanta, GA
- Traveled to various community sites and executed presentations to recruit prospective parents for minority children.
- Conducted home studies of prospective parents to determine eligibility for program.
- Placed children with families and followed up for evaluation.

1997-98   *Social Worker*
DEPARTMENT OF SOCIAL SERVICES   Atlanta, GA
- Assessed client need, developed treatment plans, and managed cases.
- Communicated with court officials in handling cases.
- Served as child advocate for court proceedings.

EDUCATION
EMORY UNIVERSITY,   Atlanta, GA
Master of Social Work, 1998

UNIVERSITY OF GEORGIA/ATHENS,   Athens, GA
Bachelor of Arts in Sociology, *cum laude*, 1996

COUNSELOR (School)

Chris Smith
178 Green Street
Fort Lauderdale, FL 38314
(305) 555-1212

PROFESSIONAL EXPERIENCE
1985-2000   AMERICAN SCHOOL OF RECIFE, Recife, Brazil
Counselor, International Primary School
- Administered psychological and educational testing for students ranging from pre-kinder-garten to fifth grade
- Counseled students, families, and teachers
- Designed remedial and therapeutic plans
- Led group activities for self-image enhancement and behavior modification
- Worked with teachers in preventive strategies for social and disciplinary problems

1983-85   INSTITUTE OF AMERICA, Sao Paulo, Brazil
Guidance Counselor
- Counseled individuals and families for students ranging from pre-kindergarten to twelfth grade
- Designed complete record-keeping system for all students
- Performed value clarification exercises with students
- Implemented behavior modification programs
- Administered achievement, vocational, and college-prep tests
- Made policy on admissions and discipline
- Worked with teachers on individual educational programs

LANGUAGE
Bilingual in English and Spanish

EDUCATION
NOVA UNIVERSITY, Fort Lauderdale, FL
Master of Arts in Counseling Psychology
Concentration: Community Clinical

BARRY UNIVERSITY, Miami Shores, Florida
Bachelor of Arts in Developmental Psychology
Associate of Arts in Human Development, *cum laude*

CREDIT ANALYST

CHRIS SMITH
178 Green Street
Grace City, OH 58445
(216) 555-5555

SUMMARY
- Five years' experience in retail banking and commercial lending.
- Adept at credit and financial analysis.
- Fluent in Dutch; knowledgeable in conversational and written German.

EXPERIENCE
WISTERIA BANK, Grace City, OH
Commercial Loan Credit Analyst, 1999-present
Provide analytical services as part of lending team. Analyze and evaluate financial statements. Develop pro forma statements and cash flow projections. Document findings; prepare independent recommendations on advisability of granting credits for corporate lenders.

Senior Personal Banker, 1998-99
Assisted in branch administration. Oversaw branch overdraft reports. Reviewed and executed consumer loans. Supervised the vault area; audited tellers; provided customer service.

Personal Banker, 1996-98
Established and serviced professional clientele accounts. Expedited investments in treasury bills, repurchase agreements, CDs, retirement accounts, and discount brokerage for bank clients. Assisted branch corporate lender weekly on a revolving commercial loan.
- Sold 16 retirement accounts in one day; resulted in an IRA sales award for branch.
- Achieved several awards for bank product sales.

COMPUTERS
WordPerfect, Lotus 1-2-3, Word

EDUCATION
OHIO STATE UNIVERSITY, Graduate School of Management, Columbus, OH
M.B.A., Concentration: Finance

B.S., Business Administration
Concentration: Accounting and Finance

CHRIS SMITH
178 Green Street
Broken Arrow, OK 74011
(918) 555-5555

SUMMARY OF QUALIFICATIONS
- Demonstrated ability in sales support services. Includes establishing client base, extensive customer servicing, telemarketing, cold calling, and sales territory development.
- Consistently met or exceeded sales goals and instituted sales programs; sales increased from $8 to $25 million.
- Possess thorough knowledge of production, assuring timely and accurate presentation of goods; adept at coordinating delivery, organizing delivery schedules, and monitoring delivery personnel.
- Extensive experience in operations—responding to customer complaints, resolving problems, interacting with credit department to ascertain customer account status. Familiar with sourcing vendors, negotiating contracts, purchasing, correspondence, account adjustments, and inventory control.

EXPERIENCE
OXBRIDGE, INC.   Broken Arrow, OK
Sales/Customer Service Representative   1997-present
Manage office operations. Interact with merchandising personnel at all levels and provide technical information on company products and services. Interact with customers, advising in selection of products.

Monitor production to ensure fulfillment of customer specifications. Coordinate delivery schedules and monitor delivery personnel. Respond to and resolve customer complaints.

Collaborate with contracting merchandisers for contract negotiation on supplies. Conduct extensive materials costing processes. Control stock and conduct purchasing procedures.

Assist sales department in establishing client base and sales territories. Organize promotional demonstration activities for home and New York marketing offices.

EDUCATION
PROPHET JUNIOR COLLEGE   Broken Arrow, OK
A.S. in Computer Operations, expected 2000

DANCER

CHRIS SMITH
178 Green Street
Las Vegas, NV 89154
(702) 555-5555 (Day)
(702) 444-4444 (Evening)

TALENTS
- Ballet
- Jazz
- Modern Dance
- Tap
- Singing
- Acting
- Choreography
- Directing

EXPERIENCE
DANCING
September 1998-present: Soloist with Mormon Youth Ensemble. Presentations include:
- "Summer Winds"—Contemporary ballet
- "Peace at Heart"—Modern piece
- "Travels Afar"—Classical ballet
- "Italian Gondolas"—Contemporary ballet
- "Two Stars"—Jazz piece
- "Clouds Above"—Dream ballet, musical
- "The Gosling"—Classical ballet
- "A Little Bit Country"—Modern ballet, musical

CHOREOGRAPHY
- Special events and shows, 1997-present
- Rocket Dance Club, Las Vegas, NV, 1998-present
- Copa Cabana Club, Las Vegas, NV, 1997-98

EDUCATION
Sierra Nevada College, Incline Village, NV
BFA in Dance and Choreography, 2000

TRAINING
- Ballet: NV Ballet, NV Academy of Ballet
- Jazz: Genevieve le Fleur, James Ivan
- Tap: Jackie Rose Studio

DATA ENTRY SUPERVISOR

CHRIS SMITH
178 Green Street
River Forest, IL 60305
(312) 555-5555

EXPERIENCE
MORTEK ANALYSTS, River Forest, IL
1998-present   **Data Analyst III**
- Collect data and analyze documents using on-line database.
- Retrieve records from the Registry of Deeds and Bureau of Vital Statistics.
- Compile and generate reports of findings.
- CAST entry and maintenance, CAPS statistical reports production (M204 system).
- Log and analyze specific calls (TOLLS).
- Act as liaison to U.S. Attorney's office.
- Gather and analyze case materials; conduct physical case reviews.
- Act as interim supervisor; train, assist, and supervise staff of 6.

1996-98   **Data Entry Supervisor**
- Supervised staff of 4.
- Processed data entry inputs and seizure/motor vehicle reports; updated personnel files and DEAS-accounting system.
- Prepared biweekly progress reports; maintained relevant records.

BLUE ANGEL ASSOCIATES, Chicago, IL
1994-96   **Data Entry Operator**
- Transcribed prescription drug data for reimbursement.
- Met goals for speed, accuracy, and attention to critical money fields.

AWARDS
- Mortek Merit Award for excellence as a supervisor
- Mortek Presidential Award for outstanding performance

EDUCATION
River Forest High School, Diploma

COMPUTER SKILLS
Lotus 1-2-3, Sybase, WordPerfect

DAYCARE WORKER

CHRIS SMITH
178 Green Street
Delaware City, DE 19706
(302) 555-5555

EXPERIENCE

Head Teacher: City Child Care Corporation, Delaware City, DE
September 1999-present
- Taught educational and recreational activities for 20 children, ages 5-10, in a preschool/playcare setting.
- Planned and executed age-appropriate activities to promote social, cognitive, and physical skills.
- Developed daily lesson plans.
- Observed and assessed each child's development. Conducted parent/teacher orientations and meetings.

Teacher: Little People Preschool and Daycare, New Castle, DE
June 1998-August 1999
- Taught educational and recreational activities for children, ages 3-7, in a preschool/daycare setting.
- Planned, prepared, and executed two-week units based on themes to develop social, cognitive, and physical skills.
- Taught lessons and activities in Mathematics, Language Arts, Science, and Social Studies.

Student Teacher: Rolling Elementary School, Newark, DE
January-May 1998
- Taught and assisted a kindergarten teacher in a self-contained classroom of 28 students. Planned and taught lessons and activities in Mathematics, Science, and Social Studies.

Teaching Intern
Freud Laboratory School, Newark, DE	January-May 1996
Green Meadow Elementary School, Newark, DE	January-May 1995
Delaware State College Daycare Centers, Dover, DE	October-December 1994

EDUCATION
University of Delaware, Newark, DE
B.A. in Early Childhood Education; GPA in Major: 3.5/4.0

CERTIFICATION
Delaware State, K-5

DENTAL ASSISTANT

CHRIS SMITH
178 Green Street
Poughkeepsie, NY 12601
(601) 555-5555

SUMMARY OF QUALIFICATIONS
- Over 5 years' experience as a Dental Assistant and as a Medical Receptionist assisting in direct patient care and patient relations.
- Honor Graduate as Medical Assistant from National Education Center.
- Sound knowledge of medical terminology and clinical procedures.
- Certified in first aid, cardiopulmonary resuscitation, and electrocardiography.
- Additional experience as receptionist/secretary with an executive search/management consulting firm, financial management company, and realty firms.

HEALTH-CARE EXPERIENCE
Dr. Herbert Dickey, M.D., Brooklyn, NY   1999-present
- Schedule patients for appointments.
- Prepare patients for surgical procedures. Record temperature and blood pressure, insert intravenous units, and administer sedatives.
- Provide postoperative care. Record vital signs every 10 minutes until patient is conscious; establish patient comfort; provide necessary information to patients regarding new medications and possible side effects.
- Handle accounts payable and receivable.

Drs. William and Joseph Janell, New York, NY   1998-99
- Began as Dental Trainee, advanced to Dental Assistant.
- Sterilized instruments, processed x-rays, scheduled appointments, maintained patient relations.

Externship   1996
Internal Medicine Associates, Brooklyn, NY
- Multidisciplinary practice, including gastroenterology, rheumatology, endocrinology, and cardiology.
- Took vital signs, performed urinalysis, EKGs, and blood chemistries. Maintained patient charts.

EDUCATION
State University of New York, Biminghamton, NY
A.S. in Biology

COMPUTERS
Word, Lotus 1-2-3

CHRIS SMITH
178 Green Street
Upper Montclair, NJ
(201) 555-5555

EMPLOYMENT

Dr. Rettman, D.M.D., Upper Montclair, NJ

Dental Hygienist   1998-present

- Provide prophylaxis treatment to patients in a variety of situations; teeth cleaning, gum massage, oral hygiene education, and periodontal scaling.
- Administer Novocaine prior to painful procedures.
- Provide secretarial assistance: telephones, paperwork, scheduling.
- Monitor radiographs.

Dr. Grohowski, D.M.D., Princeton,NJ

Dental Assistant   1996-98

- Assisted dentist in prophylactic procedures: provided necessary tools, sterilized equipment, comforted patients.
- Provided secretarial assistance, same as above.

Dr. Race Banner, Princeton,NJ

Receptionist   1995-96

- Scheduled patients, answered phones, maintained files.

EDUCATION

Kelly School of Dental Hygiene, New York, NY

A.S. in Dental Hygiene

Coursework included Chemistry, Radiology, Nutrition, Periodontology, Pathology, Anatomy, Dental Equipment, Oral Embiology, Psychology, and Pharmacology.

LICENSURE

New Jersey Dental Hygiene License
National Board Dental Hygiene Exam (written: 90)
N.E.R.B. Dental Hygiene Exam (Clinical: 93; written: 90)

DESKTOP PUBLISHER

CHRIS SMITH
178 Green Street
Revere, MA 02151
(617) 555-5555
csmith@netmail.com

EXPERIENCE

LYERLA LIFE INSURANCE COMPANY, Revere, MA   1999-present
Desktop Publisher
- Produce brochures, personnel forms, and policy pages using Word and QuarkXPress.
- Create layout and design of brochures, detailing product lines for sales representatives and convention participants. Work with sales representatives and printers regarding bid specifications and deadlines for 3-color brochures.

KANE INC., Welch, WV   1995-99
Technical Illustrator/Graphic Designer
- Created complex diagrams, schedules, charts, and signs for proposals, reports, and division communications. Designed and updated organizational charts for division.
- Designed and formatted an 8-page employee newsletter. Sized photos and used stat camera for art. Worked with outside vendors for photos and final printing of newsletter.
- Produced photo contest poster, Employee of the Year poster, booklets, brochures, and invitations promoting company events.
- Assumed management responsibility for TQM program. Prioritized assignments, delegated tasks, and planned schedules. Prepared material for presentation by TQM groups.
- Organized and led departmental meetings, resolving problems with product quality. Established department standards for artwork and documents; published handbook of standards implemented department-wide.

Junior Technical Illustrator/Technical Typist   1989-95
- Created technical drawings, diagrams, and illustrations for technical reports and proposals. Performed newspaper pasteup. Assisted photographer in photo lab.
- Typeset copy for proposals and viewgraph presentations.

COMPUTER SKILLS

Word, PageMaker, QuarkXPress, Freehand, Illustrator, Photoshop

EDUCATION

University of Tennessee, Knoxville, TN
Graphic Design Certificate

DIETARY TECHNICIAN

CHRIS SMITH
178 Green Street
Topeka, KS 66621
(913) 555-5555

EXPERIENCE

HEARTLAND OSTEOPATHIC HOSPITAL, Topeka, KS
Dietary Technician   1998-present
Supervise and coordinate activities for food-service employees. Assist with training new
employees. Plan menu selection for patients. Manage the department when dietician or
department head is absent. Keep daily record of food, refrigerator, and dish machine temperatures.

CRESCENT MOON HOSPITAL, Ottowa, KS
Nutrition Assistant   1996-98
Trained and supervised diet aides in distribution of patient trays. Consulted with patients on
diet therapy plans.

WHISPERING WOODS CHILDREN'S CENTER, Olathe, KS
Assistant Cook   1994-96
Consulted with head cook on food preparation. Planned menus in conjunction with the head
cook. Purchased food and supplies. Organized and maintained inventory.

MCPHERSON GAS COMPANY, McPherson, KS
Customer Service Representative   1992-94
Scheduled appointments for workmen. Visited sites of rehabilitated properties to inform cus-
tomers of new appliances.

EDUCATION

Washburn University of Topeka, Topeka, KS
Certificate in Food Service Preparation

Topeka Junior College, Topeka, KS
Certificate in Food Service Supervision

DIETICIAN

CHRIS SMITH
178 Green Street
Atlanta, GA 30350
(404) 555-5555

EXPERIENCE

Dietician
Ellsworth Hospital, Atlanta, GA   1999-present
- Confer with medical and multidisciplinary staffs.
- Prepare nutritional care plans.
- Interview patients.
- Maintain and document patients' medical records.
- Instruct patients and their families.
- Perform miscellaneous duties as a member of the hospital support team.

Dietary Aide
Bentley Nursing Home, Atlanta, GA   1998-99
- Assisted in preparation of patient food trays.

Internship
Dowdell County Extension Service, Atlanta, GA   Fall 1998
- Wrote weekly food advice column, "Eat Up!"
- Developed chart and gave presentation on the major nutrients.

Office Assistant
Morehouse College, Atlanta, GA   1996-98
- Served as receptionist for main office.

Library Assistant
Morehouse College Library   Summer 1996
- Worked in circulation and periodical sections.

EDUCATION
Morehouse College, Atlanta, GA
B.S. in Consumer and Family Studies, 1999   Minor: Sociology

Relevant courses: Human Nutrition; Family Financial Decision-Making; Professional
Preparation; Principles of Food I & II; The Four Food Groups; Interpersonal Communication;
Social Psychology; Human Relations.

DISPATCHER (Medical)

CHRIS SMITH
178 Green Street
Hickory, NC 28601
(704) 555-5555

Summary of Qualifications

- Four years' experience supervising service technicians, handling public's questions and complaints, and servicing patients' medical equipment.
- Effective in developing rapport with depressed patients.
- Willing to travel or relocate.

Professional Experience

1999-present   GALLIMORE HOME HEALTH CARE, Hickory, NC
Medical Technician/Dispatch Supervisor
- Schedule and supervise 12 drivers.
- Handle patients' inquiries and complaints.
- Monitor equipment and supply inventories.
- Service patients' equipment and develop rapport with them.
- Improved efficiency of driver routing and of briefing drivers on assignments.

1997-99   PHOENIX HOME HEALTH, Charlotte, NC
Medical Technician
- Set up medical equipment for patients.
- Provided general maintenance for home health equipment.

1996-97   CARE PROVISIONS, High Point, NC
Medical Technician
- Set up medical equipment for patients, same as above.

Education

JOHNSON STATE COLLEGE, Johnson, VT
Bachelor of Science in Business Management

Computer Skills

Word, WordPerfect, Lotus 1-2-3

CHRIS SMITH

178 Green Street
Birmingham, AL 35244
(205) 555-5555
csmith@netmail.com

EXPERIENCE
BANKS AND SON INC., Birmingham, AL
Senior Editor, Reference 1998-present
Evaluate general trade reference titles and assess profit potential. Acquire titles and negotiate contracts. Oversee publication, from development and editing to production, publicity, and marketing.

Serve as in-house editor for institutional authors such as the American Library Association and the *Vintage Motorcycles* newsletter.

ROMANCE NOVEL-OF-THE-MONTH CLUB, INC., Kinsey, AL
Associate Director 1995-98
Evaluated manuscripts. Oversaw pricing and inventory of club titles. Supervised initial, backlist, and premium uses. Performed budgeting and estimating for club sales. Managed 10 employees.

Managing Editor 1990-95
Evaluated manuscripts. Scheduled new and backlist titles in the *RNOMC News* and in club advertising. Supervised 2 employees.

ILL-FATED KISSES, Selma, AL
Editorial Director 1986-90
Supervised the design and production of titles for two continuity programs. Identified, developed, and acquired successful poetry and artwork.

EDUCATION
New York University, New York, NY
Completed 12 credits in the Masters in Publishing Program
Courses include Publishing Law, Finance, and Subsidiary Rights

Pace University, New York, NY
B.S., Magazine Journalism
B.A., English Literature

ELECTRICIAN

CHRIS SMITH
178 Green Street
Manchester, NH 03103
(603) 555-5555

EXPERIENCE

1987-present   MANCHESTER COMPANY, Manchester, NH
Owner/Electrical Contractor/Electrician
- Write proposals and estimates for residential and commercial wiring and perform work as requested.
- Handle advertising and bookkeeping.
- Provide electrical and general repairs, including washers, boilers, burners, and locks.
- Install outlets, switches, and wiring.
- Hire, train, and oversee assistants.

1984-87   FREELANCE
General Assistant
- Dealt with residential electrical, heating, and plumbing needs.
- Installed outlets, switches, and wiring.

1981-84   LAMPWORKS, INC., Bedford, NH
Electrical Assistant
- Demonstrated knowledge of electricity via wiring lamps; ensured proper connections and working order.

RELEVANT TRAINING/LICENSURE

MANCHESTER TECHNICAL COMMUNITY COLLEGE, Manchester, NH
Associate of Science in Electrical Technology
Journeyman Electrician State License #55329

AFFILIATIONS

Associate Member, NFPA
Associate Member, IAEI

Chris Smith
178 Green Street
Visalia, CA 93291
(209) 555-5555

QUALIFICATIONS

- Thorough knowledge of all Emergency Medical procedures.
- Certified in CPR and Heimlich Maneuver.
- Proven capabilities assisting in emergency childbirth and heart attacks.
- Demonstrated skills in applying dressings, including burn dressings, and tourniquets, oxygen, and IVs.
- Familiar with procedures for critical burns, shock, gunshot wounds, physical manifestations of child abuse, and spousal battering.
- Provide emergency treatment for rape victims while staying within the guidelines of the law.
- Excellent knowledge of all main streets and secondary routes; strong sense of direction and map-reading ability.

EXPERIENCE

DOLAN AMBULANCE SERVICES   Visalia, CA
Head Emergency Medical Technician   1998-present
Provide emergency response and care to primarily elderly patients with bone fractures, strokes, heart attacks, falls. Assist in standard hospital and legal procedures for fatalities and post-mortem crisis management.

RUSSELL AMBULANCE SERVICES   Los Angeles, CA
Emergency Medical Technician   1995-98
Assist in providing emergency response to 911 calls for patients involved in traffic accidents, heart attacks, stroke, falls, and industrial accidents.

LICENSES/CERTIFICATIONS/TRAINING

Certified, EMT License
Visalia Hospital, 1995

License #4490223
State of California, 1995

Recertification Credits
California General Hospital, 1999

CHRIS SMITH
178 Green Street
Provo, UT 84604
(801) 555-5555

EXPERIENCE

1999-present DEPARTMENT OF EMPLOYMENT AND TRAINING, Provo, UT
Supervisor
- Assign and review applications, placement, initial claims, and claims-processing adjustments.
- Supervise preparation and maintenance of statistical records. Ensure accurate reports.
- Recommend improvements in operations for enhanced public services.
- Evaluate performance of subordinates through both qualitative and quantitative analysis. Ensure compliance with established procedures.

1996-99 DEPARTMENT OF UNEMPLOYMENT, Provo, UT
Claims Adjudicator
- Interviewed employers; gathered information; determined status in claims cases.
- Analyzed and interpreted Utah Employment Security Law to ensure information completeness.
- Verified and supplemented case data through file searches and database assessment.
- Maintained weekly case log and purge files, ensuring timely handling.
- Trained new personnel.

1994-96 STEPHEN JOLIE JEWELS, Sandy, UT
Assistant Manager
- Supervised and assisted with all facets of retail and wholesale operations.
- Prepared daily balances; managed cash.
- Hired, trained, scheduled, and supervised personnel.
- Planned and implemented in-store displays and promotions.
- Coordinated advertising with media outlets.

EDUCATION
SMITH COLLEGE, Northampton, MA
B.A. in Management

AFFILIATIONS
- American Association of Business Managers
- Smith College Alumni Association
- National Conference of Women—Secretary, 1996

ESL TEACHER

CHRIS SMITH
178 Green Street
San Francisco, CA 94111
(415) 555-5555

SUMMARY OF QUALIFICATIONS
- Accomplished instructor to various populations in English and Sign Language, tutor in Chinese,
- Skilled at coordinating communication and cognitive development activities for special-needs individuals.
- Proficient at providing counseling services and initializing patients' existing motor capabilities to develop basic skills.
- Experienced in working with adults and children from diverse cultural backgrounds.
- Fluent in Chinese and English; extensive language training in French and Latin.
- Exceptional communication, interpersonal, and organizational skills.

EXPERIENCE
Ervine Prison, San Francisco, CA
Chinese and Vietnamese Interpreter   1999-present
Interpret and translate for prisoners and prison officials. Sit in on trials and probate/appellate hearings. Act as liaison between lawyers and incarcerated clients.

Chinese-American Civic Association, San Francisco, CA
Teacher   1996-99
Instruct Chinese and Vietnamese adults in English as a Second Language.

Rydell Corporation, San Francisco, CA
Counselor/Interpreter   1992-96
Conduct individual and group counseling to help eliminate inappropriate behaviors in young adults suffering from autism and cerebral palsy. Consult with psychiatrists, psychologists, and health professionals to coordinate treatment plans. Monitor clients to assess effectiveness of treatment plans. Instruct clients in basic skills, including communication, reading, writing, and math. Initiate cognitive development activities.

EDUCATION
School for International Training   Orange, CA
Master of Arts in Teaching
Concentration in Teaching of English to Speakers of Other Languages (ESOL)

University of Miami
Bachelor of Arts in Human Services   Miami, FL

EXECUTIVE ASSISTANT

CHRIS SMITH
178 Green Street
Erie, PA 16541
(814) 555-5555

EXPERIENCE
1999-present   *Redmond Computer, Inc., Erie, PA*
Administrative Assistant to the Chief Executive Officer
Coordinate and prioritize daily activities of chairman of the board. Perform administrative
functions in support of the CEO. Interact and assist in preparing for board of directors' meetings. Record and distribute minutes of management meetings.

1996-99   *Steppenwolf Associates, Pittsburgh, PA*
Administrative Assistant to the President and Chief Executive Officer
Prioritized daily activities of the CEO. Set up and maintained a "tickler system." Composed,
and edited correspondence on behalf of the president.

1992-96   *Jasmine, Rain, Inc., Beaver Falls, PA*
Administrative Assistant to the Chief Operating Officer
Interacted on behalf of the COO in sensitive customer and employee relationships. Recorded
and distributed minutes of the management committee. Maintained and distributed monthly
department reports.

EDUCATION
University of Pennsylvania Continuing Education Program, Philadelphia, PA
Courses in Management, Business, Computer Skills, Marketing, French, and Italian

Cutter College, Erie, PA
Courses in Shorthand Refresher and Medical Language

SKILLS
Computer
WordPerfect, Word, Excel

Other
Typing (60 wpm), shorthand

EXECUTIVE SECRETARY (Banking)

CHRIS SMITH
178 Green Street
Brattleboro, VT 05301
(802) 555-5555

SUMMARY OF QUALIFICATIONS
- Extensive knowledge of bank administrative policies and procedures through six years of bank experience
- Able to supervise employees and work with all levels of management in a professional, diplomatic manner
- Effective at rapidly recognizing and analyzing department problems and finding solutions
- Experienced at working on multiple projects under pressure while meeting strict deadlines and budget requirements

EXPERIENCE
BRATTLEBORO SAVINGS BANK, Brattleboro, VT
Executive Secretary to Senior Vice Present, Commercial Division 1998-present
- Set up commercial loans on computer system. Update loan files with regard to financial statements and financial information. Coordinate loan renewals with loan officer.
- Maintain appraisal files
- Prepare monthly reports for board of directors

SPARTAN TRUST COMPANY, Montpelier, VT
Executive Secretary to the Executive Vice President and Senior Loan Officer 1995-98
- Managed secretarial staff supporting the commercial loan officers
- Coordinated staff meetings and presentations to board of directors
- Prepared monthly departmental and divisional reports for distribution
- Updated and maintained policy and procedure manual

Commercial Finance Assistant 1993-95
- Prepared daily client loan advances and loan payment activity
- Maintained monthly client loan and collateral statements
- Maintained collateral availability controls by formula
- Performed analysis of client files
- Assisted in preparing departmental reports and loan agreements

COMPUTER SKILLS
WordPerfect, Lotus 1-2-3

FACILITIES ENGINEER

CHRIS SMITH
178 Green Street
Broomfield, CO 80021
(303) 555-5555

EXPERIENCE

Facilities Engineer, Breckenridge Company, Broomfield, CO   1996-present
Supervise all phases of multi-craft maintenance, utilities, engineering, and construction departments for this specialty steel company, which employs 800 and covers a 60-acre facility.

Operations
- Direct staff of 100 technicians and 10 supervisors in designing, constructing, and maintaining equipment and machinery.
- Established standards and policies for testing, inspection, and maintenance of equipment in accordance with engineering principles and safety regulations.
- Manage a budget of approximately $10 million annually.
- Participate extensively in labor relations with various trades.

Planning and Construction
- Plan and install maintenance program; direct all improvement and new construction projects, from studies for justification to project startup.
- Prepared bid sheets and contracts for construction facilities.
- Represented the company as general contractor on project and saved approximately $4 million of the original estimates submitted by outside contractors.

Project Engineer, Gibralta Corporation, Loveland, CO   1992-96
- Planned and implemented modernization program, including installation of bloom, billet, bar, rod, and strip mills, as well as the required soaking pits and reheating furnaces.
- Directed a multi-craft maintenance force of approximately 250 craftsmen and supervisors.
- Planned and installed a maintenance program that reduced equipment downtime and substantially increased cost-per-thousand savings.

AFFILIATION
Member of American Iron and Steel Engineers Association

EDUCATION
University of Colorado at Boulder, Boulder, CO
B.S., Mechanical Engineering

FAST FOOD WORKER

Chris Smith
178 Green Street
Carson City, NV 89703
(702) 555-5555

EMPLOYMENT

1999-present   THE PIZZA PALACE, Carson City, NV
Server
- Participate in opening of new store outlets.
- Assist with public relations, food service, and register control.
- Resolve conflicts in high-pressure environment.

1998-99   NEVADA TELEPHONE, Las Vegas, NV
Data Input/Repetitive Debts Collection/Commercial
- Established commercial accounts; verified records and old accounts for new service.
- Provided customer service; fielded inquiries.

Summers 1995-98   BLACKTHORN DAY CAMP, Plaston, NH
Recreation Director
- Planned, programmed, and supervised camp activities for summer outdoor education and camping services for juvenile coeds.
- Supervised cabin group, counseled, and instructed in aquatics, sports, and special events. Wrote weekly reports to parents.

1993-94   SISYPHUS GROCERY, Manchester, NH
Produce Manager
- Maintained produce inventory.
- Assisted with public relations and in-house advertising for special sales and events.

EDUCATION
MANCHESTER HIGH SCHOOL, Manchester, NH
Diploma, College Preparatory

FILE CLERK

CHRIS SMITH
178 Green Street
Cohasset, MA 02025
(617) 555-5555

EMPLOYMENT

1999-present
Brigham & Women's Hospital, Boston, MA
File Clerk
- Prepare folders and file records, observing confidentiality.
- Sort and distribute mail.
- Perform photocopying and faxing.
- Code and batch forms; prepare forms for processing.
- Handle outgoing packages to shippers and couriers.
- Type and perform other functions as needed.

1997-99
Cohasset Industries, Cohasset, MA
Clerk
- Retrieved, updated, and corrected customer files.
- Processed mail, daily reports, and correspondence.
- Coded and routed orders and billing invoices.

EDUCATION

1992-1993
The Burdett School, Boston, MA
Courses in typing, filing, and computers

SKILLS

Computer: WordPerfect, Lotus 1-2-3
Other: Typing (70 wpm)

CHRIS SMITH
178 Green Street
Los Angeles, CA 90049
(213) 555-5555

EXPERIENCE

1995-present
Freelance Writer and Videographer
- Wrote material for various Los Angeles comedians, including Sammy Krane and Jed Malone. Wrote jokes published in *Side-Splitters* magazine.
- Videotaped improvisational workshop for the L.A. Entertainment Theatre and comedy sketches for local talent.

1998-present
HOLLY CAN PRODUCTIONS, Burbank, CA
Production Assistant
- Perform general production tasks. Research and recommend prop and wardrobe choices.
- Assisted in production of *Chuck's Gals*.
- Shot and edited commercials for Swank Outfitters.

1997-98
Intern
- Observed techniques in video editing and preproduction of feature films and slide shows for corporations and universities.

WRITING
- Radio/TV commercial scripts
- 35-page comedy
- Several short narrative sketches
- Several short comedy films

EDUCATION
Bachelor of Arts in Film Production
Emerson College, L.A. program, 1998

FINANCIAL ANALYST

CHRIS SMITH
178 Green Street
Omaha, NE 68182
(402) 555-5555
csmith@netmail.com

EXPERIENCE

1998-present
BRIDELL BANK AND TRUST CO., Omaha, NE
Corporate Accounting Analyst, Comptroller's Division
Prepare and analyze income-related statements, balance sheet, and earnings schedules for $9 billion corporation and subsidiaries. Compile 10k, annual, federal reserve, management, and analyst reports. Analyze balance sheet and income statement key ratios using trend reports. Prepare GAP report; establish general ledger accounts.

1998 and Summers 1996, 1995
CARTEL BANK, Wayne, NE
Intern, Presidential Suite CSR
Serviced depositors with accounts in excess of $100,000; reconciled accounts. Handled bookkeeping, customer relations, and check verification.

1997
THE BANK OF ROME, Rome, Italy
Relationship Analyst—AIESEC Intern
Researched financial reports to support quantitative analysis of bank's relationship with foreign correspondents.

EDUCATION

UNIVERSITY OF NEBRASKA AT OMAHA, Omaha, NE
Bachelor of Science, Finance

COMPUTER SKILLS

Word, Lotus 1-2-3

CHRIS SMITH
178 Green Street
Palos Heights, IL 60445
(312) 555-5555

EXPERIENCE
1979-present
PALOS HEIGHTS FIRE COMPANY, Life Member
Firefighter, **Emergency Medical Technician**
- Ambulance Lieutenant, 1984, 1996—conduct training drills.
- Ambulance Captain, 1985
- Ambulance Auxiliary Secretary, 1985
- Photographer, 1993-present

1979-83
MIDWEST AMBULANCE, River Forest, IL
Assistant Manager/Crew
Scheduled 10 full-time and 8 part-time Emergency Medical Technicians for emergency and hospital transportation of patients. Services Burn Center at River Forest Medical Center.

AFFILIATIONS
International Fire Photographers Association, 1995-present
Deerfield Fireman's Association, 1979-present

EDUCATION
DEERFIELD COMMUNITY COLLEGE, Deerfield, IL
Emergency Medical Technician, 1994
- Certified by the Illinois Department of Health
- Illinois Association of Arson Investigators Certificate, Forensic Fire Photography
- Chicago Electric Company Fire Academy
- Gas and Electric Fire Fighting, 1980-81
- Deerfield Fire Academy, Fire Fighting I, II, III, 1979-80

TRINITY VOCATIONAL-TECHNICAL SCHOOL, Deerfield, IL
- Communications Technician, 1980-82
- Photographic Technician, 1979-80

FITNESS INSTRUCTOR

CHRIS SMITH
178 Green Street
Richmond, VA 23220
(804) 555-5555

EXPERIENCE

1999-present THE BABY BOOM, Richmond, VA
Owner/Operator
- Provide comprehensive yet responsible exercise classes for pregnant women.
- Supervise staff of 12. Hire and train employees, manage payroll, schedule work shifts, administer billing.
- Maintain steady contact with each client's physician, to ensure absolute safety for her and the baby.

1997-99 DEE DEE LEE'S FITNESS PHANTASMAGORIA, Richmond, VA
Aerobics/Calisthenics Instructor
- Taught intensive aerobics, calisthenics, and stretching to coeducational classes of up to 25 adults in all physical conditions.
- Geared program toward intermediate and advanced levels.
- Used music as a motivational tool.

1995-97 UP AND AT 'EM STUDIO, Norfolk, VA
Manager/Exercise Instructor
- Handled all sales (telephone and direct), marketing and strategy development.
- Developed client referral network.
- Motivated clients to perform intensive calisthenics, yoga, and stretching; taught techniques.
- Handled bookkeeping and all business activities.

EDUCATION

WILLAMETTE UNIVERSITY, Salem, OR
Bachelor of Arts in English, Minor in Physical Education
Studies in Physiology, Anatomy, and Nutrition
Captain of Women's Gymnastic Team

AFFILIATION

Associate member of Women in Fitness Association, Richmond Chapter

PERSONAL INFORMATION

In excellent health; perform daily aerobics, Nautilus, and Universal workouts; run 5-10 miles a day; enjoy hiking.

FLIGHT ATTENDANT (Lead)

CHRIS SMITH
178 Green Street
Troy, MI 48098
(313) 555-5555

SUMMARY OF QUALIFICATIONS
- Broad knowledge of airline safety and service procedures.
- Positive attitude; patient with challenging and difficult passengers. Excellent rapport with children, elderly, and handicapped passengers.
- Conversant in Spanish.
- Knowledgeable about fine foods and domestic wines.

EXPERIENCE
TRANS AIR BUSINESS CONNECTION, Detroit, MI   1998-present
Lead Attendant
Oversee up to 10 attendants. Greet and assist passengers boarding and leaving plane. Instruct passengers in the use of emergency equipment. Care for small children, elderly, and handicapped. Administer first aid. Assist and instruct passengers during emergencies.

Flight Attendant   1991-98
Conduct preflight procedures; ensure the safety and comfort of all passengers; serve food and beverages; stow carry-on luggage. Administer CPR/first aid if necessary.

KALEIDOSCOPE CAFE, Utica, MI   1989-91
Head Waitress and *Manager of Banquet Wait Staff*
Served as hostess and banqueting and catering assistant for elegant upscale restaurant. Seated and served patrons gourmet meals, mixed cocktails, performed cash and credit card transactions. Scheduled staff; trained minimum of 5 waitstaff.

CERTIFICATION
Trans Air Business Flight Attendant
CPR

EDUCATION
THE PERRY SCHOOL, Ann Arbor, MI. Travel Industry Program

CONCORDIA COLLEGE, Ann Arbor, MI
A.S. in Communications

FOOD INSPECTOR

CHRIS SMITH
178 Green Street
Rome, GA 30160
(706) 555-5555

EXPERIENCE

THE CITY OF ROME   1997-present
Director, Food Inspector and Public Health   Rome, GA
- Establish executive guidelines and centralized management systems for Rome restaurants, including sit-down and takeout; hospitals and health care facilities; schools and campus dining halls; airlines; and public and private cafeterias.
- Interact with Public Health, Public Safety, and food-service distributors throughout the city.
- Provide documentation and distribute warnings to establishments and distributors that fail food inspections.

GREATER ATLANTA HEALTH DEPARTMENT   1990-97
Chief Food Inspector   Atlanta, GA
- Participated in exams and regulatory inspections of food distributors, warehouses, refrigerated facilities, restaurants, supermarkets, convenience stores, and commercial buildings.
- Ensured all inspections were within regulations of the Georgia General Laws, state Sanitary Code, and local ordinances.

PLYMOUTH COUNTY HEALTH DEPARTMENT   1989-90
Internship, Food Inspectors' Offices   Hingham, MA
- Accompanied and assisted food inspectors on their rounds of food distribution warehouses, supermarkets, restaurants, and hospital kitchens.

EDUCATION

UNIVERSITY OF SOUTHERN CALIFORNIA
B.S. Environmental Health

CERTIFICATION

Registered Sanitation Inspector

GENERAL MANAGER (Printing Company)

CHRIS SMITH
178 Green Street
New London, CT 06320
(203) 555-5555

EXPERIENCE

1998-present   **Manager**
DICKENS PRINTING COMPANY   *New London, CT*
Facilitate the operation of and provide maintenance services for a combined commercial multicolor and thermographic stationery printer.
- Estimate job costs and schedule production.
- Ensure project compliance with customer specifications.
- Delegate responsibilities; train, supervise, and evaluate staff.

1996-98   **Manager**
HARDY PRESS   *Hartford, CT*
- Serviced customers, dealt with vendors, and estimated project costs.
- Scheduled projects and monitored production to ensure compliance with customer specifications.
- Delegated responsibilities; scheduled work week.
- Trained, supervised, developed, and evaluated staff.

Elected to Executive Finance Committee. Assisted in evaluating and adjusting company procedures; influential in changes that generated an increase in gross sales from $5 million to $8.5 million.

Headed standardization project, resulting in a reduction in errors and increased profits. Implemented the Profit Enhancement System for estimating and costing.

1994-96   **Project Coordinator**
COPYCAT COPIERS   *Fairfield, CT*
- Provided estimates on projects.
- Sourced vendors and conducted purchasing procedures.
- Standardized procedures for estimating, purchasing, and order documentation during a high-growth period.

EDUCATION

CONNECTICUT COLLEGE   *New London, CT*
Certified in numerous management, employee relations, and computer seminars

FAIRFIELD UNIVERSITY   *Fairfield, CT*
B.A. in Liberal Arts

GENERAL OFFICE CLERK

Chris Smith
178 Green Street
Boston, MA 02215
(617) 555-5555

EXPERIENCE

1999-present   CARTER TRUST, Boston, MA
Office Clerk

- Transcribe statements from insureds; type letters to attorneys, insureds, and other insurance companies. Type confidential material, such as employee appraisals, for the Claims Manager.
- Manage timely payment of Worker's Compensation checks and filing of Workers' Compensation forms.
- Process insurance claims, payments, and recovery checks. Print checks to insureds and vendors.
- Answer telephone inquiries from insureds, claimants, and agents.

1995-99   FEDERAL UNION INSURANCE CO., Boston, MA
Clerical Supervisor

- Supervised clerical staff, consisting of three clerical employees.
- Acted as Administrative Assistant to Claims Manager: typed letters to attorneys, insureds, and other insurance companies; handled special projects and reports from the Boston office.

1991-95   MAPLEROOT HIGH SCHOOL, Belchertown, MA
Payroll Clerk

Handled a monthly payroll for 500 salaried and hourly employees. Prepared quarterly federal withholding tax returns and labor statistics report.

EDUCATION

Certificate in WordPerfect
Certificate in Lotus 1-2-3
Mapleroot High School, Diploma

SKILLS

Computer
WordPerfect, Lotus 1-2-3, Word, Access

Other
Typing (65+ wpm)
Strong knowledge of general accounting procedures

GRAPHIC ARTIST/DESIGNER

Chris Smith
178 Green Street
Honey Grove, TX 75446
(210) 555-5555
csmith@netmail.com

DESIGN PROJECTS (selected)
- Logo for Connection Street Gallery, its storefront sign, T-shirts, jackets, business cards and stationery, advertising, and greeting cards
- Logo for *Brazen Attachment* magazine; artwork for advertising appeared in *Her View*
- Calligraphic artwork for Texas History Museum
- Cover Design for *Missed Grits: How to Cook Southern Favorites No Matter Where You Live* (Watts/Gourmet Press, 1997)

EXPERIENCE
MICHAEL JUDGE GALLERY, Dallas, TX   Spring 2000
Displayed and sold several art pieces. Illustrations used in advertisements and gallery logo.

CAROL OATES INC., Keechi, TX   1999-2000
Designed invitations, stationery, business cards, and logos for national stationery and social invitation firm.

BYRON KATZ, Kress, TX   1997-98
Contributed freelance calligraphy to national stationery company. Designed invitations and logos.

BARBARA B. DOLE, Kress, TX   1995-97
Freelance calligrapher for local clients. Designed wedding and party invitations, promotions, and advertising pieces.

EDUCATION
CONCORDIA COLLEGE, Bronxville, NY
Bachelor of Fine Arts

CHRIS SMITH
178 Green Street
Sundance, WY 82729
(307) 555-5555

EXPERIENCE

THE FIELDSTONE BANK   Sundance, WY
Bank Guard
1999-present
- Ensure safety and security of customers, bank employees, and bank assets.

WILLOW MEAD ART MUSEUM   Wolf, WY
Security Guard
1996-99
- Patrolled, performed surveillance, and controlled facilities and areas. Maintained reports, records, and documents as required.

CITY OF ROCK SPRINGS POLICE DEPARTMENT   Rock Springs, WY
Property Clerk
1993-96
- Supervised security, transfer, and storage of personal effects and properties as evidence in trial and court cases.

CITY OF GILLETTE SCHOOL DEPARTMENT   Gillette, WY
Transitional Aide
1989-93
- Ensured safety of students and security of school property at Madison Park High School.

THUNDERBEAT CONSTRUCTION   Crowheart, WY
Weigher of Goods/Track Foreman
1988-91
- Weighed materials and supervised track construction at University of Wyoming.

EDUCATION
UNITED STATES COAST GUARD, Miami, FL
Certificate, Interactive Query Language
Certificate, Advanced PMIS
Certificate, Coast Guard WP School
Winter Park High School, Winter Park, FL

HAIRSTYLIST

CHRIS SMITH
178 Green Street
Menoken, ND 58558
(701) 555-5555

SUMMARY OF QUALIFICATIONS
- Skilled in various hair cutting techniques, such as texturizing
- Experienced with permanents, body waves, and spiral perms
- Named "Most Promising Hairstylist" by the *Bismarck Gazette*
- Coordinated promotional events with local radio stations, including The First Annual Much Ado About Hair-Do's and Don'ts

EXPERIENCE
1998-present
The Hair Studio, Mandan, ND
Hairstylist
- Cut client's hair in requested styles.
- Use prepared dyes or create coloring or streaking as desired.
- Perform waxing.
- Answer phones and schedule appointments.
- Style hair for local fashion shows: French braids, twists, floral weaves.
- Doubled base clientele within first 2 months.

1995-98
Hair America, McKenzie, ND
Hairstylist
- Performed duties as above.
- Manicured nails.
- Independently sold hair-care products.

EDUCATION
National Hair Academy, Bismarck, ND
Hair Styling Certification

HEALTH CLUB MANAGER

CHRIS SMITH
178 Green Street
Anchorage, AK 99502
(907) 555-5555

EXPERIENCE

MUSCLE MANIA, Anchorage, AK

Manager   1999-present
- Initiate and execute sales, marketing, and promotional efforts for corporate membership packages.
- Plan budget for facility operations, supplies, and equipment.
- Schedule and train personnel in sales and service.
- Implement programs and operations.

Program Director   1997-99
- Designed comprehensive health and fitness evaluation, incorporating components of strength, flexibility, cardiovascular and muscular endurance, and cardiac risk factors.
- Organized and instructed fitness classes for special interest groups (pre- and postnatal exercise, aerobics for learning-disabled children, and exercise for the elderly).
- Developed and administered monthly seminars, workshops, and special-interest-group meetings to enhance public relations.

ACCOMPLISHMENTS
- National Wrestling Champion, 1996.
- Consultant for the U.S. Olympic Wrestling Team, 1998.
- Certified in CPR/first aid.

EDUCATION

UNIVERSITY OF MAINE AT ORONO
B.S. in Physical Education, 1997
Major—Exercise Physiology
Minor—Recreational Sports Management
Activities: Wrestling (team captain), weightlifting trainer

CHRIS SMITH
178 Green Street
Fairbanks, AK 99508
(907) 555-5555

EXPERIENCE

1999-present   VEDDER COMMUNITY HEALTH PLAN, Fairbanks, AK

Multi-Specialty Float

Currently trained in nine departments to ensure smooth operations in medical assisting and administrative work. Departments include Internal Medicine, Nutrition, Pediatrics, Visual Services, OB-GYN, Radiology, Pharmacy, Main Desk, Building Services.

- Member, *Leadership Committee* for unification and cooperation of interpersonal relations among management and staff.
- Member, *Diversity Committee* to promote awareness of the similarities in values despite diversities among multicultural staff.

1997-99

Hospital Admissions Coordinator

Scheduled examinations and surgeries, including emergencies. Set up operating rooms. Coordinated inpatient hospital rooms and physicals. Interviewed patients for information before surgery and examinations. Informed patients of necessary requirements before surgery.

- Received Dunstable Award for highly developed level of responsibility and commitment to member satisfaction.
- Received Gold Star Award for implementing new practices and procedures that remain a permanent part of hospital admissions.

1995-97

Medical Assistant

Scheduled appointments for gynecology and obstetrics. Booked appointments exclusively for OB-GYN specialist. Answered and screened patient phone calls, channeled them to proper doctor. Maintained records, input data.

1990-95   THE LEE HUANG RESIDENCE, Fairbanks, AK

Childcare Governess

Provided quality homecare for two children in their parents' absence. Oversaw general supervision of home. Creatively organized activities.

EDUCATION

UNIVERSITY OF ALASKA, Fairbanks, AK   Candidate for M.Ed., 2000
ALASKA PACIFIC UNIVERSITY, Anchorage, AK   B.A. Liberal Arts

HOME HEALTH AIDE

CHRIS SMITH
178 Green Street
Decorah, IA 52101
(319) 555-5555

EXPERIENCE
HOMECARE INCORPORATED, Decorah, IA
1999-present   *Case Administrator*
- Manage the daily clinical operation of CPMS (Clozaril Patient Management System), monitor laboratory results, and manage staff. Recruited to program at its inception to develop, test, and implement new home-care system.
- Coordinate patient services, including blood draws and drug delivery. Monitor and report lab results to physicians for review and documentation. Assisted in selecting and developing office and pharmacy.
- Establish and maintain service schedule for staff consisting of RNs, LPNs, phlebotomists, and pharmacists. Assist in recruiting, selecting, and evaluating RNs, LPNs, and phlebotomists. Administer training and orientation for clinical staff.
- Generate monthly Quality Assurance reports and audit records and computer files. Identify and resolve service-related incidents. Report and maintain record of incidents as described by quality assurance guidelines. Support marketing and sales teams of pharmaceutical companies.

1998   *Nurse Clinician*
- Provided professional nursing support for homebound patients in need of infusion therapy. Worked closely with Nursing Supervisor, agency staff, and referring physicians.
- Attended to full range of patients, including those with AIDS. Provided patient and family/caregiver education. Educated members of nutrition support, oncology, and IV teams in providing professional services.

SIOUX CITY HOSPITAL, Sioux City, IA
1994-98   *Staff nurse* for the medical/surgical units
- Assessed condition of primary-care patients. Planned and implemented services, evaluated patient outcomes.
- Acted as resource nurse for staff of a 50-bed unit, with immediate responsibility for 12–15 patients.
- Supervised LPNs and ancillary staff.

LICENSE
Registered Nurse, State of Iowa, #379526

EDUCATION
SIOUX CITY HOSPITAL SCHOOL OF NURSING, Sioux City, IA
B.S. in Nursing

HOSPITAL ADMINISTRATOR

CHRIS SMITH
178 Green Street
Detroit, MI 48203
(313) 555-5555

EXPERIENCE
THE DETROIT MEDICAL CENTER, Detroit, MI
Hospital Director, 1998–present
- Supervise and coordinate administrative services for city's public health care program.
- Handle health care and hospitalization for indigents, low-income, and welfare patients consistent with care afforded to insurance and fee-for-service patients.
- Resolve staff and general administration conflicts and issues.
- Resolve policy issues; develop reports and documents for budgeting proposals and expenditure control.

Central Administrator, Emergency Services, 1992–98
- Coordinated all administrative details of Emergency Room health care.
- Assisted medical team in providing prompt support services.
- Supervised floor secretaries, interpreters, and ancillary personnel.
- Prepared budget and monitored expenditures.

Unit Manager, 1990–92
- Provided administrative support to Intensive Care Units, Operating Rooms, and Medical/Surgical Floors.
- Supervised secretarial staff and ancillary personnel.
- Handled vendor relations and inventory control.

ADDITIONAL EXPERIENCE
- Central Administrator, Night Admitting Manager, and Floor Secretary, 1982–90.

EDUCATION
UNIVERSITY OF DETROIT MERCY, Detroit, MI
M.S. in Health Service Administration

MICHIGAN HOSPITAL ASSOCIATION, Detroit, MI
Certificate in Management Development

MICHIGAN STATE UNIVERSITY, East Lansing, MI
B.A. in English

BOARD MEMBERSHIPS
Elected to Board of Directors, Department of Public Health, 1996-present.

HOTEL CLERK

CHRIS SMITH
178 Green Street
Halstead, KS 67056
(316) 555-5555

EXPERIENCE

THE OLIVER HOTEL, Whitewater, KS   1999-present
Hotel Clerk
- Provide for guests' needs.
- Control reservation input, using EECO computer system.
- Handle incoming calls.
- Maintain daily reports involving return guests, corporate accounts, and suite rentals.
- Inspect rooms.

WALDEN HOTEL, Walton, KS   1996-99
Hotel Clerk
- Trained personnel.
- Handled bookings from telephone, international fax, and telex.
- Maintained daily and monthly reports tracking demands and guaranteed no-show billing.
- Utilized APTEC computer for inputting group bookings and lists.

READ ALL ABOUT IT, Newton, KS   1994-96
Sales Associate
- Assisted customers.
- Maintained stock.
- Opened and closed shop.
- Tracked bestselling novels, made recommendations to customers.

BETHEL COLLEGE, North Newton, KS   1991-93
Secretary
Performed general clerical duties. Resolved inquiries. Assisted in locating guest speakers.

EDUCATION

BETHANY COLLEGE, Lindsborg, KS
Bachelor of Science in Sociology

Chris Smith
178 Green Street
Milwaukee, WI 53233
(414) 555-5555

EXPERIENCE
JAMESON HOTEL, Milwaukee, WI
Concierge, 1999-present
- Promoted to establish Concierge Department in 350-room luxury hotel. Manage 40-person hotel staff, including concierge department assistants, mail and information clerks, bell staff, doormen, valet parking and hotel garage staff, and telephone operators. Diplomatically and effectively resolve guest grievances and problems; compose responses and make follow-up phone contact.
- Assist in setting tone and image of hotel through providing guest services, including tourist information and arranging for tours, hotel and airline reservations, car rentals and limousine hires, theater and symphony tickets. Make restaurant recommendations and dinner reservations based on comprehensive knowledge of and contact with area restaurants and management. Handle and route guest mail and faxes.
- Assist in hotel promotions and marketing strategies; coordinate all Bridal Package arrangements. Administer emergency lifesaving procedures as necessary. During hotel's promotion, handled all guests from check-in to check-out; coordinated 2,500 museum tickets, consulting with guests on preferred times.

Bell Captain, 1998-99
- Supervised all Bellman and Doormen. Acted as Concierge prior to establishment of Concierge Department.

Doorman/Bellman, 1997
- Greeted guests; fostered positive impression of establishment.

EDUCATION
Sorbonne University, Paris, France: Summer 1992
Marquette University, Milwaukee, WI: 1991-93

SKILLS
Language: French
Other: Certified in CPR and first aid

HOTEL MANAGER (Front Desk)

CHRIS SMITH
178 Green Street
Phoenix, AZ 85021
(602) 555-5555

EXPERIENCE
1998-present
DESERT SANDS HOTEL, Phoenix, AZ
Front Desk Manager
- Manage front desk operations for this 500-room, three-star hotel.
- Provide guest services, including tours, travel reservations, car rentals, theater and restaurant reservations.
- Interview, hire, and supervise a staff of 15.
- Book and coordinate local and national business conventions and seminars.
- Designed and implemented a guest survey to gauge satisfaction with the hotel, its staff, and services.

1996-98
LE MIRAGE HOTEL, Phoenix, AZ
Front Desk Clerk
- Handled reservations, guest check-in and checkout.
- Handled cash and credit card transactions for 250 rooms.
- Resolved guest complaints.

1993-96
GOTTA FLY TRAVEL, Tucson, AZ
Travel Agent
Assessed client needs. Handled plane reservations and hotel bookings.

COMPUTER SKILLS
Word, Excel, SABRE

EDUCATION
UNIVERSITY OF ARIZONA, Tucson, AZ
Bachelor of Science in Business Administration, 1992

HUMAN SERVICES WORKER
(Juvenile and Family)

Chris Smith
178 Green Street
Elmhurst, IL 60126
(312) 555-5555

SUMMARY OF QUALIFICATIONS
- Knowledgeable at assessing cases, developing clinical treatment plans, facilitating crisis intervention, and conducting informal family therapy.
- Exceptional counseling skills, motivating several individuals to enter programs for substance abuse treatment.
- Extensive experience and familiarity with child abuse and neglect cases.
- Excellent rapport with children.

EXPERIENCE
1998-present   **Investigator/Ongoing Case Manager**
SOCIETY FOR THE PREVENTION OF CRUELTY TO CHILDREN   Chicago, IL
Conduct assessments and develop treatment plans for family caseload. Maintain ongoing documentation of contracts. Provide crisis intervention and informal family therapy. Advocate for clients in court and with community agencies.

1996-97   **Intern**
FARMINGTON JUVENILE COURT   Farmington, IL
Established monitor contacts and composed monitor reports. Tracked abuse and neglect cases to ensure that status reports and petitions were filed accurately and on time. Observed court hearings and trials and established court expectations.

1995-96   **Intern**
PEORIA JUVENILE COURT   Peoria, IL
Provided individual and group counseling for juvenile offenders in detention. Reviewed case files and incident reports.

1994   **Intern**
DEPARTMENT OF MENTAL HEALTH   Gardena, IL
Assisted retarded adults in enhancing motor skills; encouraged development of self-esteem and self-sufficiency.

EDUCATION
BRADLEY UNIVERSITY   Peoria, IL
Bachelor of Science in Human Services, 1997

INFORMATION SUPPORT SPECIALIST

CHRIS SMITH
178 Green Street
Evansville, WY 82636
(307) 555-5555
csmith@netmail.com

EXPERIENCE
Kimball Equipment Corp., Casper, WY
1999-present
Information Support Specialist
- Offer formal and informal training and assistance for end-user computing hardware and software, particularly Lotus 1-2-3, WordPerfect, and Windows.
- Work with user department personnel to ensure adherence to office automation/end-user computing guidelines, standards, and procedures.
- Coordinated with other Information Services staff to provide appropriate education, hardware, software, and data required to effectively assist users.
- Analyze and resolve problems via help desk.

1994-98
Supervisor, Word Processing, Word Processing Center
- Planned and supervised stenographic, clerical, word/information processing services, and company telephone operators.
- Supervised 13 full-time employees.
- Determined material, personnel, and budgeting needs.
- Designed workflow systems, defined operating standards, and evaluated effectiveness.
- Established cost and quality controls.

1992-93
Word Processing Specialist, Word Processing Center
- Formatted and produced complex documents; processed records.
- Met high-priority deadlines.
- Analyzed requirements for and handled special projects.
- Trained personnel in use of equipment.
- Acted as administrative support specialist and supervisor in their absence.

EDUCATION
University of Wyoming, Laramie, WY
Associate in Business Management

INSURANCE AGENT

CHRIS SMITH
178 Green Street
Erie, PA 16505
(814) 555-5555

EXPERIENCE
SENIOR SUPERVISOR CLAIMS
1999-present
Bimscala Risk Management
Pittsburgh, PA

- As Senior Supervisor, Claims, was accountable for all claims service provided by the Workers' Compensation and Liability units. Oversaw the delivery of a quality product that developed client confidence in the claims-handling ability of Bimscala.
- Responsibilities encompassed direct claims handling, reporting and negotiating high-exposure claims, and conducting periodic claims reviews and loss-report reviews.
- Established all opening reserves on cases and advised adjusters of specifics needed. Instituted authority levels. Reported claims to excess carrier.

DIRECTOR OF RISK MANAGEMENT
1998-99
Aspenwood and Co.
Scranton, PA

- Analyzed risk of potential loss to clients' assets and revenues.
- Consulted on property and casualty insurance for clients of various industries.
- Interacted directly with corporate financial and general management officers to establish insurance policies and procedures.

CLAIMS MANAGER
1997-98
Jared Barkly, Inc.
Reading, PA

- Administered Workers' Compensation claims for regional district; processed claims, hired independent adjusters, physicians, and attorney.

EDUCATION
Grove City College, Grove City, PA
Master of Arts in Speech and Business Communications, 1997
Mansfield University, Mansfield, PA
Bachelor of Science in Visual and Verbal Communications, 1995

LICENSE
Licensed Insurance Agent, State of Pennsylvania, #1068

INSURANCE UNDERWRITER (General)

CHRIS SMITH
178 Green Street
Tempe, AZ 85287
(602) 555-5555

EXPERIENCE
SCRIMSHAW INSURANCE CO., Tempe, AZ
Underwriter, Personal Lines Insurance, 1994-present
Underwriting
- Analyzed all personal lines of business to determine acceptability and to control, restrict, or decline, according to company guidelines.
- Supervised all personal lines of business for Arizona and New Mexico.
- Handled computer- and manually-issued policies.
- Resolved client grievances.

Training
- Kept current with changing policies, rates, and procedures, explaining coverage, rules, forms, and decisions to agents, staff, and insured.
- Assisted in training administrative and technical personnel, either directly or by setting up training schedules.

Assistant Supervisor, Manual Rating and Policy Writing, 1990-92
- Delegated responsibilities, set objectives, and monitored work. Evaluated performance. Established supervisory controls.
- Conducted audits.
- Implemented new programs through staff briefing, ongoing training, and updating materials.

Senior Rater, 1990
- Rated and coded all lines of business for personal lines.
- Trained other raters and introduced the merit rating surcharge program for Arizona Automobile (Commonwealth of Arizona).

EDUCATION
- Underwriter Trainee, 1992-93
- Completed program at Jones Underwriting School in Phoenix, Arizona, and trained for 1 year to become an underwriter.
- Ongoing education has included the following classes: Effective Letter Writing, How to Conduct an Interview, Career Workshop, Speed Reading, Xerox Sales Course, Underwriting School (6-week program), Senior Underwriting Seminar, Listening Seminar, Supervisory Seminar.

INTERIOR DESIGNER

Chris Smith
178 Green Street
Murfreesboro, TN 37129
(615) 555-5555

EXPERIENCE

1998-present
MERRIMONT BUSINESS SETTINGS, INC., Jackson, TN
Senior Interior Designer
- With team of 6 designers, produce space plans and interior finishes for corporate offices, schools, libraries, and banks.
- Apply expertise in field measuring, architectural planning, inventory, product specification, finish selection, renderings and presentation boards, and supervising installation.
- Enjoy extensive client contact throughout design process, including problem resolution.
- Plan budgets, make estimates, and negotiate final sales agreement with client.
- Train and supervise junior designers.

1995-98
LAWRENCE LOWFERN ASSOCIATES, Nashville, TN
Junior Interior Designer
- Conducted preliminary inventory work; site measurement; drafting of space plans; 1/4-scale details; elevations; choosing and pasting up finishes on presentation boards; budgets; writing specifications; and follow-up.
- Provided customer relations support.
- Provided administration support.

Summers 1993, 1994
BAKER'S DESIGN, Nashville, TN
Secretary
- Answered phones, filed, and provided customer service.

EDUCATION
MEMPHIS COLLEGE OF ART, Memphis, TN
Bachelor of Fine Arts in Interior Design

JOB PLACEMENT OFFICER

CHRIS SMITH
178 Green Street
Kensington, MN 56343
(313) 555-5555

EXPERIENCE
The Now Division, Kensington, MN
Job Placement Officer   1999-present
Establish and maintain contact with prospective employers, union, public and private agencies, and associations, to develop job opportunities for community residents. Participate in developing vocational training, on-the-job training, and equal-employment opportunities. Participate in staff activities, community meetings, and conferences; prepare in-depth reports on proceedings. Recruit trainees; instruct them in good grooming and proper procedures for applying for a position.

Emmanuel Agency, Minneapolis, MN
Job Placement Officer   1996-99
Counseled underprivileged youths, individually and in groups, to develop positive attitudes and conduct for entering the job market. Studied information on current labor trends and investigated areas of referrals. Maintained liaisons with available placement agencies throughout the city.

Borden's Boy's Club, Minneapolis, MN
Athletic Director   1994-96
Developed and implemented recreational programs for 700-800 boys, ages 7-15. Supervised staff of 10. Maintained all equipment and materials; established excellent relationships with participating children, parents, and other community agencies.

AFFILIATIONS
National Association of Human Resource Administrators
National Association of Job Placement Officers

EDUCATION
Clarke College, Dubuque, IA
Bachelor of Arts in Psychology

CHRIS SMITH

178 Green Street
College Park, MD 20742
(301) 555-5555
csmith@netmail.com

EXPERIENCE

1992-present **FREELANCE JOURNALIST AND PHOTOGRAPHER**

Cover a variety of current events and general-interest topics, including political protests in Washington, DC, and town meetings around Virginia and Maryland. Articles have appeared in the *Washington Post, New York Times, Newsweek,* and *Harper's,* among others.

1999-present **UNIVERSITY OF MARYLAND,** College Park, MD
Lecturer

Teach English Composition and "Ethics and the Media" 18 hours a week to first-, second-, and third-year journalism students.

1997-99 **SMITH COLLEGE,** Northampton, MA
Librarian

Coordinated undergraduate library assistance. Organized fundraising and library activities.

1995-97 **READER'S PARADISE,** Boston, MA
Contributing Editor and Columnist

Wrote articles on international politics and a biweekly column, "Washington Update," tracking legislation proposed in Congress.

1993-95 **PALE MOON PUBLISHING CO.,** Boston, MA
Contributing Editor

Wrote postscripts and flaps for books, corresponded with authors. Researched and co-authored almanac of resumes for publication in trade market.

EDUCATION

Wardell College, Boston, MA
Master of Arts in Journalism

Georgetown University, Washington, DC
Bachelor of Arts in Photography

AWARDS
Springfield Society

Received scholarship for being "most likely to contribute to the field of publishing."

CHRIS SMITH
178 Green Street
Boise, ID 83725
(208) 555-5555

EMPLOYMENT HISTORY
SPUD TRUST, Boise, ID
Junior Accountant 1999-present
- Supervise the accounts payable unit. Prepare monthly journal entries, oversee cash disbursements, expense recording, and petty cash reconciliation. These responsibilities are in addition to the Accounting Technician position.

Accounting Technician 1995-99
- Process accounts payable, agency commissions, and policyholder refunds for five companies. Print vendor, claims, refund, and agency commission checks. Code invoices. Process 1099 forms.
- Perform month-end closing.
- Respond to vendor calls. Handle correspondence in reply to telephone inquiries.
- Prepare travel and entertainment reconciliations for vice president's expenses and reconciliation spreadsheets for company telephone charges.
- Support the secretary for the Vice President of Accounting.

Secretary to Vice President of Finance 1993-95
- Type correspondence and memos. Type, proofread, and distribute financial statements. Handle incoming calls to Accounting and Data Processing department and schedule appointments. Assist in processing policyholder refunds, claims, and agency commission checks. File accounts payable backup.

EDUCATION
The Computer Network, Boise, ID
- Completed word processing certificate program
- Fluent in Spanish

COMPUTER SKILLS
Word, Lotus 1-2-3

LAB TECHNICIAN

CHRIS SMITH
178 Green Street
Hoxie, Kansas 67740
(913) 555-5555

EXPERIENCE
KANSAS GENERAL HOSPITAL, Topeka, KS
1999-present   **Medical Media Technical Coordinator**
- Coordinate, set up, and implement media services for hospital personnel and medical school students and faculty.
- Supervise 3-8 media technicians, complex medical and educational photography, processing, and slide reel setup.
- Direct setup of medical videos and video equipment.
- Set up, operate, and demonstrate medical equipment to medical students.
- Diagnose and resolve problems.
- Conduct hematological and seratological medical testing.

1996-present   **Laboratory Supervisor**
- Coordinated laboratory operations, including media technology, analysis of test results, reporting, and record keeping.
- Resolved departmental problems.

1995-96   **Laboratory Technician**
DAMON CORPORATION, Shawnee Mission, KS
- Conducted hematology and serology testing, as well as test-sample photography.
- Recorded, analyzed, and communicated results to physicians, patients, and their families.

1990-93   **Media Research Technician**
MAYFARB INSTITUTE, Wichita, KS
- Produced synchronized audio and slide programs on medical and medical educational topics.
- Conducted cancer research.
- Served as a reference and research guide for institute staff and Harvard Medical School affiliates.

EDUCATION
University of Kansas, Lawrence, KS
B.A., Media and Communications

LABOR RELATIONS SPECIALIST

CHRIS SMITH
178 Green Street
New York, NY 10027
(212) 555-5555

PROFESSIONAL EXPERIENCE

THE CITY OF NEW YORK DEPARTMENT OF HEALTH   1997-present
Labor/Management Relations Analyst
- Represent over 4,000 employees. Investigate and mediate disciplinary actions taken by supervisors against employees; conduct grievance hearings. Collect, compile, and evaluate labor and economic data; write reports; present findings at City Hall hearings.
- Provide assistance in planning, implementing, and disseminating policy. Aid and advise management staff with interpreting and applying collective bargaining agreements, supplemental agreements, personnel policies and practices, and grievance policy.
- Act as liaison with union representatives. Research and determine appropriate adherence to labor contract terms. Prepare documentation for evidence; mediate in hearings.
- Interact with staff members, union representatives, and management; develop recommendations; design agreements.

NEW YORK COMMISSION AGAINST DISCRIMINATION   1996-97
Field Representative
- Investigated alleged discrimination practices. Used paralegal training and analytical writing skills. Wrote recommendations and case dispositions.

NEW YORK HISPANIC LEGISLATIVE CAUCUS   1994-96
Legislative Assistant
- Served as liaison between Hispanic community, state legislators, and business interests. Liaison responsibilities extended statewide to over 200 agencies.
- Organized and conducted legislative research. Interacted with senior staff researchers.
- Cooperated with Caucus in implementing community outreach goals and general counseling needs.

LANGUAGE
Fluent in spoken and written Spanish

EDUCATION
FORDHAM UNIVERSITY, Bronx, NY
B.A. in Government

LABORATORY ASSISTANT

CHRIS SMITH
178 Green Street
Manchester, NH 03102
(603) 555-5555

EDUCATION

NOTRE DAME COLLEGE, Manchester, New Hampshire
Master of Science in Microbiology, 1999

ST. ANSELM COLLEGE, Manchester, New Hampshire
Bachelor of Science in Biology, 1997
- Dean's List
- Natural Sciences Department Award
- Senior Class President
- Named to *Who's Who in American Colleges and Universities*

EXPERIENCE

1999-present
ST. ANSELM COLLEGE, Manchester, New Hampshire
Laboratory Assistant to Microbiology Department Head
- Prepare media and cultures for microbiology classes.
- Order supplies for department; monitor inventory.
- Act as informal tutor.
- Clean glassware.
- Make sure equipment is in good working order.
- Assist with experiments to be included in research paper for leading biological journal.

1997-99
DURHAM MEDICAL ASSOCIATES, Durham, NH
Laboratory Technician for four physicians
- Initiated running of laboratory; organized equipment and materials.
- Ran tests for patients, reported on same-day basis.
- Ordered supplies; maintained inventory.

LABORATORY TECHNICIAN

CHRIS SMITH
178 Green Street
Dayton, Ohio 45469
(513) 555-5555

SUMMARY OF QUALIFICATIONS
Laboratory Expertise
- Proven ability in analysis, scientific theories, and procedures.
- Experience collecting and studying data from various biological sources.
- Proficient at producing and processing blood components.
- Skilled at performing tissue experiments using electron microscopy.
- Quickly and accurately learn and perform complicated tasks.
- Member, American Association of Clinical Pathologists.

Technical Writing
- Experience organizing, writing, and editing detailed reports and research papers.

Training
- Trainer for biochemists in routine blood-banking procedures.

EMPLOYMENT
1994-present   American Red Cross, Cleveland, OH
Laboratory Technician
Produce and process blood components. Label and release for transfusion and manufacture.
Perform viral immunology testing and irradiation of blood products.

1999-present (part-time)   College of Wooster, Wooster, OH
Clinical Research Technician
Perform hormonal assays using RIA, ELISA, and nucleic acid hybridization in clinical
research of fertility patients.

1991-93
Research Assistant   Roma Color, Cincinnati, OH
Conducted research and development in organic pigments.

LANGUAGES
Fluent spoken and written French, Spanish, and Italian

EDUCATION
Nebraska Wesleyan University, Lincoln, NE
Bachelor of Science, Biology/Chemistry

CHRIS SMITH
178 Green Street
Albuquerque, NM 87104
(505) 555-5555
csmith@netmail.com

EXPERIENCE

JEFFERSON MANUFACTURING CORP., Albuquerque, NM   1998-present

Documentation Development Coordinator

Analyze application software requirements for engineering LAN; develop and maintain software. Provide training and user support for all applications to LAN users. Maintain departmental PC workstations, including software installation and upgrades.

Achievements
- Reduced data entry errors and process time by developing an online program that allowed program managers to submit model number information.
- Replaced time-consuming daily review-board meetings by developing a program that allowed engineers to review and approve model and component changes on-line.
- Developed an on-line program that reduced process time, standardized part usage, and allowed engineers to build parts lists for new products and components.

Computer Systems Analyst   1994-98

Analyzed and designed database management systems; maintained and repaired workstations, and managed the company LAN.

Achievements
- Reduced process time and purchasing errors by developing an on-line program that allowed the purchasing department to track the status of all purchasing invoices.
- Developed a purchase-order entry program for the purchasing department that improved data entry speed and reduced the number of data entry errors.

EDUCATION

University of Notre Dame
Associate in Electronics Engineering Technology

COMPUTER SKILLS

Operating systems: DOS, Windows, Macintosh, UNIX
Programming: C++, Java, Visual Basic
Writing/publishing: Word
Financial: Excel, Lotus 1-2-3
Online help: RoboHELP

LAW CLERK (Corporate and Contract Law)

CHRIS SMITH
178 Green Street
Romeoville, IL 60441
(312) 555-5555 (work)
(312) 444-4444 (home)

EDUCATION
DEPAUL UNIVERSITY SCHOOL OF LAW, Chicago, IL
J.D., May 1999
Specialized coursework: Environmental Law

ILLINOIS WESLEYAN UNIVERSITY, Bloomington, IL
B.A. in Political Science, May 1996
GPA: 3.2/4.0

EXPERIENCE
1999-present
Law Clerk, Hall & Gotes, Chicago, IL
Research and write appellate briefs; draft motions, complaints, and answers.
Research and prepare memoranda on corporate and contract law. Assist in
attorney-client conferences by describing the law as it pertains to the client's
suit.

1996-99
Research Assistant, Attorney Barbara Cady, Elgin, IL
Researched and investigated important new issues in environmental law.

Summer 1995
Law Clerk, Justice Lori O'Connor
Supreme Court of Illinois, Chicago, IL
Researched and drafted decisions on motions; prepared and wrote memo-
randa on various issues. Participated in pretrial conferences.

Summer 1994
Congressional Intern, Rep. Wendy Millbauer (D-OH), Washington, DC
Conducted research for legislative bills, reviewed and reported on committee
hearings, corresponded with constituents.

LEGAL ASSISTANT

CHRIS SMITH
178 Green Street
Chicago, IL 60605
(312) 555-5555

EDUCATION
ROOSEVELT UNIVERSITY, Chicago, IL
Bachelor of Arts, *cum laude,* 1998
Major: Political Science; Minor: Economics

EXPERIENCE
MUNICIPAL ASSOCIATION, Chicago, IL
Legal Assistant   1999-present
Research impact of reduced state revenue sharing on municipal public safety staffing. Assist in needs assessment, strategy planning, community outreach, interviewing, data collection, analysis, and reporting.

CHICAGO DISTRICT ATTORNEY'S OFFICE, Domestic Violence Unit, Chicago, IL
Victim Witness Advocate   1998-99
Interviewed victims and witnesses, prepared documents and organized information for court appearances. Assisted attorneys during trials.

ILLINOIS PUBLIC DEFENDERS, Chicago, IL
Legal Intern   1996-98
Researched and drafted motions on criminal law and procedural issues. Interviewed clients at Illinois correctional institutions. Argued bail motions in several state district courts. Negotiated plea and bail agreements for defendants accused of misdemeanors. Attended criminal trials and depositions.

PRO BONO LEGAL ADVISORS COMMITTEE, Chicago, IL
Legal Intern   Summer 1996
Advised mentally handicapped clients on aspects of mental health law, including guardianship, commitment, discharge, and civil rights. Drafted motions, complaints, and discharge petitions for clients. Devoted part of time to advising clients at the Central Square Homeless Shelter.

ATTORNEY DANIEL BANNEN, Oak Park, IL
Legal Secretary   Summer 1995
Greeted clients. Prepared documents for legal proceedings involving real estate transactions. Entered client information into computer system.

COMPUTER SKILLS
WordPerfect, Word, FileMaker Pro

LEGAL SECRETARY (Civil Law)

CHRIS SMITH
178 Green Street
Danville, KY 40422
(606) 555-5555

SUMMARY OF QUALIFICATIONS
- 15 years' experience as a legal assistant/secretary in civil litigation.
- 10 years' part-time experience in general practice.
- Supervisory skills, delegating and distributing workload evenly among secretarial staff.
- Notary public.

EXPERIENCE
1999-present   LAW OFFICES OF LANGSTON & GREY, Lexington, KY
Legal Secretary
Organize pre-deposition conferences with doctors, attorneys, and involved parties. Schedule court hearings; prepare motions and trial papers. Research files for necessary documentation. Proofread and notarize legal documents.

1989-97   THEODORE F. LOGAN, Danville, KY
Legal Secretary
Part-time duties in general-practice law office involved scheduling clients and court appearances; typing legal documents; and drafting wills, letters, and complaints.

1985-88   CUMBERLAND INSURANCE, Lexington, KY
Secretary
Performed general secretarial tasks: typing correspondence and reports, filing, answering phone.

COMPUTER SKILLS
Word, Excel, FileMaker Pro

EDUCATION
CENTRE COLLEGE, Danville, KY Paralegal Studies, 1998-99
Also participated in Communications Skills Workshop for Paralegals.

DANVILLE COMMUNITY COLLEGE, Danville, KY
Relevant training and coursework in legal issues and computers.

CHRIS SMITH
178 Green Street
Burlington, VT 05401
(802) 555-5555

EXPERIENCE

KATHRYN F. BELL LIBRARY   Burlington, VT
Librarian, 1986-present
Reference
Answer reference questions and maintain a reference search file. Assist patrons in use of the computerized catalog, computers and Internet access, and audiovisual equipment. Obtain and send books through the interlibrary loan system. Select and order new books and other library materials. Catalog incoming materials.

Circulation
Check out materials at the circulation desk. Shelve incoming library materials. Compile statistics on door count, photocopies, and reference questions.

Managerial
Develop and manage a $90,000 budget; hire, train, and supervise staff and volunteers. Write grant proposals for state funds, resulting in $8,000 in grants for books on health, computers, and business reference. Contact corporate computer donors, who provided 4 new PCs and software for a study room. Contract for painting and recarpeting the library.

Community
Coordinate and publicize library reading and film series, which draw an average of 12 and 35 people, respectively, per evening. Circulation of library materials has increased 16% since these programs began.

EAST CATHOLIC HIGH SCHOOL   Rutland, VT
Librarian/Audiovisual Coordinator, 1980-86
Supervised library and aided staff. Maintained audiovisual equipment; instructed teachers on equipment use; scheduled equipment use.

EDUCATION

SIMMONS COLLEGE, Boston, MA
Master of Library Science

BURLINGTON COMMUNITY COLLEGE, Burlington, VT
Bachelor of Arts in English

LOAN ADMINISTRATOR

CHRIS SMITH
178 Green Street
Collister, ID 83706
(208) 555-5555

EXPERIENCE

1998-present   Bank of Boise, Collister, ID
Loan Administrator, Commercial Real Estate Division.
- Disburse, track, and service loans.
- Administer accounts.
- Maintain close contacts with customers, legal firms, and contacts within bank and in the Pocatello office.

1995-97   Garden City National Bank, Garden City, ID
Bank Reconciliation Clerk
- Edited journal entries prior to posting.
- Processed invoices for payment.
- Determined proper budget account for coding of receipts.
- Reconciled bank accounts in U.S. currencies.
- Communicated with banks to clarify and resolve outstanding items.

1992-94   The Tyler Corporation, Narupa, ID
Accounting Assistant, Finance Department
- Verified accuracy and proper authorization of bills prior to payment.
- Processed bills.
- Reconciled accounts and wrote journal vouchers.

EDUCATION
College of Idaho, Caldwell, ID
Associate in Accounting

COMPUTER SKILLS
Word, WordPerfect, Lotus 1-2-3

MANAGEMENT ACCOUNTANT (Restaurant)

CHRIS SMITH
178 Green Street
Killington, VT 05751
(601) 555-5555

EXPERIENCE

1998-present   **THE SIZZLER STEAK HOUSE**, Killington, VT
Management Accountant
Managed accounting operations and accounts payable department. Ensured use of correct accounts payable control factors. Reconciled bank and credit card accounts. Reviewed the general ledger and made adjustments for inter-company transactions. Prepared road tax documents for trucks throughout New England states. Monitored inventory transfers among branch locations.

1995-97   **DIAL TONES**, Burlington, CT
Manager
Performed business and technical activities. Provided supervision, performance evaluation, and training for technical staff of 7, delegating authority to collect revenues while maintaining equipment. Reconciled bank accounts and handled administrative record keeping.

1992-95   **MAPLE TREE ARENA**, Burlington, VT
Manager
Directed concession activities for consecutive seasons, including financial record keeping, bank account reconciliation, and food preparation. Directly supervised staff of 20 employees.

VOLUNTEER
The Burlington Soup Kitchen, Burlington, Vermont
Vermont Volunteer Income Tax Assistance, Burlington, VT

EDUCATION
University of Vermont, Burlington, VT
Bachelor of Science in Accounting

COMPUTER SKILLS
WordPerfect, Lotus 1-2-3

CHRIS SMITH
178 Green Street
Westhampton, MA 01027
(413) 555-5555
csmith@netmail.com

EXPERIENCE
1999-present
Management Consultant, Kimberly Neumann, Inc., Westhampton, MA
Provide assessment and consult in the areas of human resources, health care, administration, and economic development, with emphasis on full use of staffing, capital equipment, and all other resources. Served as Chief Project Officer for firm with emphasis on marketing, coastal zone planning, and intergovernmental relations services.

1996-99
Staff Consultant/Political Scientist, National Commission for the Protection of Animals in Scientific Experiments, Hadley, MA
Developed and implemented general surveys regarding animal experimentation in social and behavioral sciences. Managed agenda for National Animal Experimentation Conference, securing over 25 scholarly research papers.

1989-96
Executive Director, Northampton Health Clinic, Northampton, MA
Directed operations of a federally funded ambulatory care center offering medical, dental, and mental health services. Reduced agency debt by more than $250,000 by reorganizing billing system.

1987-89
Executive Director, William Stoughton Children's Center, Springfield, MA
Established collaborative in mental health services with an area program, using funding from national and local nonprofit organizations.

EDUCATION
VANDERBILT UNIVERSITY, Nashville, TN
Master of Arts in Political Science

UNIVERSITY OF THE SOUTH, Sewanee, TN
Bachelor of Arts in Political Science

AFFILIATION
National Management Organization (NMO)

MANAGER (Computers)

CHRIS GREEN
178 Green Street
Berkeley, CA 94720
(415) 555-5555
csmith@netmail.com

SKILLS PROFILE
- Over 10 years' management experience, encompassing personnel functions, client relations, and facilities management.
- Demonstrated planning and leadership skills.
- Human resource skills include determining staffing needs, selecting, hiring, assigning, and supervising.
- Articulate and expressive speaker. Presenter of numerous well-received client seminars on product features.

EXPERIENCE
TOUCHSTONE SYSTEMS, INC., Berkeley, CA
Manager   1998-present
- Direct all aspects of customer service operations for the Norwalk branch office.
- Determine office staffing needs, write and place employment ads, interview and select qualified personnel. Provide orientation and training in company policy and practices and customer service techniques. Conducted intensive onsite training sessions for clients and installation staff.
- Administer property management budget with sensitivity to cost control.

QUARTERMAIN CONTRIBUTORS, INC., San Diego, CA
Branch Manager   1996-99
- Provided leadership and direction for TS systems installers and trainers outside the San Diego metropolitan area. Selected, trained, directed, and evaluated the performance of technical support staff, ensuring compliance with highest-quality standards.

PERCELL ASSOCIATES, Los Angeles, CA
Manager   1994-96
- Managed and oversaw office functions encompassing the control of annual operating budgets. Sourced and negotiated purchasing of cost-effective, quality equipment and supplies.

EDUCATION
Pepperdine University, Malibu, CA
Bachelor of Science in Management

COMPUTER SKILLS
Word, Lotus 1-2-3

MANAGER OF NETWORK ADMINISTRATION

CHRIS SMITH
178 Green Street
Cranston, RI 02920
(401) 555-5555
csmith@netmail.com

EXPERIENCE
Travis Computer, Inc.   Cranston, RI
Manager of Network Administration 1999-present
- Manage staff of three network administrators and network of 100+ UNIX machines and 250+ users. Network consists of 10 servers, 30+ UNIX workstations, dialin and dialout lines, uucp, T1 connection to a West Coast company, many X terminals, and exabyte backup.
- Serve on team to transition Travis into several spin-off companies. Entails network design, execution, and subsequent move to new locations.

Network Administrator 1998-99
- Administered UNIX network, including enhancing and modifying tools, solving problems, performing maintenance. Created accounts, facilitated mail and news traffic, and installed and upgraded systems.
- Wrote proposal for security and a general plan to carry the network into the future.

Lafayette Donlin Laboratory   Easton, PA
Member Assistant Staff 1995-98
- Software engineer for real-time integrated airborne radar system.
- Wrote code that operated hardware over a DVL bus.

Pollack and O'Keefe   Bethlehem, PA
Computer Systems Coordinator 1993-95
Administered systems used by CAD, Accounting, Word Processing, and Engineering departments.

COMPUTER SKILLS
Hardware
Travis, IBM, Cayman Router, Macintosh
Software
Operating systems: DOS, Windows, Macintosh, UNIX
Programming: C++, Java
Other: Word, Lotus 1-2-3

EDUCATION
Pennsylvania State University   University Park, PA
B.S. in Applied Mathematics

MANUFACTURER'S REPRESENTATIVE

Chris Smith
178 Green Street
Douglasville, GA 30134
(404) 555-5555

KEY QUALIFICATIONS
- More than 10 years of successful experience in professional sales and marketing to manufacturers throughout New England. Experience includes prospecting, telemarketing, key account sales, customer follow-up and relations, product management and sales, as well as related aspects of sales administration and contract negotiation.
- High aptitude for acquiring new product sales and marketing technologies.
- Experience includes production and operational areas of management, such as scheduling, distribution, purchasing, inventory management, personnel supervision and relations, labor management relations and negotiations, and related aspects of business operations.

EXPERIENCE
1999-present   Blackwell Manufacturing Corp.
AREA MANUFACTURING REPRESENTATIVE
Atlanta, GA
- Hired to explore and develop unmarketed territory for expanding clothing manufacturer.
- Developed territory in declining market area from $0 to annual volume of over $500,000.
- Handled all aspects of professional sales, from cold calling, market research, and follow-up on referrals and customer inquiries to networking customer base and assisting with styling and complete design of product to customer specifications.

1994-99   Birmingham Corp.
AREA MANUFACTURING REPRESENTATIVE
Decatur, GA
- Opened and developed Southeastern territory from $0 to annual sales of $600,000.
- Sold belts and children's clothing to accounts throughout the Southeast.
- Established and maintained good working relationships with all major manufacturers in the Southeast.

EDUCATION
Oglethorpe University, Atlanta, GA
Bachelor of Science, Business Administration
Minor: Economics

MANUFACTURING ENGINEER

CHRIS SMITH
178 Green Street
Seattle, WA 98103
(206) 555-5555

TECHNOLOGY
- Type 1 (SMT both sides), type II (SMT both sides and PTH), and type III (SMT single side and PTH) PWB assemblies.
- High-density, large (22" x 11"), 6-mil lines and spaces, micro via, high-aspect ratio, fine-pitch, 0.093" thick, dry-film solder mask, impedance-controlled PWBs.
- Range of SMT components includes PQFPs (fine-pitch technology), PLCCs, SOPs, and discrete chips.
- Futurebus+/Metral and HD+/Litton interconnection technologies.

EXPERIENCE

1999-present   Kai Pacific Computer Inc., Seattle, WA
Manufacturing Engineer
Design
Review and modify design of assemblies for manufacturability. Specify the fabrication and assembly process and create assembly instructions for PWBs. Improved PWB design and manufacturability by creating design guidelines.

Manufacturing
Manage PWB fabrication and assembly vendors. Evaluated and prepared Kai Computer's vendors in Japan for volume manufacture of new products, which entailed travel to Japan. Improved PWB assembly quality and turnaround time by influencing the vendor to add new equipment. Managed and coordinated prototype PWB fabrication and assembly vendors to bring in eight different surface-mount PWB assemblies built to an aggressive schedule.

Testing
Design tooling and fixturing required for assembly and repair of new products. Improved in-circuit/ATE testability of PWBs by reducing tooling-hole tolerance and increasing test-pad diameter. Wrote the specification for and managed the design and build of a test station for boundary scan and functional testing and debug of PWB assemblies.

1995-99   Saturn Computer Inc., Auburn, WA
Manufacturing Engineer
Purchased tooling and fixturing required for production and repair of existing products. Solved design, production, and material availability problems of existing products through initiating engineering change orders (ECOs) and temporary variance authorizations (TVAs).

EDUCATION
University of Iowa, Iowa City, Iowa
Bachelor of Science in Mechanical Engineering (BSME)

MARKETING ASSISTANT

Chris Smith

178 Green Street
Terre Haute, IN 47804
(812) 555-5555

EXPERIENCE

Marketing Assistant, The Art Lover's Institute
Indianapolis, IN   1999-present
- Temporary position assisting the manager of public information.
- Distributed exhibit posters and organized development of merchandising displays to promote the exhibit at local retailers.
- Coordinated press clippings and releases about the exhibit.

Assistant Box Office Manager, Terre Haute Performing Arts Center
Terre Haute, IN   1998-99
- Managed daily operations for a staff of 20 operators responsible for customer service and the sale of all tickets in a theater seating 5,000.
- Compiled all financial statements on a daily and monthly basis for each performance in the theater, averaging 10 performances per month, including daily deposits and revenue from outlet sales on secondary ticketing systems.

Gallery Assistant/Window Exhibit Coordinator, Jim Cannon's Art Implosion
Bourbon, IN   1997-98
- Developed marketing plan for fine-art prints and coordinating notecards.
- Developed client base and serviced accounts.
- Coordinated special events relating to current exhibits, opening receptions, and artist signings. Handled press releases.

EDUCATION

Valparaiso University, Valparaiso, IN
B.A, Arts Administration, 1999 Concentration in Marketing/Communications

COMPUTER SKILLS

Word, WordPerfect, Excel, dBASE, PageMaker

CHRIS SMITH
178 Green Street
Hawthorne, FL 32640
(904) 555-5555

EXPERIENCE

1999   Hawthorne Management, Hawthorne, FL
Consultant—Market and Strategic Management Research
Conducted large-scale quantitative research projects based in customer satisfaction measurement and total quality implementation, including design, coordination, statistical analysis, and report generation. Specialized in business-to-business services and health care.

1997-98   Scott, Wilder, Johanson and Rolfe, Archer, FL
Research Associate—Public Relations and Market Research
Managed behaviorally-based research projects, including proposal writing; methodology, instrument and sample development; field coordination; data coding, analysis and interpretation; report writing. Projects included customer and employee studies, communication audits, market analysis, name and logo testing, constituency relations research, positioning, and purchaser/user studies.

1996   International Research Group, Gainesville, FL
Management Consultant—Public Relations
Provided counsel in areas of marketing, behavior, and research. Participated in internal and external strategic planning for Fortune 500 companies, government agencies, nonprofit organizations, and health-care providers.

1995   Webber and Sons, Inc., Ocala, FL
Research Assistant—Market Research
Conducted onsite survey groups, interviews, intercepts, and telephone interviews. Recruited focus groups and pre-screened samples. Participated in project execution, coding, and analysis.

EDUCATION

Stetson University, De Land, FL, 1995
Advanced Graduate Certificate Marketing Management. GPA 3.8

Georgetown University, Washington, DC, 1993
M.A. Applied Psychology Concentration in Health Care research. *GPA 3.6*

Central Connecticut State University, New Britain, CT, 1990
B.A. Psychology, minor *Business Administration.* Field work in Puerto Rico.

MARKETING MANAGER

CHRIS SMITH
178 Green Street
El Paso, TX 79925
(915) 555-5555

EXPERIENCE
DENNISON PRESS, El Paso, TX
Trade Division
Marketing Coordinator   1999-present
Develop and supervise implementation of Dennison marketing plans with the sales and marketing departments.
- Prepare and manage the annual marketing budget of $2 million.
- Manage scheduling and production of sales and marketing materials.
- Supervise marketing assistant.
- Provide marketing information at biennial sales conferences.

Professional Division
Children's Books Department
Editorial Administrator   1997-99
- Managed revisions from manuscript preparation to bound book. Resolved author questions and problems. Ensured manuscript conformity to budgetary and scheduling constraints.
- Directed supplement program of over 70 books from budget management to project completion, with emphasis on electronic manuscript preparation.
- Provided information to marketing department for direct-mail promotions; reviewed copy for accuracy.

Children's Books Department
Editorial Coordinator   1994-97
- Supervised the supplement program.
- Conducted editorial market research and assessed results with senior editors.

Children's Books Department
Editorial Assistant   1993-94
- Provided general support for senior editors.
- Fulfilled various author requests.

EDUCATION
Baylor College, Waco, TX
B.A., English; Economics minor

SKILLS
Computer: Word, WordPerfect, Lotus 1-2-3, QuarkXPress
Languages: French

MEDICAL TECHNOLOGIST

CHRIS SMITH
178 Green Street
Milwaukee, WI 53201
(414) 555-5555

SUMMARY
A Certified Medical Technologist seeking a challenging position in a private laboratory setting.

PROFESSIONAL BACKGROUND
1996 to present   MILWAUKEE HOSPITAL, Milwaukee, Wisconsin
Senior Medical Technologist
- Conduct laboratory tests and operate equipment at night for all departments in hospital, especially Chemistry and Hematology departments.
- Perform data entry via CRT to obtain test results.

1994-96   BIOCARE, Ashland, WI
Medical Technologist
- Conducted laboratory tests at Children's Hospital in Ladysmith, WI.
- Operated Nova for electrolytes, Coulters, and Fibrometer.

1991-94   KIPLING HOSPITAL, Ripon, WI
Medical Technologist
- Conducted testing for several departments and operated Astra, Coagamate, and ELT.

1988-90   DIALTEK, De Pere, WI
Medical Technologist
- Operated Coulters and utilized computer information in Hematology Department.
- Fielded calls for entire department.

1986-88   AL KARTOUM M.D., La Crosse, WI
Private Hematologist Intern
- Operated hematology laboratory using haemacount machine, leitz photometer, and EKG Machine.

EDUCATION
UNIVERSITY OF WISCONSIN AT MADISON, Madison, WI
A.S. in Medical Technology

PROFESSIONAL LICENSES
H.E.W. Certified Medical Technologist #3259050
Certified Laboratory Assistant #BID01359

MIS MANAGER

CHRIS SMITH
178 Green Street
Cambridge, MA 02139
(617) 555-5555
csmith@netmail.com

TECHNICAL SUMMARY

Hardware Platforms:	PCs, workstations, mainframes, servers
Operating Systems:	DOS, Windows, UNIX
Networks:	TCP/IP
Approaches:	OODB, client-server, remote data access, RDB, CAD/CAM

EXPERIENCE
NILES CORPORATION

Ultrix Systems and Software, MIS Manager 1999-present
Developed and implemented an overall information architecture for the manufacturing and engineering operational units of the low-end business. Managed 24 professionals and an annual budget of $2.7 million, as well as a computer resource group that serviced 1,200 customers.

Consultant and Information Systems Marketing 1996-99
Served as MIS expert in development of courses to educate senior sales and software service staff in MIS functions and problems and Niles's solutions. Designed and implemented seminars and symposiums to educate customers. All these activities resulted in increased sales and new service accounts.

Field Service Logistics (FLS) IS Manager 1994-96
Directed the design, development, and implementation of the New Business Process. Directed and managed a staff of senior MIS professionals implementing the MRPII application in multiple locations. The result was an inventory savings of 25% and expense reductions of $10 million.

MIS Manager, Low-End Business Center 1993-94
Directed MIS activities in support of high-volume order-processing unit. Analyzed the operation, hired staff, proposed investments, and drove solutions. The result was smoother operations and reduced indirect labor costs.

EDUCATION
Massachusetts Institute of Technology
M.S. in Computer Science

Boston University
Bachelor of Business Administration in Accounting
Currently enrolled in the Certified Financial Planning program

MODEL

CHRIS SMITH
178 Green Street
Acworth, GA 31707
(912) 555-5555

Height: 5'9"	Age Range: 18-30	Bust: 36"
Weight: 120 lbs	Dress Size: 5	Waist: 28"
Hair Color: Auburn	Shoe Size: 7	Hips: 35"
Eye Color: Green		

TRAINING
Rick Bass Casting, Modeling and Acting
Joy DeVivre, Modeling and Acting

EXPERIENCE
Fashion Shows
BRYDIE'S BRIDAL SHOP, Atlanta, GA   Fashion Show, May 2000

RAYANNE'S FASHIONS, Albany, GA   Runway Show, July 1999

Film
EBONY'S FINE ARTS SCHOOL, Alphoretta, GA   Summer 1998
Modeled for photography class

GOLD MORNING PRODUCTIONS
Extra for three scenes in *Morning Serenade*, Boston, MA   October 1998

Competition
EVAN HAWKE MODELING CONTEST, Atlanta, GA   December 1999
First place

SPECIAL SKILLS
Sports: swimming, ice skating, snow and water skiing, bicycling, baseball, basketball, tennis, jogging, aerobics
Dancing: jazz, tap, ballet
Play classical piano
Comfortable working with animals, including large and exotic species

EDUCATION
Georgia County Community College, Atlanta, GA
Chemical Engineering studies

NANNY

Chris Smith
178 Green Street
Livermore, CO 80536
(303) 555-5555

EXPERIENCE

1999-present   Private residence, Livermore, CO
NANNY
Care for twin boys from the age of two months through two years. Assist in selecting toys and equipment, provide environmental stimulation, personal care, and play.

1997-99   Baby Bear Preschool, Keystone, CO
TEACHER
Taught infant, preschool, and after-school programs. Planned curriculum, organized activities, communicated with parents and staff regarding children's growth and development. Suggested equipment to enrich children's experiences and helped create a stimulating environment.

1995-97   This Little Piggy Daycare Center, Dove Creek, CO
TEACHER
Planned and implemented curriculum for infants. Communicated with parents and other staff regarding daily progress of children.

1993-95   The Kid Corral, Wild Horse, CO
TEACHER
Planned and implemented curriculum for toddler program. Enriched children's experiences through play, music, and art.

1991-93   Ivywild Coalition for Retarded Citizens, Ivywild, CO
CAREGIVER
Provided care in clients' homes, administering physical therapy when necessary. Planned activities to stimulate and improve children's skills and environment.

EDUCATION
Metropolitan State College, Denver, CO
Completed 30 credits in Education, with an emphasis on the daycare setting.
Minor: English.

SKILLS
Valid driver's license; perfect driving record
CPR/first aid certified
Skiing, reading, music, arts and crafts

NURSE (Home Health Care)

Chris Smith
178 Green Street
Yukon, MO 65589
(314) 555-5555

EXPERIENCE

1999-present **AIDS Clinical Coordinator/Home Infusion Nurse**
THE LAMONT CENTER Yukon, MO
- Provide case management, teaching, and follow-up for AIDS patients receiving home infusion therapies.
- Identify appropriate candidates for high-tech home infusion therapies.
- Train patients and families to safely conduct these complex therapies at home.
- Therapies include total parenteral and enteral nutrition, IV antibiotic therapy, infusion chemotherapy, parenteral pain management, and IV hydration.

Achievements
- Identified need for study on the infection rate of venous access devices in AIDS patients; currently collecting pertinent data.
- Appointed to the Lamont Center Home Care Committee.

1993-99 **Senior Staff Nurse (Level II)**
Oncology Division
- Functioned as primary nurse coordinating care for acute and chronic patients.
- Provided nursing care for chemotherapy and pain-management patients.
- Facilitated discharge planning with home-care agencies.
- Acted as coordinator for autologous bone-marrow transplant program.
- Conducted inservices for staff on procedural updates and progress of program.
- Served as hospital oncology resource for care of central venous catheters.

Achievements
- Developed orientation program for new staff members.
- Served as chair of the Family Education Committee.

LICENSE
Registered Nurse, State of Missouri #794791

EDUCATION
Building Professional Skills to Work with Intravenous Drug Users
AIDS Program for Clinical Nurses

RENDALL HOSPITAL SCHOOL OF NURSING, Saint Louis, MO
Diploma: Registered Nurse

NUTRITIONIST

Chris Smith
178 Green Street
Winchester, MA 08190
(617) 555-5555

EXPERIENCE

Laboure College   Winchester, MA
Lecturer   1999-present
- Instruct future dieticians and dietetic technicians in the science of foods and nutrition.
- Lecture on the role of dietetics in public and home health agencies, daycare centers, health and recreation clubs, and government-funded food programs for the poor, elderly, malnourished, disabled, pregnant and nursing women, and children.
- Train dietetic technicians to perform nutritional screenings and assessments, cholesterol reduction, and portion control.

O'Donnell Medical Center   Winchester, MA
Nutritionist   1986-present
- Train, supervise, and coordinate all menus for patients for cardiac, renal, diabetic, weight reduction and gain, and postsurgical patients; plan menu selections.
- Analyze patient dietary needs; ensure menu adheres to dietary needs.
- Consult with facility cook concerning food preparation; assist in budgeting and purchasing foods.

Massachusetts General Hospital   Jamaica Plain, MA
Dietary Technician Supervisor   1980-86
- Supervised and coordinated activities for food-service employees. Trained new hires and diet aides in distribution of patient trays.
- Assisted in planning patients' menus.
- Took daily inventory of food. Monitored refrigerator and dishwasher temperatures.

LICENSE

American Dietetic Association (ADA)
Registered Dietician

EDUCATION

Boston University, Boston, MA
B.S., Public Health, *cum laude*

Laboure College, Dorchester, MA
Certificate in Food Service Supervision

OCCUPATIONAL THERAPIST

CHRIS SMITH
178 Green Street
Topeka, KS 66621
(913) 555-5555

EXPERIENCE

1998-present
DIXON REHABILITATION CENTER   Hillsboro, KS
- Independently assessed clients with stroke and head trauma, ages 10-60.
- Initiated treatment and implemented therapy, using standard disability interventions and physical management techniques.
- Monitored, identified, and resolved client behavioral problems.
- Performed notation, billing, and statistical recording. Assisted in training an O.T. aide.
- Participated in rehab and clinical rounds and family conferences.
- Facilitated community field trips. Co-led a shopping and community reentry group.

1996-98
WILD THORN CHILDREN'S CENTER   Sterling, KS
- Led dyadic groups for E.D. preadolescents with diagnoses of conduct, personality, and affective disorders.
- Structured developmental group with parallel/project format using cooking, games, leather, and woodworking.
- Observed, monitored, and reported individual/group interaction.
- Drafted weekly progress notes.

1993-96
CURTIS SCHOOL FOR THE BLIND   Wichita, KS
- Evaluated, planned, and established treatment for clients with congenital disabilities and MR, Rubella, CP, Lebers, and FTT diagnoses.
- Used neurodevelopmental, biomechanical, SI, and developmental methods.
- Coordinated program aids to implement treatment and wrote quarterly progress notes.

EDUCATION
NEW YORK UNIVERSITY, College of Allied Health   New York, NY
Master of Science in Occupational Therapy, 3.8 GPA

PROFESSIONAL AFFILIATIONS
Member, American Occupational Therapy Association
Member, Kansas Association for Occupational Therapists

OFFICE MANAGER (General)

CHRIS SMITH
178 Green Street
Wayne, NE 68787
(402) 555-5555
csmith@netmail.com

EXPERIENCE

1999-present   EMERSON ASSOCIATES, Wayne, NE
Office Manager
Arrange logistics for office expansion and relocation. Establish office procedures and systems. Actuate/implement filing system, client billing system, and bookkeeping. Order supplies; maintain inventory. Handle word processing and receptionist responsibilities.

1990-99   RUNNING FAWN HOUSING COMMISSION, Primrose, NE
Administrative Assistant
Functioned as principal support staff person to Executive Director, providing comprehensive administrative and clerical support services. Organized/managed work schedule. Coordinated communications flow with commissioners, staff, Mayor's Office, public and private officials, and general public. Prepared Director's scheduled events; organized/presented information in a useful format. Administered work-flow.

1985-90   COMMISSION ON JEWISH AFFAIRS, Table Rock, NE
Administrative Assistant
Typed, recorded minutes at commission meetings, handled incoming calls, assisted general public, and maintained office supplies. Coordinated information release to press, legislators, and interested individuals.

1982-1985   PAUA SHELL HOSPITAL, Broken Bow, NE
Personnel Assistant
Provided administrative support to Personnel Recruiter and Personnel Representative. Screened applicants; checked references; scheduled interviews. Prepared candidates for typing tests. Answered incoming calls. Typed all office materials and correspondence.

SKILLS
Computer: Word, Excel
Language: Fluent in Spanish

EDUCATION
Broken Bow High School, Broken Bow, NE
Diploma

OPERATIONS MANAGER (Distributor)

CHRIS SMITH
178 Green Street
Upper Arlington, OH 43221
(614) 555-5555

EXPERIENCE

ORMON EQUIPMENT COMPANY, Columbus, OH
Operations Manager, 1997-present
Ormon is a medium-sized distributor of machinery.
Direct all administrative functions. Manage accounts payable and receivable
and financial statements. Improved collection of outstanding accounts.
Coordinate sales reports with available inventory.

Generate sales to national and Midwest clients. Work with purchasing agents;
expedite customer service needs. Provide information to engineers on appropriate equipment to meet their needs, within budgetary limits.

Hire, motivate, and evaluate staff of 75 in office, sales, and warehouse. Order
all equipment and supplies.

Schedule shipments, ensuring on-time delivery. Supervise fleet vehicle purchase and maintenance, driver staffing, and safety.

HATTRICK EQUIPMENT RENTALS, Grove City, OH
Assistant Supervisor, 1992-97
Oversaw rental stock and replacement. Dealt with customers, recommending
appropriate equipment and explaining terms of contract. Handled billing,
accounts payable and receivable, and equipment depreciation writeoff.
Supervised staff of 12.

EDUCATION

CAPITAL UNIVERSITY, Columbus, OH
Bachelor of Arts in Accounting

ORDER ENTRY CLERK

CHRIS SMITH
178 Green Street
Lincoln, NE 68522
(402) 555-5555

EXPERIENCE

THE BULLFROG COMPANY, Lincoln, NE   1999-present
Order Entry Clerk, Parts Department
- Process and ship orders within 12 hours of receipt to Bull Group Field Engineers in the U.S. and abroad.
- Consistently meet or exceed daily deadlines.
- Coordinate with multiple departments and shippers to ensure timely delivery.
- Establish and maintain functional files.
- Use computer to track orders and determine parts status and availability.
- Generate daily reports on status of orders.
- Use reports to identify and resolve order processing problems.
- Investigate and resolve complaints from Field Engineers.

K.T., INC., Norfolk, NE   1997-99
General Office Administrator
- Typed letters and reports, maintained files, answered inquiries about customer accounts.
- Received payments and balanced statements. Posted accounts receivable and payable.
- Supervisor said I had displayed one of the finest first years she had ever seen.

EDUCATION

Marcelle Junior College, Omaha, NE
B.A., Computer Science, expected 2001.

COMPUTER SKILLS

Writing: Word, WordPerfect
Financial: Lotus 1-2-3, Excel
Other: Various proprietary database and order entry systems

PARALEGAL (Civil Law)

CHRIS SMITH
178 Green Street
Santa Fe, NM 87501
(505) 555-5555

SUMMARY OF QUALIFICATIONS
- Outstanding case research and writing skills; compiled training manual.
- Revamped accounting and debit and credit systems.
- Skilled at interviewing, negotiation, and mediation.

EXPERIENCE

LAW OFFICES OF BRENDAN ELLIS
Civil Litigation Specialist/Office Manager

Santa Fe, NM
1998-present

- Manage entire office and staff of 3 secretaries. Ensure smooth operation of small law firm.
- Interview clients; prepare files and discovery.
- Request and review medical documentation; ascertain evidence information and process all with the appropriate parties.
- Negotiate and settle cases with defense attorney and insurance companies.
- Attend mediations and conciliations.
- Prepare clients for depositions and trials.
- Control and maintain law office accounts.

BROWNINGTON, INC.
Administrative Assistant

Albuquerque, NM
1993-98

- Confirmed all manpower hours and prepare monthly logs to bill various sites.
- Provided clerical support to 24 software engineers.
- Recognized for "Excellence in Customer Satisfaction—Southwest Region."

WILD RAIN EXOTIC GIFTS
Owner/Operator

Silver City, NM
1990-93

- Sold art and memorabilia on consignment. Hired, trained, and supervised 8 sales personnel. Handled accounts, managed incoming and outgoing orders, created promotions.

EDUCATION

SAINT JOHN'S COLLEGE
B.S., Resource Management
Numerous seminars on Insurance Reform and Personal Injury Law

Santa Fe, NM

PAYROLL MANAGER

CHRIS SMITH
178 Green Street
St. Paul, MN 55105
(612) 555-5555

EXPERIENCE
1998-present   JASMINE HEART, INC., St. Paul, MN
Jasmine Heart is a well-known apparel and home decor company.

PAYROLL MANAGER
- Manage payroll for 150 shops in North America and 10 shops in Canada. Supervise tax payments, filings, journal entries, accounts payable, and wire transfers for direct deposits.
- Serve as liaison between Finance, Human Resources, corporation executives, and outside vendors.
- Act as systems administrator for combined Human Resources and payroll system, producing 5,500 W-2s and 200 T-4s annually.

Accomplishments
- Maintained operation of payroll department in Newark, New Jersey, while transferring department operations to new St. Paul headquarters.
- Oversaw all human resources payroll-related issues.

1994-98   ADAGIO LEASING, INC., Mankato, MN
PAYROLL MANAGER
Supervised department team of 7. Coordinated a $40 million payroll for 3,000 employees. Managed 18 multi-state payrolls: 10 weekly and 8 biweekly.

Accomplishments
- Organized, corrected, and implemented 18 separate payrolls.
- Converted existing manual-worksheet system to full on-line computerized system.
- Revised procedures for customer audits, increasing revenue.

EDUCATION
State University of New York at Cortland
B.S. in Education

COMPUTERS
Word, Lotus 1-2-3, Managistics on-line payroll system

CHRIS SMITH
178 Green Street
Denver, CO 80208
(303) 555-5555

EXPERIENCE

National Equipment Corporation   **Denver, CO**
Personnel Consultant, Software, Inc.   *1995-present*
- Provide consultation to and leadership for senior staff members and their management teams. Advise on organization and business issues, including needs assessment, diagnosis, transition planning, and problem solving.
- Develop positive and proactive employee relations, effective communications, employee advocate role, participative management, third-party negotiation, interpretion of company policies and procedures, employee development, compensation and benefits, and training design.
- Recommend organizational design and reorganization to maximize utilization of work-force. Design and/or facilitate group development activities, i.e., team-building programs. Communicate Affirmative Action/EEO policies and procedures, including profile, climate, goal-setting, identifying problem areas, and planning.

Training Consultant, Sales Training Development, Barnes and Rogers   *1989-94*
- Consulted with product groups and other clients to determine training needs. Performed needs analysis and established program objectives. Recommended training solutions.
- Identified methods of introducing new information to increase job competence. Devised and documented training. Developed basic training materials and coordinated efforts of outside consultants and vendors. Determined effective instructional technique. Assembled and organized materials into course design.
- Arranged for design and printing of material and preparation of audiovisual aids. Assisted in conducting pilot programs to train instructors.

State of Colorado   **Denver, CO**
Staff Assistant, Bureau of Employment   *1989*
- Devised in-service staff development programs for state employees. Coordinated implementation with union and management. Planned career ladder education programs for upward mobility for state employees.

EDUCATION
University of Denver Graduate School of Education, Denver, CO
M.Ed., Administration, Planning and Social Policy Program

Colorado College, Colorado Springs, CO
B.A. in History

PHOTOGRAPHER

CHRIS SMITH
178 Green Street
Burlington, VT 05405
(802) 555-5555

PHOTOGRAPHIC PROJECTS (selected)
- Location photography of Men's Swim Team for U.S. Olympic Committee
- Hard-line advertising and marketing brochures and corporate portraits, Kenerson Industries, Burlington, VT
- Promotional photography for ballet recital, University of Vermont, Burlington, VT
- Photos in several issues of *National Stamp Collector* magazine
- Photographs for portfolio reproductions and theatrical head shots at Goddard College
- Photo essay for Jake's Fisheries: "A Day Offshore"

SKILLS
Cameras: 35mm; medium-format cameras; large-format view cameras (4 x 5, 8 x 10)
Film: Accomplished at developing and printing in black-and-white and color (negative and direct-positive processes)
Lighting: Proficient at studio and location lighting equipment setups
Effects: Familiar with special effects, multiple imagery, conventional and electronic manipulation techniques
Computer: Pagemaker, QuarkXPress, Photoshop, Freehand, Illustrator

EXPERIENCE
Photographer/Assistant   1997-present
Executed a variety of location and studio assignments. Interpreted layouts, designed and constructed sets for complete on-figure fashion shoots. Performed extensive layout and shooting of hard-line advertising.

Photography Instructor   1997-present
University of Vermont, Burlington, VT
Developed curriculum and instructed photography classes.

Photographic Assistant   1993-present
- Frank Zanna, still life, Hubbel Pen, Dom Champagne, 1998-present
- Jack Camp, still life, Merry Maids, 1997-present
- Les Meyers, location editorial, Goddard College, 1993-97

EDUCATION
Goddard College, Plainfield, VT
Bachelor of Fine Arts in Visual Arts, 1997
Concentration: Photography

PHYSICAL THERAPIST (Orthopedic)

CHRIS SMITH
178 Green Street
Franklin, IN 46131
(317) 555-5555

EXPERIENCE
MIDWEST MEMORIAL HOSPITAL, Indianapolis, IN
Orthopedic In- and Outpatient Clinic   1999-2000
- Develop treatment plan for 10-patient caseload.
- Work extensively with chronic-pain and cardiac patients.
- Present in-service on hip and knee prostheses.

DEARBORN COUNTY HOSPITAL, Richmond, IN
Cardiac Rehabilitation   1998-99
- Acted as program coordinator for exercise regimen.
- Provided individualized treatments using ultrasound, electric stimulation, massage therapy, and stretching/strengthening exercises.
- Coordinated aquadynamics program for chronic-pain patients.

CINNAMON MOUNTAIN, Mishawaka, IN
Pediatric Rehabilitation   1996-98
- Coordinated the treatment of amputee children and children with congenital birth defects.
- Created the "Alive with Pride" program now functional at 30 national hospitals.
- Encouraged regular exercise by developing child-oriented play program.
- Directed teacher workshops at local elementary schools.

SPECIAL PRACTICUM
INDIANA UNIVERSITY, Bloomington, IN
- Performed independent research evaluating back and shoulder strength of musicians who were suffering from tendinitis or bursitis.
- Presented findings to Physical Therapy Department; later published in the *Indiana Journal of Medicine* (Vol. X, pp. 20-24, August 1998).

EDUCATION
INDIANA UNIVERSITY, Bloomington, IN
Bachelor of Science in Physical Therapy
Coursework included Pediatric Therapy and research in the application placement of vibrator and effects of TVR.

PHYSICIAN ASSISTANT

CHRIS SMITH

178 Green Street
Topeka, KS 66614
(913) 555-5555

SUMMARY OF QUALIFICATIONS

- Developed interpersonal skills, having dealt with a diversity of professionals, clients, and staff members.
- Administrative abilities in legal and business environments.
- Self-motivated.
- Function well in high-pressure atmosphere.
- Clerical skills include typing, word processing, and computer literacy.

EDUCATION

MEDICAL EDUCATION CENTER, Topeka, KS
Medical Assisting Diploma, 1999
Specialized in Vital Signs EKG, Lab Procedures, Patient and Examining Room Preparation, Instrument Setups, CPR, and First Aid.
Trained in front-office procedures and typing. Completed 170 hours' practical experience Externship.

LEDGER WORD PROCESSING CENTER, Topeka, KS
Certificate, 1992
12-week training program in typing, word processing, office procedures, accounting, and communications.

EXPERIENCE

BRYMAN ASSOCIATES, Topeka, KS   1998-99
Receptionist
Typed legal documents, merchant agreements, and contracts. Handled filing, incoming and outgoing mail, general office equipment, and PBX telephone system.

MASTER PRESS, Topeka, KS   1993-98
Receptionist
Dealt with incoming calls, mail, and monthly reports. Typed correspondence and manuscripts. Managed varied aspects of final book production. Prepared shipping orders.

VANDELAY INDUSTRIES, Topeka, KS   1990-93
Receptionist
Handled general office functions, arranged meetings, issued payroll.

POLICE OFFICER (Campus)

CHRIS SMITH
178 Green Street
Baltimore, MD 21210
(410) 555-5555

EXPERIENCE

1995-present   JOHNS HOPKINS UNIVERSITY POLICE DEPARTMENT, Baltimore, MD
Patrolman
- Protect life and property on and about the campus of Johns Hopkins University.
- Patrol on foot and via automobile; utilize strong observational skills.
- Uphold laws and codes of the State of Maryland and Johns Hopkins University.
- Cooperate with other law enforcement agencies; act as Deputy Sheriff, Essex County.
- Maintain community relations; give seminars on drunk driving.

1993-95   BUCKMAN ASSOCIATES, Bethesda, MD
Head of Security
- Managed all aspects of security for hotels and adjoining properties.
- Hired, scheduled, supervised, and evaluated personnel.
- Provided all policing functions, with emphasis on defusing potentially violent situations.
- Cooperated extensively with Baltimore and Bethesda Police Departments.
- Promoted from starting position as Patrol Officer.
- Received standing offer of return for emergency or full-time employment.

1988-92   TOWN OF ROCKVILLE POLICE DEPARTMENT, Rockville, MD
Patrolman
- Performed all abovementioned policing functions.
- Oversaw proper use of Chapter 90 sheets and citations.
- Interacted and communicated with town officials.
- Kept records; maintained data.

EDUCATION AND TRAINING

Graduate, Baltimore Police Academy, 1995
Graduate, Rockville Police Academy, 1988

CERTIFICATION AND LICENSURE

- License to carry firearms
- Emergency Medical Technician, National Certification
- Certification in radar usage, Breathalyzer, and Identi-Kit systems

PROGRAM COORDINATOR

CHRIS SMITH
178 Green Street
Alexandria, VA 22311
(703) 555-5555

SUMMARY OF QUALIFICATIONS
- Accomplished coordinator of all production activities associated with fundraising through mass-mailing programs.
- Experienced at grant proposal preparation.

PROGRAM COORDINATOR
1999-present   Watercrest Developers, Alexandria, VA
- Provide direct assistance to the director of fundraising programs, particularly the direct-mail aspect of the annual giving program.
- Coordinate planning, copywriting, production, analysis of results, and in-house consultant reports.
- Streamlined procedures for mailings of 80,000 pieces; saved 40% in printing costs through vendor survey and negotiation.
- Conduct market research; supervise telemarketing activities and other functions involved in expediting 16 annual mailings totaling approximately 300,000 pieces while managing a $600,000 budget. Overall results, 1999, $3.1 million.

FUNDRAISER/SUPERVISOR
1997-99   Nathan Hawke Associates, Manassas, VA
- Directed fundraising team responsible for initiating and developing contacts with political contributors for progressive parties and organizations.
- Interviewed, trained, and supervised staff of 20 while coordinating workflow.
- Assisted in preparing promotional letters for campaign-fund solicitations.

DEVELOPMENT/ADMINISTRATIVE ASSISTANT
1996-97   Appleton Art Abode, Appleton, WI
- Assisted in preparing grant proposals; prepared and reviewed proposals for events at Art Center while organizing and providing production support for publication of the *Appleton News*.

EDUCATION
Lawrence University, Appleton, WI
Bachelor of Arts in Political Science

PROJECT MANAGER

CHRIS SMITH
178 Green Street
Rocky Mount, NC 27804
(919) 555-5555
csmith@netmail.com

PROFESSIONAL EXPERIENCE
Quonto Information Systems, Rocky Mount, NC
Senior Systems Analyst, 1998-present

- Member of a team selected to establish Quonto in the U.S., reporting directly to the Chief Executive. Oversee specification, development, and installation of a sales/marketing and accounting application used in conjunction with the company-developed Property Management System.

- Evaluate and develop applications development tools.

- Hire, train, monitor, and supervise programming staff.

- Write software using C++ and BASIC.

- Coordinate and deliver sales presentations and maintain a positive and professional relationship through cooperative interaction.

Milton Data Processing, Reading PA
Systems Analyst, 1995-98

- Designed, programmed, and acted as project leader for developing patient administration system.

- Evaluated and marketed patient administration and laboratory systems, including composition of technical proposals and cost-benefit analyses.

Programmer, 1988-95

- Functioned as part of a team responsible for developing accounting software for microcomputers.

COMPUTER SKILLS
Operating systems: DOS, Windows, UNIX
Programming: C++, Visual Basic
Other: Word, Excel

PROOFREADER

CHRIS SMITH
178 Green Street
Hope, AR 71801
(501) 555-5555
csmith@netmail.com

EXPERIENCE

1999-present   Vigilant Widow Publishers, Hope, AR
Proofreader
- Proofread for small press.
- Mark for typographical errors and page makeup using standard proofreading symbols.
- Query suspected errors.
- Proofread bluelines prior to publication.
- Capable of rush jobs or longer-term assignments.

1995-99   Sapphire Business Forms, Walnut Ridge, AR
Proofreader
- Proofread outgoing business forms, pamphlets, booklets, and direct-mail pieces.
- Rewrite and copyedit if necessary.
- Proofread company Web site.

1993-95   Walsingham Press, Birmingham, AL
Secretary
- Answered phones, typed letters and memos, and provided customer service.
- In addition to secretarial functions, proofread outgoing business forms, pamphlets, and booklets.

EDUCATION
Krakotoa State Community College, Eureka, IL
B.A. in English

SKILLS
Computer
Word, WordPerfect, PageMaker

Other
Knowledge of *Chicago Manual of Style*

CHRIS SMITH

178 Green Street
Syracuse, NY 13213
(315) 555-5555
csmith@netmail.com

EXPERIENCE

BIG APPLE NATURAL FOODS, Syracuse, NY

Special Events Coordinator   1998-present
- Create and coordinate special events and promotions.
- Select and write event advertising, promotional materials, and publicity.
- Manage $425,000 marketing budget.
- Handle charity fundraising, corporate image positioning, and community outreach activities.

Assistant to the Director of Public Relations   1997-98
- Assisted in promotion and publicity of special events.
- Drafted press releases.
- Developed press kits; maintained media relations.
- Compiled publicity files.
- Researched prospective consumer markets.
- Created direct-mail lists; updated media lists.

SYRACUSE UNIVERSITY, Syracuse, NY   1996-97
Teacher's Assistant
- Assisted professor in editing *Working with the Media.*
- Developed lesson plans.
- Graded midterm and final exams for class of 18 students.

ABC KID CARE, Syracuse, NY   Summers, 1995, 1996
Coordinator
- Organized daily activities program for 45 children.
- Supervised 3 counselors.
- Developed promotional and advertising strategies for potential markets.

COMPUTER SKILLS

Word, WordPerfect, PageMaker, FileMaker Pro

EDUCATION

SYRACUSE UNIVERSITY, Syracuse, NY
Bachelor of Arts in Public Relations, *magna cum laude*

CHRIS SMITH
178 Green Street
Omaha, NE 68114
(402) 555-5555

SUMMARY OF QUALIFICATIONS
- Recognized for ability to plan and direct successful programs for fundraising, public relations, and education.
- Administrative experience with major voluntary health agency.
- Extensive volunteer recruitment experience.
- Experience representing agency interests to legislators.
- Supervisory experience with both professional and nonprofessional staffs.

EMPLOYMENT EXPERIENCE
Nebraska Heart Society, Inc., Omaha, NE
Public Relations Manager, 1997-present
Organizing
Serve as consultant to the 7 state chapters regarding campaign problems and activities. Organize statewide and regional campaign meetings; speak at several campaign conferences.

Lobbying
Review state legislation regarding the Heart Society and bring specific bills to the attention of the proper committee or individual. Staff the Legislative Advisory Committee and follow through on specific bills.

Fundraising
Develop fundraising programs (bequests). Conducted the previous two annual campaigns for the newly merged Central Chapter (Antelope County). Currently serve as chairman for the Nebraska Independent Health Agency Committee and secretary for the Combined Federal Campaign.

Training
Assisted in developing four 2½-day orientation courses held for new employees; acted as training coordinator.

Directorial Assistant (Greater Omaha Chapter), 1995-97
Supervised chapter campaign duties and assisted the Executive Director with administrative responsibilities, such as personnel and budget.

EDUCATION
Dillard University, New Orleans, LA
M.S. in Public Relations
University of Michigan at Flint
B.A. in Government

PUBLICIST

CHRIS SMITH
178 Green Street
Pullman, WA 99164
(509) 555-5555
csmith@netmail.com

EXPERIENCE

CNBS TELEVISION, "Confrontations," Pullman, WA   1998-present
Production Assistant
Book main guests and panelists. Generate and research story ideas. Conduct video research. Edit teasers for show. Organize production details for studio tapings. Troubleshoot equipment malfunctions. Monitor lighting and TelePrompTer. Coordinate publicity ads in local newspapers.

BARSTOW COMPANY, Seattle, WA   1996-98
Publicity Assistant
Publicized new books and authors. Assisted in booking media tours (TV, radio, and print). Wrote and designed press releases. Fulfilled review copy requests. Conducted galley mailings and performed general office work.

WNBN-TV, Tacoma, WA   1995-96
Production Intern
Assisted producers of a live, daily talk show. Researched and generated story ideas. Pre-interviewed possible guests. Logged tapes. Went out on shoots and wrote promotional announcements. Produced 5 of my own segments for the show.

THE BENEDICT COUNCIL, UNIVERSITY OF WASHINGTON, Seattle, WA   1994-95
Promotional Assistant
Implemented promotional campaigns for concerts on campus. Wrote and designed promotional advertisements. Initiated student involvement with program.

THE CHERRY HAIKU, INC., Seattle, WA   1993-94
Art Assistant
Produced pasteups and mechanicals. Operated Photostat camera; coordinated logistics for photo shoots. Participated in brainstorming sessions with creative team.

EDUCATION
UNIVERSITY OF WASHINGTON, Seattle, WA
B.A. in Communications, *cum laude*
Minor in English

PURCHASING AGENT

CHRIS SMITH
178 Green Street
Bountiful, UT 84040
(801) 555-5555

EMPLOYMENT

PURCHASING AGENT   1999-present
Data Basix, Westwood, MA
- Purchase Montgomery, Sprint, and Miyako products, PCs, laptops, and peripherals.
- Maintain open-order status reports for Montgomery, Sprint, and Miyako products and expedited orders, as necessary, pertaining to inventory control.
- Return defective and obsolete inventory products.

PURCHASING AGENT   1998-99
Radlett, Inc., Lark, UT
- Purchased Wellsville 1068, Moore laptop PCs, and peripherals. Interacted with sales and marketing departments; oversaw order processing, scheduling, and inventory control. Purchased general supplies for entire company.

REGIONAL DISTRIBUTION SUPERVISOR   1997-98
Rybell Corporation, Teasdale, UT
- Purchased Grinfeld, KRT, Willard, and Moore laptop computers as well as software and peripherals to be sold to individuals and companies. Supervised and trained a staff of 8 in buying, order processing, and billing, and 5 in warehouse administration and maintenance for the Western Region.
- Started as a buyer, responsible for annual purchases of $17 million in microcomputer equipment and peripherals, monitoring inventory, and preparing forecasts for a perpetual inventory system. Company sold to Rybell; was promoted to Regional Distribution Supervisor by new management.

BUYER   1994-97
O'Donnell Corporation, Oasis, UT
- Purchased electronic components from manufacturers and local distributors for a collision-avoidance radar system used by both commercial and military shipping. Functioned as assistant to the mechanical buyer. Purchased all office and miscellaneous supplies.
- Started as a purchasing secretary responsible for administrative support to purchasing agent and liaison to outside vendors. In 1995, based on performance, was promoted to position of buyer.

EDUCATION
University of Colorado at Boulder
B.A., Business Administration

Chris Smith
178 Green Street
Las Vegas, NV 89154
(702) 555-5555
csmith@netmail.com

EXPERIENCE
1999-present
Lakinakis Corporation, Wendover, NV
Customer Service Receiver
Quality Assurance Test Technician
Received computer workstation units that failed in the field; tested and repaired; ran diagnostic tests and handled troubleshooting on the sub-assembly level.

1998-99
Ostow Stores, Search Light, NV
Area Specialist/Department Manager
Managed retail camera and electronics department. Hired, trained, and supervised staff of three. Sold, troubleshot, and repaired cameras, radios, and other electronic goods.

1996-98
Woodruff Electronics, Las Vegas, NV
Field Service Technician
Repaired PCs onsite. Performed preventive maintenance and customer service.

EDUCATION
New York University, New York, NY
B.S. in Computer Science, candidate, expected 2000
Maintaining GPA of 3.9.

1994-96
Colgate University, Hamilton, NY
Physics Major
Successfully completed 4 semesters toward a B.A. Achieved a 3.8 GPA before transferring to New York University for completion of studies.

1993-96
Spinack Data Institute, Brooklyn, NY
Electronics Technology
Received a Certificate in Electronics Technology. Achieved honors for maintaining a 95+ average.

QUALITY CONTROL INSPECTOR

CHRIS SMITH
178 Green Street
Crittenden, KY 41030
(505) 555-5555

EXPERIENCE
NEWPORT NAVAL SHIPYARD, Newport, RI
Boiler Systems Inspector, Quality Assurance Office   1996-2000
Accountable for all phases of inspection of surface ship propulsion systems and main boiler plants, requiring full knowledge and experience of boilermaker duties combined with additional certifications and training.

Conduct working audits on final systems operational tests performed by all shops. Certify acceptance of systems whose testing was audited. Perform inspections on handholds, manholes, pressure parts, piping, condensers, pressure fuel-oil tanks, and support machinery.

Investigate and report on problems and special projects. Submit reports and recommendations on all work on systems. Maintain files, charts, and reports on work in progress and inspections.

Boilermaker/Boilermaker Foreman   1995-96
Manufactured and overhauled surface ship propulsion systems and main boiler plants to close tolerances, adhering to strict quality control.
- Performed shipfitter and structural steel work to assemble cylinders, pipes, tank heads, condenser heads, and shells.
- Produced pipefitting for boiler hookups, tanks, and pressure chambers.
- Used mason and insulator skills to install fire brick, insulating brick, calcium silicate block, burner tiles, and baffle tiles.

EDUCATION AND SPECIALIZED TRAINING
Steam Generating Plant Inspector
San Francisco, CA
U.S. Navy Main Propulsion Steam Generating Plant Certificate, 1996

American Society for Quality Control
New York, NY
Inspection Gaging Workshop, 1995

Newport Naval Ship Yard Apprentice School
Newport, RI
Boilermaker Apprentice, 1991-95

REAL ESTATE APPRAISER

CHRIS SMITH
178 Green Street
Winona, MN 55987
(507) 555-5555

SUMMARY OF QUALIFICATIONS
Professional experience includes the following areas:
- Assessing property and real estate value for insurance claims, adjustments, and repair.
- Successfully marketing services to Fortune 500 companies.
- Project and office management, supervising estimators, superintendent, and construction crew.
- Demonstrating estimating software in Northern regions and following up with problem-solving assistance.

EXPERIENCE
1998-present   WINONA CONSTRUCT, Winona, MN
Vice-President/Appraiser
- Manage 2 estimators, a superintendent, and 20-member construction crew, assessing damages, preparing estimates and proposals for insurance companies, and supervising reconstruction activities.
- Achieved average annual sales of $950,000 with new clients.
- Provide demonstrations and training to groups of 10-30 in estimating software package, traveling to Maine, Florida, Georgia, and Massachusetts. Followed up with problem-solving services.
- Traveled to Los Angeles area to write estimates for apartment complexes damaged by 1994 earthquake as special assignment.

1994-98   NORTHERN STAR RESTORATION COMPANY, Minneapolis, MN
General Manager
- Worked closely with management companies and apartment complexes, managing restoration work for new company, hiring and supervising subcontractors, and supervising jobs from start to finish.

1991-94   ST. PAUL LIFE & CASUALTY, St. Paul, MN
Property Claims Representative
- Appraised all types of residential properties and investigated all types of damages to home, including water, fire, vandalism, and natural disasters. Determined value of claim and prepared report.

EDUCATION
BROWN UNIVERSITY, Providence, RI
Bachelor of Arts in Education

CHRIS SMITH
178 Green Street
Laramie, WY 82071
(307) 555-5555

EMPLOYMENT
MARSTON CONVENT, Laramie, WY, 1998-present
Receptionist
Answer phone, greet visitors, and provide information, tours, and literature. Record and monitor thank-you notes for all received donations. Perform light typing, filing, and word processing.

RINALDO RANCH, Laramie, WY, 1993-98
Secretary
Provided word processing, customer relations, some accounts payable processing. Implemented new system for check processing; increased prompt payment of client bills.

WOMANPOWER INC., Laramie, WY, 1990-93
Secretary
Acted as liaison between public and CEO.

STATE HEALTH COALITION., Laramie, WY, 1986-90
Statistical Typist
Prepared health record documentation of infectious disease patients at State hospital. Trained new hires.

SKILLS
Computer
Word, WordPerfect, Excel, Lotus 1-2-3

Other
Typing (65 wpm), statistical typing, shorthand, dictaphone, multi-line phones/switchboard, bookkeeping, credit checks

EDUCATION
TRAINING, INC., Boston, MA
Office careers training program in bookkeeping, typing, reception, word processing, and office procedures
ST. JOSEPH'S ACADEMY, Portland, Maine   Diploma

RECEPTIONIST (Salon)

CHRIS SMITH
178 Green Street
St. Louis, MO 63130
(314) 555-5555

EXPERIENCE

DIETER'S SALON, St. Louis, MO   1999-present
Receptionist/General Clerk
Answer incoming calls; schedule appointments
Handle customer payments and weekly payroll
Perform clerical duties, including some accounting, inventory maintenance, and filing

FRED'S SALON, St. Louis, MO   1997-99
Receptionist
Same as above.
Opened and closed salon and tallied the day's receipts.

CHANTILLY LACE APPAREL, Winslow, MO   1996-97
Receptionist
Provided customer assistance; registered sales; responded to telephone inquiries, deposited
checks.

BALZAC'S, St. Charles, MO   1994-96
Sales Associate/Cashier
Provided customer assistance; registered sales; responded to telephone inquiries. Security-
related functions included daily pre-opening check of employee and fitting rooms.

SKILLS
Computer
WordPerfect, Lotus 1-2-3

Other
Typing (40 wpm)
Accounting; adept with figures

EDUCATION
St. Charles High School, St. Charles, MO   Diploma

CHRIS SMITH
178 Green Street
New London, CT 06320
(203) 555-5555

EXPERIENCE
NORMAN DEPARTMENT STORES, New London, CT
Manager of Executive Recruitment, 1996-2000
- Oversaw college recruiting process—annual budget $75,000.
- Presented campus recruitment workshops; developed internship program.
- Hired support and merchandising staff.
- Organized senior executive involvement.
- Received award for overall achievement and outstanding performance in human resources.

Department Manager, 1994-96
- Merchandised children's clothing and accessories.
- Analyzed and marketed $2 million inventory.
- Coordinated inventory control.
- Trained and developed staff of 15 sales associates in customer-service skills and selling techniques.
- Achieved 20% sales increase over one-year period.
- Chosen manager of the year for excellence in execution of responsibilities, 1995.

SEINFELD'S, Redding, CT
Selling Supervisor Trainee, 1995
- Coordinated merchandising and overall appearance of Men's Department.
- Evaluated sales data.
- Controlled inventory and placement of incoming merchandise.
- Executed price revisions.

EDUCATION
CONNECTICUT COLLEGE, New London, CT
B.A., Spanish Modified with Government Studies

CHRIS SMITH

178 Green Street
Greenville, SC 29613
(803) 555-5555
csmith@netmail.com

WRITING
- Superior Scholar Award for "Jack-O-Lantern Dreams," a creative-writing senior project, comprised of seven poems and four prose pieces about growing up in a Jehovah's Witness family. Spring 1999
- "Amazon Expedition" (article), accepted by *Charleston Record* travel section. Sept. 1998
- Researched and wrote historical articles for *The Insider's Guide to Greenville (1997)*.
- Published 3 short stories in *Gnashings,* the Furman student literary magazine, 1997-99.

EDUCATION
FURMAN UNIVERSITY, Greenville, SC
Bachelor of Arts in English, 1999
SYRACUSE UNIVERSITY, Sydney, Australia, Fall 1997
Concentration: Language and History

EXPERIENCE
EYE ON GREENVILLE, Greenville, SC   Summer 1999
Reporter/Editor
- Researched and wrote articles; assisted in determining editorial content.

English Peer Tutor   Spring 1999, Fall 1997
- Provided one-on-one interaction in basic writing with a freshman student; emphasized grammar and writing skills.

POINT MAGAZINE, Charleston, SC   Summer 1998
Intern
- Assisted writers in research; prepared media kits for potential advertisers.

REACH, Furman journal of student scholarship   Spring 1997
Member, Editorial Committee
- Evaluated and selected articles.

COMPUTER SKILLS
Word, Lotus 1-2-3, PageMaker

RESEARCH ASSOCIATE

CHRIS SMITH, Ph.D.
178 Green Street
Los Angeles, CA 90041
(213) 555-5555

EXPERIENCE

1999-present   SUN LABORATORIES, Los Angeles, CA
Manufacturing Research Associate II
- Develop expertise in research through production via process experimentation and operation of pilot plant equipment
- Perform large-scale fermentation, protein purification, and other processes under GMP regulations
- Develop system for preparing media
- Perform related protein assays

1984-94   GRAYSON RESEARCH CORPORATION, Los Angeles, CA
Research Technician, Cell Propagation Department
- Optimized growth parameters of fibroblast and epithelial cell lines
- Scaled up culture from 25 cc T-flasks up through 40-L fermentor microcarrier cultures; worked independently
- Established media unit for exclusive use of department
- Set up perfusion system

Technician-2, Media Department
- Filtered and sterilized various media under GMP regulations

Assistant Supervisor, Glassware Department
- Supervised department of 15 employees
- Prepared, sterilized, and distributed tissue culture glassware to different departments

EDUCATION

Ph.D. in Biology, 1999
California Institute of Technology, Pasadena, CA
Course: Biochemistry, Molecular Biology, Protein Chemistry

Master of Liberal Arts in Biology, 1996
Occidental College, Los Angeles, CA
Concentration: Immunology

Bachelor of Science in Agricultural Engineering, 1984
Huntingdon College, Montgomery, AL

RESTAURANT MANAGER (Fast Food)

Chris Smith
178 Green Street
Colchester, VT 05446
(802) 555-5555

EXPERIENCE

1999-present   BURGER CHEF, Colchester, VT
Manager
Schedule and supervise staff, control inventory, deposit cash, maintain physical plant and lockbox, complete daily and weekly reports. Supervise up to 20 employees per shift.
- Completed management training program.

1996-98   BLACK DIAMOND ICE CREAM CORPORATION, Mount Snow, VT
Shift Supervisor
Same responsibilities as in current position.

1994-96   GRIMSHAW LOUNGE, South Burlington, VT
Manager
Supervised staff of 30 employees per shift. Monitored food costs, filed reports. Planned weekly menu, made changes where necessary.

1993-94   THE YEE HAH RESTAURANT, Brattleboro, VT
Manager
Supervised night shift, special function catering, and kitchen personnel. Hired and trained staff, monitored payroll, supervised banquets.

EDUCATION

CHURCHILL CULINARY ARTS SCHOOL
- Completed 2-year course of study.

UNITED STATES AIR FORCE
- Completed Class A & C Cooking School.
- Honorably discharged.

COMMUNITY ORGANIZATIONS
- Volunteer time and cooking skills at Snacks on Tracks and the Boys Club of Colchester.

CHRIS SMITH
178 Green Street
Baltimore, MD 21227
(301) 555-5555

EXPERIENCE
CALVIN CLOTHES COMPANY, Baltimore & Bethesda MD, Washington DC

1997-present   **Buyer**—Junior Apparel Departments, Baltimore
- Developed sales volume from $5.5 million to $7.5 million, 1997-99. Consistently achieved net operating profit of 5%—highest in company.
- Implemented promotional strategies and developed key classifications directly responsible for volume increase.
- Developed a wide range of communication networks that not only supplied product knowledge to sales staff but also affected strategic planning of vendor programs.
- Chosen as Merchant of the Month, October 1998.

1995-97   **Divisional Sales Manager**, Bethesda
- Handled furniture, electronics, lamps, and basement store. Total volume in 1995 reached $5.6 million.
- During mall expansion, was instrumental in holding store sales volume within plan by achieving 12% increase. Priorities included constant evaluation of stock levels and content, goal setting, development of key personnel, and achieving a high motivational level.

1991-95   **Assistant Buyer**, Washington, DC
- Handled men's coordinates, coats, swimwear, and activewear.
- Interpreted, analyzed, and responded to reports, including OTB, selling reports, and seasonal plans.
- Acted as liaison with vendors and warehouse to assure timely merchandise delivery.

1985-91   **Store Manager**, Washington, DC
- Promoted from trainee to manager within 18 months.
- Conceptualized and implemented employee training and effectiveness program.

EDUCATION
UNIVERSITY OF DELAWARE, Newark, DE
B.S., Marketing

CHRIS SMITH
178 Green Street
Los Angeles, CA 90035
(310) 555-5555

EXPERIENCE
SPINNER RECORDS CORPORATION, Los Angeles, CA
Manager   1999-present
- Manage Spinner's largest-volume store (approximately $50,000/week). Handle all merchandising, inventory control, ordering, cash control, and maintenance. Direct sales floor activities. Prepare daily sales reports. Hire, train, and coordinate a staff of 26.
- Assist in developing local marketing and advertising strategies. Coordinate special promotions and events.

Achievements
- Won two merchandising display contests.
- Received the "Super Spinner" Sales Award for exceeding sales goals

Assistant Manager   1997-99
- Fulfilled all management responsibilities. Opened and closed store; handled customer service complaints and cash control. Supervised and motivated employees. Assisted in merchandising.

SANTA ANA SHOPS, Santa Ana, CA
Assistant Manager   1995-97
- Handled hiring, merchandising, and cash control for this convenience store. Opened and closed market. Prepared bank deposits and daily sales reports. Supervised 15 employees.

LENNY'S TOYS, Santa Ana, CA
Assistant Manager   1994-95
- Hired, trained, and supervised shifts of four people.
- Tallied the day's receipts and made bank deposits.
- Maintained inventory levels; ordered merchandise.

SALES ADMINISTRATOR

CHRIS SMITH
178 Green Street
Shreveport, LA 70460
(318) 555-5555

EXPERIENCE

SOUTHERN TRAVEL, Shreveport, LA   1999-present
Sales Administrator to Regional Vice President
- Assist sales personnel with outside sales and telemarketing to National and Group Associations.
- Create and proof camera-ready ads and color brochures.
- Act as liaison for sales staff and passengers.
- Process travel orders and correspondence.
- Direct incoming invoices, outgoing commission checks, and passenger payments.
- Maintain records.
- Serve as availability coordinator for travel programs.
- Provide customer service.
- Use Trans-National Reservation System.

BEAUREGARD'S BRIGADE, Baton Rouge, LA   1997-99
Sales Manager
- Managed all facets of $1.1 million annual volume men's clothing business.
- Hired, trained, and motivated 18-member staff.
- Achieved 19% increase in sales over 1-year period.

Manager   1995-97
- Managed daily operations for national video store, including selection, training, and evaluation of 10 sales associates.
- Successfully introduced profitable line of creative slogan T-shirts.
- Coordinated advertising and displays.

ORSON'S PRIDE, New York, NY   1992-95
Manager
- Managed accessories department of this $2.2 million international women's clothing store.

EDUCATION

FORDHAM UNIVERSITY, College at Lincoln Center
New York, NY
B.A. in Marketing, 1995

SALES ASSISTANT (General)

Chris Smith
178 Green Street
Fort Worth, TX 76112
(817) 555-5555

EXPERIENCE

1999-present   REGENCY CORPORATION, Dallas, TX
Sales Assistant
Act as liaison between customer and sales representative. Provide customer service via telephone. Ascertain order accuracy. Track and expedite orders. Cooperate in team endeavors.

1996-99   THE MUSIC MAKER, Inc., Houston, TX
Sales Assistant
Coordinated sales efforts of a staff of 6 for a large musical instruments dealership. Developed and maintained working relationships with manufacturers and customers. Supported top account executives. Maintained open files to ensure greatest customer satisfaction.

1994-96   CITY OF DALLAS, TREASURERS DEPARTMENT, Dallas, TX
Research Assistant
Assisted in the collection of delinquent real estate, personal property, and motor vehicle excise taxes. Matched instrument of taking against daily tax-title receipts. Processed petitions of foreclosure for the legal section and title searches.

1993-94   TRAFFIC AND PARKING DEPARTMENT, Dallas, TX
Senior Claims Investigator
Investigated and expedited claim settlements relating to ticket disputes and information requests.

1992-93   SHERMAN BANK FOR SAVINGS, Sherman, TX
Bank Teller
Interacted with customers, processed money and check transactions, balanced transactions at the end of each shift. Developed a working knowledge of money market funds and IRA accounts.

EDUCATION

Austin College, Sherman, TX
A.S., Business Management

Texas Institute of Banking
Completed courses in Bank Organization and Business English

SALES REPRESENTATIVE (Computers)

CHRIS SMITH
178 Green Street
Salt Lake City, UT 84102
(801) 555-5555
csmith@netmail.com

SUMMARY OF QUALIFICATIONS
- Knowledgeable in sales services, account acquisition, and management.
- Proficient at reactivating dormant accounts and developing successful sales techniques.
- Consistently meet and exceed sales quotas.
- Over 6 years' experience within a major hardware and software company.

EXPERIENCE

1999-present   *Sales Representative*
GRASSVILLE SYSTEMS
Salt Lake City, UT
- Sell Panasonic, Hewlett Packard, IBM, and compatible desktops, laptops, and peripherals to corporate accounts and dealer channels.
- Acquire new accounts; maintain and reactivate existing accounts. Coordinate cold calling; process orders and sell service accounts.
- Devise solutions for customer microcomputer needs and after-sales support.

1996-99   *National Sales Representative*
NIMBUS COMPUTERS
Provo, UT
- Sold IBM, Macintosh, Hewlett Packard, Compaq, and compatible desktop and laptop systems.

1993-96   *Sales Associate*
SUEDE BOGGS COMPANY
Salt Lake City, UT
- Facilitated promotional activities; provided customer service.

EDUCATION
NEW HAMPSHIRE COLLEGE, Manchester, NH
Bachelor of Arts: Communications

COMPUTERS
Word, Lotus 1-2-3, Excel, Access, QuarkXPress

SALESPERSON

Chris Smith
178 Green Street
Lancaster, PA 17064
(717) 555-5555

EDUCATION
LESLEY COLLEGE, Cambridge, MA
B.A., Politics and History, 1997
Minor: English

SALES EXPERIENCE
PETIE'S PET LAND, Pittsburgh, PA   1997-99
Salesperson
Sold merchandise, increasing sales volume by 6% in first 3 months. Developed ongoing customer relationships, enhancing future sales. Developed special seasonal sales. Handled cash transactions and kennel care.

THE TIRE BARON, INC., Beaver Falls, PA   Summer 1994
Upper Bay/Lower Bay Technician
Sold merchandise. Provided customers with technical advice. Trained new employees. Received Employee of the Month award in July 1997 for highest sales volume in 7 stores.

THE SUBVERSIVE PAGES BOOKSTORE, Erie, PA   Summer 1993
Salesperson
Sold merchandise. Provided customer service. Purchased materials and monitored books.

OTHER EXPERIENCE
UNITED PACKAGERS, Boston, MA   Summer 1996
Material Handler

LESLEY COLLEGE, Cambridge, MA   Summer 1995
Maintenance Technician, Buildings and Grounds

ACCOMPLISHMENTS
Fluent in French
Student Government Representative, 1995-96
Founder, Debate Team, 1996

SECRETARY (Hospital)

CHRIS SMITH
178 Green Street
Washington, DC 20057
(202) 555-5555

EXPERIENCE
JENNINGS HOSPITAL, Washington, D.C.
Secretary, Radiation Therapy Department   1998-present
- Answer phones, schedule appointments, greet patients and visitors, prepare and file charts.
- Type and print invoices and requisitions.
- Supervise inventory and general office organization.
- Serve as liaison between physicians, staff, and patients.

Senior Birth Registrar   1994-98
- Recorded live births. Prepared and processed birth certificates, infant data, and associated documentation.
- Served as liaison between physicians, staff, and patients regarding legal documentation.
- Inaugurated a pilot program to facilitate networking between hospital and Registry of Vital Statistics.

Purchasing Assistant   1992-94
- Assisted in purchasing chemical and equipment requisitions.
- Controlled inventories and distribution.
- Implemented procedure enhancements.

Patient Observer   1991-92
- Provided emotional support and observation for at-risk patients.
- Program was administered through the Nursing Office.

EDUCATION
TRIBORO JUNIOR COLLEGE, Denver, CO
A.S., Business, Major in Executive Secretarial Sciences

COMPUTERS
Word, Excel, WordPerfect, Lotus 1-2-3

SOCIAL WORKER (Juvenile)

CHRIS SMITH
178 Green Street
Chalmette, LA 70043
(504) 555-5555

EDUCATION
TULANE UNIVERSITY   New Orleans, LA
Master of Social Work   1997

LOYOLA UNIVERSITY   New Orleans, LA
Bachelor of Arts in Psychology   1995
Research assistant to Dr. Sophie Dillon. Project involved studying intrinsic and extrinsic motivation in children.
Dean's List

EXPERIENCE
CHALMETTE CHILDREN'S HOSPITAL,
Early Intervention Program   Chalmette, LA
Social Worker/Case Manager   1997-present
As member of interdisciplinary team, service children who are at environmental and/or biological risk. Provide clinical, concrete, and supportive services, family education, and developmental stimulation for children. Services provided via home visits and participation in classroom team for children.

NEW ORLEANS TEEN CLINIC   New Orleans, LA
Intern   1996-97
Provided social work to children and adolescents, including pregnant teens and foster parents. Cooperated with Department of Social Services regarding treatment and placement of children in foster care.

VETERANS' ADMINISTRATION HOSPITAL OF NEW ORLEANS   New Orleans, LA
Intern   1995-96
Performed medical and psychiatric social work at outpatient clinic. Provided direct patient care for individuals and groups. Coordinated with nationally recognized pain team at New Orleans Outpatient Clinic.

PROFESSIONAL INTERESTS
Adolescent Behavior, Gifted Children, Neuropsychology

SPEECH PATHOLOGIST

Chris Smith
178 Green Street
Providence, RI 02918
(401) 555-5555

EXPERIENCE

1996-present   ST. CHRISTOPHER'S HOSPITAL, Providence, RI
Clinical Supervisor, Bennet Hospital Satellite Speech and Language Program
- Started and direct Speech and Language program under aegis of Bennet Hospital. Evaluate, diagnose, and treat inpatients and outpatients, adults and children, with a variety of communication disorders. Provide supportive and educational counseling.
- Develop policies and procedures, perform various managerial and administrative tasks. Hire, instruct, and supervise employees, graduate students, and clinical fellows. Conduct quality assurance; appraise performance.
- Develop augmentative communication systems for nonverbal population. Conduct aural rehabilitation for elderly. Provide in-service consultation to hospital staff, students, various agencies, and organizations.

1993-96   BENNET HOSPITAL, Providence, RI
Staff Speech-Language Pathologist, Speech, Hearing and Language Center
- Evaluated, diagnosed, and treated inpatients and outpatients, adults and children, with a variety of communication disorders, including apraxia, aphasia, dysarthria, head injury, fluency, voice, neurological impairments, language, mental retardation, phonology, laryngectomy, dialectal variances, hearing impairments, cleft palate, and cerebral palsy.
- Ran preschool language group.
- Participated on Stroke Team.
- Provided in-service consultation to staff and agencies.

1990-93   PRIVATE PRACTICE, Cape Town, South Africa
Speech Pathologist
- Assessed, diagnosed, and treated adults and children exhibiting a variety of communication disorders.
- Conferred with physicians and schools.
- Provided supportive and educational parent counseling.

EDUCATION

Brown University, Providence, RI
Master of Education in Human Development and Reading

Cape Town University, Cape Town, South Africa
Bachelor of Arts with Honors in Speech Pathology and Audiology

STAFF ASSISTANT

CHRIS SMITH
178 Green Street
Clinton, MS 39058
(601) 555-5555

EXPERIENCE

1999-present   AUGUSTUS TELEPHONE COMPANY, Clinton, MS
Staff Assistant, Human Resources Department
- Administer personnel and support activities relating to management job evaluation and compensation support.
- Develop and maintain internal procedures.
- Control management salary guide.
- Research and analyze significant data.
- Coordinate, direct, and codify reports and procedures.

1998-99   BRAINCHILD, INC., Jackson, MS
Staff Assistant
- Reviewed, prepared, and processed job and employee change reports for all general departments.
- Interpreted salary policy.
- Interacted with Human Resources Department and upper-level management.

1995-98   TECHNIQUES, INC., Lorman, MS
Staff Assistant, Human Resources Department
- Maintained employee database.
- Prepared data on employee exit interviews for analysis.
- Provided general support services.

EDUCATION

Mississippi College, Clinton, MS
B.A. in Communications

COMPUTER SKILLS

Word, Excel

STENOGRAPHER

CHRIS SMITH
178 Green Street
Redford, MI 48239
(313) 555-5555

QUALIFICATIONS AND ACHIEVEMENTS
- Strong shorthand and speed writing skills at 130 wpm
- Excel at Gregg Simplified and Diamond Jubilee methods; proficient with the Pitman method
- Area of expertise is transcribing, editing, and interpreting stenographic characters into clear, concise, and precise English
- Typing skills include word processing (80 wpm) and typewriter production (65 wpm)
- Recipient of the *Shorthand Award* and *Stenographer of the Year Award* from the Pitman method archives
- Consistent recognition from the Gregg Simplified Method archives for excellence in Gregg-style character performance

EMPLOYMENT
1997-present
Harvard University, Cambridge, MA
Head Stenographer, Admissions Department

1993-97
John Ervine Mutual Life Insurance Co., Boston, MA
Stenographer

PUBLICATIONS
Stenographer's Notes, coauthor with D. D. Sweeny
Whole Word Publishing, Boston, MA 1996

Gregg Shorthand Made Simple, coauthor with D. D. Sweeny
Whole Word Publishing, Boston, MA 1994

EDUCATION
Salem State College, Salem, MA
A.A Secretarial Sciences

Katherine Gibbs Secretarial School, Boston, MA
Executive Secretarial program

SUBCONTRACTOR (Programming)

CHRIS SMITH
178 Green Street
New York, NY 11215
(212) 555-5555
csmith@netmail.com

Computer Skills
Operating systems: DOS, Windows, Macintosh, UNIX
Programming: C++, Java, Pascal, COBOL, Visual Basic
Writing/publishing: Word
Financial: Excel, Lotus 1-2-3
Database: Access, Oracle
On-line help: RoboHELP

EXPERIENCE
New York Department of Public Welfare, New York, NY   1999-present
Subcontractor
Designed and developed programs for new reporting system and performed maintenance programming on existing reporting system.

Rowe Street Bank and Trust, New York, NY   1998-99
Subcontractor
Performed maintenance programming on the Trust Accounting System to add tax withholding on interest and dividend income.

New York Hospital, Hempstead, NY   1996-98
Subcontractor
Designed and developed program for the existing Medicaid billing system.

New England Life Insurance Co., Elmira, NY   1994-96
Subcontractor
Performed maintenance programming to handle year-end changes to the agent commission system.

Atwood Corporation, Amherst, NY   1992-94
Programmer/Analyst
Performed programming and design on a portfolio-management system.

EDUCATION
Houghton College, Houghton, NY
B.S. in Computer Science

SURVEYOR

CHRIS SMITH
178 Green Street
Billings, MT 59102
(406) 555-5555

EXPERIENCE

Surveyor   1999-present
Maintain a private practice handling site surveys, real estate development layout, and topographical surveys.

Public Works Department, Billings, MT
Chief Surveyor   1999-present
Perform highway, watershed, and topographical surveys. Supervise preparation of plans and specifications for all county highways, bridges, park buildings, and related structures.

Office Engineer   1997-99
Developed standard designs, still in use, for retaining walls and reinforced concrete bridge abutments.

Job Works Program, Billings, MT
Seminar Teacher   1999-present
Instruct construction foreman in construction methods and leadership.

LICENSES

Professional Engineer, Montana
Surveyor, Montana
Builder, Montana

EDUCATION

Montana State University, Bozeman, MT
B.S. in Civil Engineering, *cum laude*, 1999
Additional coursework in concrete design, BASIC programming, and computer-aided design. Maintain state-of-the-art skills through extensive reading on construction and business topics.

SYSTEMS ANALYST (Industrial)

CHRIS SMITH
178 Green Street
Appleton, WI 54912
(414) 555-5555
csmith@netmail.com

EXPERIENCE

1999-present   **Systems Analyst**
DEVLIN INDUSTRIES, Appleton, WI
Devise new ways of making the computer system more efficient. Create or change programs
to generate new reports and new ways of retrieving information.

Achievements
- Set up minicomputer-to-PC interface to archive daily receipts onto optical disks.
- Created a device driver for a new disk system and a new operating system to handle the new driver.
- Qualified all Devlin software onto a new computer system.
- Built a new method of handling orders into the system.
- Rewrote the accounts receivable program system to handle long-term notes.

1995-99   **Production Assistant**
PRICE COMPUTER, Madison, WI
Worked in Production Department on board repair and revectoring, equipment assembly,
basic production on electronic manufacturing. Suggested an improvement in board revectoring that was subsequently implemented.

COMPUTER SKILLS
Operating systems: DOS, Windows, UNIX
Programming: C++, Java, Pascal, COBOL, Visual Basic
Writing/publishing: Word
Financial: Excel, Lotus 1-2-3
Database: Access, Oracle
Online help: RoboHELP

PROFESSIONAL AFFILIATION
Association of Computing Machinery

EDUCATION
Milwaukee School of Engineering, Milwaukee, WI
B.S. in Computer Science/Systems
B.S. in Applied Physics/Astronomy

SYSTEMS ENGINEER

CHRIS SMITH
178 Green Street
Charlotte, NC 28214
(704) 555-5555
csmith@netmail.com

BACKGROUND
- Extensive and diversified computer hardware and software knowledge in personal computers.
- Expertise in prototype computer testing.
- Excellent investigative and research skills.
- Self-taught in many programming languages, word processors, operating systems, database and spreadsheet software applications.

COMPUTER SKILLS
Operating systems: DOS, Windows, Macintosh, UNIX
Programming: C++, Java, Pascal, COBOL, Visual Basic
Writing/publishing: Word, WordPerfect
Financial: Excel, Lotus 1-2-3
Database: Access, Oracle
On-line help: RoboHELP

EXPERIENCE

Maximilian Data Systems, Charlotte, NC   1998-present
Systems Engineer
Co-authored Maximilian software test plan for computer prototypes; received plaque acknowledging outstanding efforts. Researched, wrote, and edited test procedures. Developed computer engineering test tools. Wrote database application to track and generate reports on problems found during development. Organized preproduction testing of prototypes.

Analyzed requirements for new work-related quality processes to improve product testing. Created software applications that automated work-related processes, such as generating status- and engineering-change request reports.

Gilford College, Greensboro, NC   1997-98
Instructor
Taught computer programming, systems, and testing.

EDUCATION
Georgia Institute of Technology, Atlanta, GA
B.S. in Computer Science

SYSTEMS PROGRAMMER

CHRIS SMITH
178 Green Street
Little Rock, AR 72209
(501) 555-5555
csmith@netmail.com

PROFESSIONAL EXPERIENCE

1999-present   **Systems Programmer**
Little Rock, AR
PUBLIC AUTHORITY FOR CIVIL INFORMATION
- Maintained over 300 assembler modules and developed 75.
- Formulated screen manager program, using Assembler and Natural languages, to trace input and output to the VTAM buffer.
- Developed program to monitor complete security control blocks, using Assembler and Natural.
- Produced a standalone IPL and created a backrest on IBM 3380 DASD.

1991-99   **Partner/Technical Manager**
Fayetteville, AR
- Initiated start-up and implemented operations.
- Designed and managed implementation of a network providing the legal community with a direct line to Supreme Court cases.
- Developed a system that catalogued entire library's inventory.
- Used C++ to create a registration system for a university registrar.

EDUCATION

ARKANSAS TECH UNIVERSITY   Russellville City, AR
Completed coursework in Advanced IBM 370 Assembler, SNA Fundamentals, MVS/ESA Architecture, Natural 2 Programming Language, MVS/XA Concepts and Facilities, MVS/XA Job Control Language, MVS/XA System Problem Determination, ACF/VTAM Concepts, MVS/XA Using Utility Programs, MVS/XA Using and Creating Procedures.

UNIVERSITY OF ARKANSAS AT PINE BLUFF
Bachelor of Science: Mathematics and Computer Science

COMPUTER SKILLS

Operating systems: DOS, Windows, UNIX
Programming: C++, Java, Visual Basic, Assembler, Natural
Database: Access, Oracle, dBASE
On-line help: RoboHELP
Other: Word, Excel, Lotus 1-2-3

TEACHER (Elementary School)

CHRIS SMITH
178 Green Street
Charleston, SC 29424
(803) 555-5555

EMPLOYMENT

IMMACULATE CONCEPTION SCHOOL, Charleston, SC
1995-present   Fifth Grade Teacher

- Develop and implement curricula, lesson plans, special projects, and exercises to increase dexterity, alertness, and coordination.
- Assisted in setting up new curriculum; selected materials, designed learning area, and advised on physical setup of classroom.
- As a member of the Handbook Committee, compile, write, and analyze school policies and regulations.
- Chair committee for school accreditation ceremony.
- Serve as director of school bowling league, 1996 to present: recruit chaperones, set and collect dues, organize outings, and coordinate total program for 125-190 students, grades 4-8. Served as league treasurer and chaperone, 1995-99.
- Organize and coordinate annual Sports Banquet.
- Plan and supervise class field trips.
- Supervise summer program for low-income youths.

1993-95   Fourth Grade Teacher

- Developed curricula and lesson plans and instructed in reading, mathematics, science, spelling, language, art, religion, and history.
- Participated in and conducted parent-teacher conferences, advising parents on children's progress and how best to reinforce education.
- Planned and supervised annual field trip to Charleston Historical Museum.

EDUCATION

CLEMSON UNIVERSITY, Clemson, SC
Bachelor of Science in Early Childhood Education

- Minor in Mathematics/Educational Mathematics

CERTIFICATION

- South Carolina teaching certificate

TEACHER (High School)

CHRIS SMITH
178 Green Street
Tacoma, WA 98416
(206) 555-5555

EXPERIENCE
TACOMA HIGH SCHOOL, Tacoma, WA
Chairperson, Mathematics Department, 1984-present
- In addition to responsibilities as math instructor described below, serve as director of the Math Evaluation Committee.
- Develop report for submission to the National Association of Schools and Colleges.
- Report details and assess goals, programs, plans, and professional performance and development.
- Develop and monitor budget; approve purchases.
- Select and approve departmental texts; write and upgrade course descriptions as necessary.
- Evaluate staff teachers; advise on contract renewal and new hires.

Mathematics Instructor, 1979-present
- Instruct grades 9-12 in trigonometry, algebra I & II, geometry, pre-calculus, and business math.
- Develop curricula and lesson plans, select texts, and design tests.
- Initiated remedial math program and after-school tutorial sessions for problem math students.
- Conduct summer-school sessions in remedial math and SAT preparation (8 weeks each).

EDUCATION
UNIVERSITY OF WASHINGTON, Seattle, WA
M.S. in Secondary Education

EVERGREEN STATE COLLEGE, Olympia, WA
B.A. in Mathematics, cum laude

CERTIFICATION
Teaching Certificate, Washington State

TEACHER (Preschool)

CHRIS SMITH
178 Green Street
Summerfield, OK 74966
(918) 555-5555

EXPERIENCE

MISS NICOLE'S DAYCARE, Summerfield, OK   1999-present
Head Teacher—Toddlers, ages 3 and 4

- Design a developmentally sound curriculum to enhance the social, physical, and intellectual well-being of the children.
- With assistance from childcare coordinator, design and arrange space for a variety of activities to promote children's independence.
- Supervise teacher, assistant teacher, and other support staff; conduct weekly meetings for planning and supervision.
- Hire and train new staff as necessary.
- Prepare menus and documentation for the nutrition program, according to state guidelines; order food, and plan and serve snacks.
- Coordinate arrangements for field trips and for meeting or pickup of children from bus stops and classrooms.
- Maintain classroom safety and inform childcare coordinator when repairs are needed.

SUMMERFIELD SCHOOL SYSTEM, Summerfield, OK   1998-99
Substitute Teacher

- While attending college, taught classes in various school systems at elementary and secondary levels.
- January 1999–June 1999, worked as a permanent substitute with the Summerfield School System.
- Prepared teaching outline for course of study, lectured, demonstrated, and used teaching aids to present subject matter to class.
- Prepared, administered, and corrected exams.

EDUCATION

University of Massachusetts, Boston, MA
Bachelor of Science in Elementary Education

CERTIFICATION

Elementary Education, Grades K—6

TECHNICAL INSTRUCTOR

CHRIS SMITH
178 Green Street
Alpha, NJ 08865
(609) 555-5555
csmith@netmail.com

EXPERIENCE

The Race Bannen Company, Rockaway, ME

Program Management Training Specialist/Network Administrator   1999-present

Prepare and teach classes in program management techniques and the use of program management software. Manage and maintain the computer network for the department of Program Management. Reconfigured the computer network, resulting in 60% increase in the efficiency of the electronic mail system. Developed course material for 7 classes and presented them to over 300 employees.

Program Manager Computers   1997-99

Coordinated all efforts going into the development of computer products, from their inception through their discontinuance. Managed electrical and mechanical engineering, publications, purchasing, and regulation. Successfully managed 6 computer models to market, including the company's first 83962-based portable.

Marketing Support Engineer   1994-97

Applied working knowledge of all Race Bannen computer products. Represented the company at computer trade shows. Answered technical questions from dealers, distributors, and prospective customers. Field tested computer products and performed other "continuing engineering" functions.

Software Documentation Writer   1991-93

Authored documentation for computer products, including a complete revision of the original manual.

EDUCATION

Ramapo College of New Jersey, Mahwah, NJ
M.S. in Physics

COMPUTER SKILLS

Operating systems: DOS, Windows, UNIX
Programming: C++, Basic, Assembly
Writing/publishing: Word, QuarkXPress, FrameMaker
Financial: Excel
Database: Access, Oracle

TECHNICAL SUPPORT SPECIALIST

CHRIS SMITH
178 Green Street
Fairbanks, Alaska 99775
(907) 555-5555
csmith@netmail.com

SASQUATCH HEALTH CARE, Fairbanks, AK
1998-present   TECHNICAL SUPPORT SPECIALIST
- Structure the submission of test files for electronic billers according to the required specification manual, which imposed significant changes in physicians' reimbursements. Developed and designed test data formats for telecommunications claim billers relative to internal technical operations and equipment.
- Monitored effective working relationships with external credentialing groups, linking users to meet shared objectives. Formulated and edited technical user specification manual. Submitted weekly patient accounting checkwriting jobs.

1997-98   INTERNAL SUPPORT SPECIALIST
- Communicated with physician and health providers desiring to submit patient billing claims on the professional line of business, Medicaid, including initiating activities related to their acceptance and approval of tape, diskette, and telecommunications billers.
- Acted as corporate liaison, communicating and monitoring the providers fraud list for active, suspended, or deceased physicians. Reviewed contracts for credentials of providers anticipating technical billing authorization and a physician provider identification code.

1995-97   DATA CONTROL ANALYST
- Serviced local and regional billing agents who submitted weekly hardware on tapes and diskettes for printing and cutting of a weekly checkwriting voucher file. Created and maintained a database on the facility line of business for input files. Distributed hard copies of vouchers for health-care services provided by hospital facilities, to aid as balance control documents.
- Allocated missing data that controlled the mechanisms for billing tape submissions; analytically identified and resolved data processing problems and communicated the solution. Promoted from statistical analyst and keypunch operator.

EDUCATION
FAIRBANKS COMMUNITY COLLEGE, Fairbanks, AK
Associate of Arts, Computer Science, 2000, GPA: 3.7

ALASKA INSTITUTE OF COMPUTERS, Fairbanks, AK
Diploma, Computer Programming, 1997, GPA: 3.6

TECHNICAL WRITER

CHRIS SMITH
178 Green Street
Melrose, FL 32666
(904) 555-5555
csmith@netmail.com

EXPERIENCE

1999-present   RIZZO ASSOCIATES, Melrose, FL
Technical Writer/Project Administration
- Research data and accurately describe the installation, removal, erection, and maintenance of all military hardware.
- Outline wiring diagrams and draw part breakdowns for illustrators.
- Serve as administration lead for specific projects in A-3, EA-3, and EP-3E programs.
- Work on IPB, MIM, and IFMM for all maintenance levels.
- Read from various source materials, including engineering drawings and wiring diagrams.

1994-99   CAPABIANCO PUBLISHING, Winter Park, FL
Technical Writer
- Performed duties as above for military hardware. Served as project lead, including editing, layout, and corrections. Started in Report Storage/Administrative Assistance; promoted to technical writer.

1992-94   DARK WILLOW ENGINEERING CORPORATION, Killarney, FL
Editor/Writer
- Edited and wrote large proposals for government contracts. Designed format and coordinated production. Organized and maintained up-to-date dummy book through several revision cycles. Interpreted client RFP requirements and determined applicability of proposal response to RFP.

EDUCATION

Curtis College, Winter Park, FL
B.S. in Civil Engineering
Coursework in English Composition, Drafting, and Computer Science.

COMPUTER SKILLS

Writing: Word, WordPerfect
Financial: Lotus 1-2-3, Excel
Other: CAD

TELECOMMUNICATIONS MANAGER

CHRIS SMITH
178 Green Street
Bremerton, WA 98310
(206) 555-5555
csmith@netmail.com

EXPERIENCE

THE SHERWOOD CORPORATION, Bremerton, WA
Telecommunications Director 1999-present
Manage 80 problem-resolution telephone representatives. Develop and
implement customer service procedures. Reported year-end positive variance of $5.2 million budget.

Manager, Problem Resolution Center 1997-99
Developed rotational instruction for inbound telephone managers and
supervisors. Areas included Account Analysis, Trading Support,
Management Support, and Payments.

Manager, Telephone Operations 1996-97
Planned and scheduled 24-hour operations and ongoing training for 600
telephone representatives at new operations center in Bremerton. Relocated
from Vermont as part of start-up team.

Supervisor, Retail Sales, Woodstock, VT 1995-96
Promoted to supervisor of 15-30 representatives. Improved individual and
group performance and productivity.

Telephone Representative 1994-95
Provided customer service as one of the first Sherwood telephone representatives to be fully cross-trained in sales, customer service, and mutual fund
trading.

EDUCATION

Heritage College, Toppenish, WA
Bachelor of Science candidate, History and Political Science,
expected December 2000

TELEMARKETER

Chris Smith
178 Green Street
Saint Petersburg, FL 33713
(813) 555-5555

QUALIFICATIONS
- Outstanding selling and closing capabilities with proven track record.
- Excellent listener; patient and sensitive to clients' needs.
- Calm under pressure; meet deadlines; meet all sales quotas.
- Proven problem-solving skills.

EXPERIENCE
1998-present   ESP Telecommunications, Saint Petersburg, FL
Telemarketing Professional
Cold-called residential consumers, discovered their domestic and international
calling needs, recommended programs. Consistently achieved at least 125% of sales
goals.

1997-98   Kaybee Education Group, Miami, FL
Marketing Assistant
Cold-called high school and college students; sold diagnostic college and graduate
school entrance exams.

1996-97   Bill Wonka Quality Car Wash, Cambridge, MA
Bookkeeper
Performed bank reconciliations, trial balances, and general ledger.

AWARDS AND ACCOMPLISHMENTS
- Inducted into national club of Top Ten Percent, 1999.
- Awarded Golden Ring Award for meeting sales goals throughout 1997.

EDUCATION
Quincy College, Quincy, MA
Courses in Accounting and Finance

COMPUTER SKILLS
Word, Lotus 1-2-3

TELEPHONE OPERATOR

CHRIS SMITH
178 Green Street
Pompano Beach, FL 33063
(305) 555-5555

EXPERIENCE

Southern Bell Telephone/SBT
Pompano Beach, FL
1997-present
Operator
- Using OSDI equipment, process customer calls that cannot be direct-dialed.
- Log repair orders and transmit to main office.
- Refer emergency calls to police or fire department, ascertaining necessary information from caller.
- Assist all callers in a timely, courteous fashion.
- Received customer service award twice.

1995-97
411 Directory Assistance Operator
- Provided telephone numbers for callers.
- Consistently met quotas while ensuring numerical accuracy.

EDUCATION AND TRAINING

Winter Park High School, Winter Park, FL
Diploma

Southern Bell Telephone Company Directory Assistance Operator Seminar

SKILLS

Computer: Word, data entry
OSDI telecommunications equipment
Typing (45 wpm); high accuracy

TRAINING SPECIALIST

CHRIS SMITH
178 Green Street
Winter Park, FL 32789
(305) 555-5555

EXPERIENCE
ALLSAFE INSURANCE AGENCY, Orlando, FL
1998-present
Training Specialist
- Oversee employment process for assigned departments. Conduct employment interviews; make hiring recommendations; network to maintain and expand base of contacts.
- Administer employee benefit programs, including Short/Long Term Disability and Medical/Dental programs.
- Develop and conduct a variety of training programs emphasizing system instruction for all levels of employees.
- Develop and evaluate positions according to a point system. Assign salary grades; analyze and conduct periodic salary surveys.
- Recommend appropriate resolutions to employee relations problems. Interpret company policies to management and staff.

1997
Human Resources Assistant
- Handled Worker's Compensation filings and temporary placements.

1996
Human Resources Clerk
- Provided office support.

EDUCATION
ROLLINS COLLEGE, Winter Park, FL
Certificate in Human Resources Management

ECKERD COLLEGE, St. Petersburg, FL
B.A. in Sociology

CHRIS SMITH
178 Green Street
Joliet, IL 60435
(815) 555-5555

SUMMARY OF QUALIFICATIONS
- Four years' experience acquired during employment and educational training within the travel industry.
- Thorough knowledge of various reservation transactions, including booking, bursting, ticketing, sales, customer service, and dealing with contracted vendors to ensure customer reservation specifications.
- Familiar with SABRE reservations system.
- Proficient at general office duties.

PROFESSIONAL EXPERIENCE

SURGE AND SIEGE TRAVEL, INC., Joliet, IL   1999-present
Air Coordinator
Coordinate air ticketing requests and tour departures using APOLLO and SABRE systems. Resolve client problems and special requests. Verify international and domestic fares; input pricing data. Issue tickets and final itineraries. Maintain and file pertinent materials. Assist with special projects; prepare reports.

GOTTA FLY TOURS, Wheaton, IL   1997-99
Computer Operator/Supervisor
Executed all SABRE operations. Administered ARC ticket stock and accountable documents. Managed office accounting. Supervised personnel. Served as group leader for Caribbean familiarization trips. Implemented system to eliminate SABRE computer costs.

QUICK TRIP TRAVEL, Evanston, IL   1996-97
Travel Consultant
Arranged individual and group travel. Generated invoices.

EDUCATION
MIDWEST TRAVEL SCHOOL, Chicago, IL
Graduated third in class, 1996.

DEPAUL UNIVERSITY, Chicago, IL
Bachelor of Arts, History, 1995.

WINDY CITY COMMUNITY COLLEGE, Chicago, IL
Associate of Arts, Geography, 1993.

CHRIS SMITH
178 Green Street
Bel Air, MD 21015
(301) 555-5555

EDUCATION
Loyola College, Baltimore, MD
Bachelor of Arts in English: Professional Writing, *cum laude,* 1998
GPA: 3.21/4.0. Dean's List, 6 semesters

EXPERIENCE
Goden Academy, Baltimore, MD   January 1999-present
Tutor
Teach English to a Japanese senior 6 hours a week, concentrating on grammar and composition.

Ridge Heights Elementary, Baltimore, MD   November 1998-present
Teaching Assistant
Instruct group of 5 second- and third-grade students in writing and creative expression.

WPIT, Boston, MA   September 1998
News Intern
Spent a week in the newsroom, field reporting, and attending music and promotional meetings at Boston's #1 radio station. Communicated with traffic center and sourced news stories.

Loyola College, Baltimore, MD   Summer 1998
Writing Skills Tutor
Assisted students with writing and managed writing skills center during daily hours.

Camp Lalcota, Bethesda, MD   Summer 1997
Special Needs Counselor
Planned and supervised daily events. Assisted in care and feeding of campers ages 6-15.

Loyola College, Baltimore, MD   September 1997-May 1998
Peer Counselor
Assisted students in social and personal development regarding adjustment to college life.
Led group and individual counseling sessions.

COMPUTERS
Word, Lotus 1-2-3

TYPIST

CHRIS SMITH
178 Green Street
Tampa, FL 32714
(813) 555-5555

EXPERIENCE
Contemporary Data Systems, Tampa, FL, 1997-present
Secretary and Clerk Typist I-III
- Transcribe and distribute reports; prepare other documents.
- Type purchase orders and expense reports.
- Log, file, and retrieve Component Engineering Reports.
- Coordinate and distribute part numbers for engineering departments.
- Serve as department receptionist.
- Answer and direct incoming phone calls and messages.
- Send and distribute fax messages.
- Make travel arrangements and reservations.
- Order office supplies for department.
- Record and distribute petty cash.

Tampa Sporting Goods, Tampa, FL, 1997-98
Sales Clerk (part-time)
- Responded to customer inquiries for products and information.
- Performed cash transactions.
- Stocked shelves, conducted inventories; maintained inventory levels.
- Participated in showroom reorganization and presentations.

SKILLS
Computer
Word, Excel, Access

Other
Typing (70 wpm)

EDUCATION
University of Tampa, Tampa, FL
B.A. candidate

VETERINARIAN

Chris Smith, D.V.M.
178 Green Street
New York, NY 02135
(212) 555-5555

EDUCATION

TUFTS UNIVERSITY, Medford, MA
D.V.M., 1999

NORTHEASTERN UNIVERSITY, Boston, MA
B.S., Pre-Med/Biology, 1993

EXPERIENCE

DR. JAMES HERRIOTT, D.V.M.
Boston, MA
Animal Technician/Surgery   1995-99
- Administered, assisted, and maintained anesthesia during surgery.
- Performed duties with animal patients in ICU under doctor's orders, including oral, IV, IM, SQ, fluid therapy, radiology, hematology, immunology, chemotherapy.

LUCKY DOG PET FOODS, INC.
Boston, MA
Animal Technician/Manager Assistant, Research Center   1993-95
- Directed hygienic procedures on 300 animals, including surgery and necropsies.
- Conducted research on pet food products and analyzed studies on nutrition, zinc, urine, feces, fluid therapy, medication, breeding, and artificial insemination.
- Collaborated in testing new vaccine for feline leukemia.
- Provided and submitted reports to government entities for FDA approval.
- Supervised and scheduled 20 center and union employees in conducting research.

NEWMAN ANIMAL CARE CLINIC
Medford, MA
Surgery Staff Nurse   1991-93
- Prepared animals for surgery.
- Administered antibiotics.

VETERINARY ASSISTANT

CHRIS SMITH
178 Green Street
Marylhurst, OR 97036
(503) 555-5555

EXPERIENCE
PIAGETTI ANIMAL CARE CLINIC

Marylhurst, OR
Neonatal Intensive Care Nurse   1999-present
- Monitor patients and schedule work, personnel, and supplies. Perform pre- and postoperative care and emergency care.
- Monitor ventilation and vital statistics of premature and critically ill animals. Serve on Emergency Ventilation Team.
- Collect and ship blood samples, perform intravenous and arterial catheterization, intubation of endotracheal and nasogastric tubes.
- Organize labs for veterinary students and for clinical instruction.

Surgery Staff Nurse   1997-99
Administered pre- and postoperative surgical care. Prepared animals for surgery. Administered antibiotics.

Rotating Staff Nurse   1995-97
- Assisted clinicians and students in treating patients.
- Provided room nursing and pre- and postoperative care.

CERTIFICATIONS
Licensed Animal Health Technician, 1995
Veterinary Medicine, University of Portland, 1999
Applied Dentistry for Veterinary Technicians, 1999

EDUCATION
University of Oregon, Eugene, OR
B.A. in Animal Health Technology, 1999
University of Portland, Portland, OR
A.S. in Animal Health Technology, 1995

CHRIS SMITH
178 Green Street
Kaneohe, HI 96744
(808) 555-5555

EXPERIENCE

THE PALMS, Kaneohe, HI   1998-present
Head Waiter
- Managed, opened, and closed high-volume restaurant.
- Hired, trained, scheduled, and supervised wait staff.
- Reconciled cash intake.

PALUA SAILS RESTAURANT, Kaneohe, HI   1996-98
Head Waiter
- Provided efficient service to full bar and serving area.
- Trained new waitstaff.
- Chosen Employee of the Month.

CANDLE IN THE WIND, Honolulu, HI   1995-96
Barback
- Handled customer service and cash intake.
- Assisted with liquor inventory.
- Performed security services.

BLUE HAWAII RESTAURANT, Honolulu, HI   1994-95
Busboy
- Organized large dining room.
- Trained new bus people.

ADDITIONAL TRAINING
- Certified in the SIPS program for responsibly serving alcohol.
- Attended Restaurant Association training session: "Customer Satisfaction in the 90s."

EDUCATION
HAWAII LOA COLLEGE, Kaneohe, HI
B.A. in Liberal Arts, candidate, expected 2000

WAREHOUSE MANAGER

CHRIS SMITH
178 Green Street
Hoboken, NJ 07030
(201) 555-5555

SUMMARY OF QUALIFICATIONS
Experience in the following areas:
- Large-volume warehouse operations
- Special-handling requirements
- Inventory, quality control, and sanitation
- Truck fleet operations

EXPERIENCE
AMERICAN CRYSTAL COMPANY, Hoboken, NJ

1999-present   **Warehouse Manager**
- Manage a 25,000-square-foot warehouse with 7 bays and 3 forklifts.
- Service company-owned retail locations as well as a variety of distributors.
- Direct rerouting and management of a 12-truck delivery fleet.
- Supervise staff of 17. Schedule employees.
- Handle special-handling freight requirements.
- Oversee rate negotiations and breakage and inventory control.

1998-99   **Warehouse Supervisor**
- Operated and directed activities in four warehouse operations.
- Supervised 32 people, including 4 managers, and 35,000 square feet of warehouse space.
- Resolved problems.
- Reviewed managers' weekly reports regarding productivity numbers, expenses, overtime, and overall operations.

CORNUCOPIA SHOPS, Hoboken, NJ

1996-98   **Assistant Warehouse Superintendent**
- Supervised 175 warehouse employees in a 50,000 square foot warehouse.
- Worked with both inbound and outbound dry groceries and nonfoods; shipments totaled over 50 trailers a day, moving 275,000 cases per week.
- Oversaw shipping, receiving, and inventory control.

EDUCATION
Hoboken Community College, Hoboken, NJ
A.S., Business Administration

Index

EVERYTHING

The Everything Cover Letter Book
by Steven Graber

The *Everything Cover Letter Book* includes over 200 examples of cover letters. This informative and up-to-date book covers every situation, including:

- Response to a classified ad or a blind ad
- Cold letter to employers
- Letter to employment agencies
- Thank you letters
- Follow-up letters
- And plenty more

The Everything Get-a-Job Book
by Steven Graber

Whether you're looking for a job or just trying to find a better one, *The Everything Get-a-Job Book* will give you the practical job search advice you need. From creating a polished resume that effectively presents and sells your candidacy, to smoothly handling stressful interview questions, *The Everything Get-a-Job Book* will help you stand out from the crowd.

We Have EVERYTHING

OVER TWO MILLION EVERYTHING BOOKS SOLD

More Bestselling Everything Titles Available From Your Local Bookseller:

Everything **After College Book**
Everything **Astrology Book**
Everything **Baby Names Book**
Everything **Baby Shower Book**
Everything **Barbeque Cookbook**
Everything® **Bartender's Book**
Everything **Bedtime Story Book**
Everything **Beer Book**
Everything **Bicycle Book**
Everything **Bird Book**
Everything **Build Your Own Home Page Book**
Everything **Casino Gambling Book**
Everything **Cat Book**
Everything® **Christmas Book**
Everything **College Survival Book**
Everything **Cover Letter Book**
Everything **Crossword and Puzzle Book**
Everything **Dating Book**
Everything **Dessert Book**
Everything **Dog Book**
Everything **Dreams Book**
Everything **Etiquette Book**
Everything **Family Tree Book**

Everything **Fly-Fishing Book**
Everything **Games Book**
Everything **Get-a-Job Book**
Everything **Get Published Book**
Everything **Get Ready For Baby Book**
Everything **Golf Book**
Everything **Guide to New York City**
Everything **Guide to Walt Disney World®, Universal Studios®, and Greater Orlando**
Everything **Guide to Washington D.C.**
Everything **Herbal Remedies Book**
Everything **Homeselling Book**
Everything **Homebuying Book**
Everything **Home Improvement Book**
Everything **Internet Book**
Everything **Investing Book**
Everything **Jewish Wedding Book**
Everything **Kids' Money Book**
Everything **Kids' Nature Book**
Everything **Kids' Puzzle Book**
Everything **Low-Fat High-Flavor Cookbook**
Everything **Microsoft® Word 2000 Book**

Everything **Money Book**
Everything **One-Pot Cookbook**
Everything **Online Business Book**
Everything **Online Investing Book**
Everything **Online Shopping Book**
Everything **Pasta Book**
Everything **Pregnancy Book**
Everything **Pregnancy Organizer**
Everything **Resume Book**
Everything **Sailing Book**
Everything **Selling Book**
Everything **Study Book**
Everything **Tarot Book**
Everything **Toasts Book**
Everything **Total Fitness Book**
Everything **Trivia Book**
Everything **Tropical Fish Book**
Everything® **Wedding Book, 2nd Editio**
Everything® **Wedding Checklist**
Everything® **Wedding Etiquette Book**
Everything® **Wedding Organizer**
Everything® **Wedding Shower Book**
Everything® **Wedding Vows Book**
Everything **Wine Book**